SECRETS WE KEPT

SECRETS

THREE WOMEN OF TRINIDAD

WE KEPT

KRYSTAL A. SITAL

W. W. NORTON & COMPANY

Independent Publishers Since 1923

NEW YORK ~ LONDON

For information about permission to reproduce selections from this book, write to Permissions, W. W. Norton & Company, Inc., 500 Fifth Avenue, New York, NY 10110

For information about special discounts for bulk purchases, please contact W. W. Norton Special Sales at specialsales@wwnorton.com or 800-233-4830

Manufacturing by LSC Communications
Book design by Fearn Cutler de Vicq
Production manager: Beth Steidle

ISBN: 978-0-393-60926-4

W. W. Norton & Company, Inc., 500 Fifth Avenue, New York, N.Y. 10110
www.wwnorton.com

W. W. Norton & Company Ltd., 15 Carlisle Street, London W1D 3BS

1 2 3 4 5 6 7 8 9 0

This book is for you, Mom and Gramma.
May the words we've breathed life into live on forever,
no longer an oral tale carried to the depths of the ocean.

To my partner, Pawel Grzech,
who believed in me always and supported me when
I didn't have the energy to do it myself. Your dedication and kindness
have shown me over and over again what love truly is.

And to the three stars in our lives
—Amelia, Emelina, and Grayson—
I hope this book reminds you of how you came to be.
May you grow to be brilliant, kind, and patient, my three warriors.

CONTENTS

SECRETS WE KEPT

TRINITY

WE ARE OF TRINIDAD—my grandmother, my mother, and I.

Our island is located in the Lesser Antilles of paradise, a dot on the map that is often forgotten. *It like ah drop ah oil,* some say, *as doh somebody forget to wipe it ahwey.*

The bodies of water that seep into the island are as much a part of the island's identity as they are a part of ours, and everywhere we have come to settle after abandoning home has been with the proximity of the seaside in mind. Perhaps the openness of the sea soothes the inner turmoil of us island women, or perhaps it shows the island's inability to contain us.

While attending school in Trinidad—*hwome,* as we will call it for the rest of our lives, though we are all now settled in America—we're taught how Christopher Columbus discovered it in 1498. That the Carib and Arawak tribes were indigenous didn't stop historians from calling it a discovery. In conversation with Americans, I've heard my grandmother and mother draw the same facts from our elementary education, the same ones I mention to others today. *Do you know why it's called Trinidad? It's because of the three hills along the southern coast of the island— Morne Derrick, Gros Morne, and Guaya Hill. When Columbus first spotted the land on July 31 in 1498 he was inspired to name it after the three hills—La Trinidad, the Trinity. These ternate hills that peak* above the clouds in mottled greens, picturesque, majestic, form a wall that breaks the patterns of the most ferocious hurricanes, a natural protection that no other island in the Caribbean owns. The Trinity represents our most powerful guardians.

Rising with elegance along the bluffs, the supple branches of immortelle trees stretch wide, their leaves on fire against the backdrop of a perfect Caribbean sky. Native to Venezuela, just off the coast of Trinidad, these mountain trees shine emerald all year round in their natural habitat. Once they were brought to Trinidad to cast shade over the cocoa plantations in the nineteenth century, they too, like all else touched by the islands, changed. Their roots burrowed deep, and they exchanged their greenery for fire petals that flicker orange and red along the regions of Trinidad and Tobago. Sown into the very history of the terrain, we choose what of the island we will share with others, and so the beak of a hummingbird dipping into the beaded nectar of an immortelle flower creates the ambiance for the stories we choose to tell. And so, like the fingers of a hand skimming the water of a glassy tide pool, you touch but the surface.

What we never say is how historians call the naming of Trinidad a "historical hoax." Columbus had every intention of baptizing the next land he found La Trinidad. Its having three hills was either mere coincidence or a miracle. It depends on how one chooses to tell the story.

Most people shake their heads in confusion when we tell them where we're from. *Where?* they ask. *Where exactly is that?* And sometimes those who have a vague familiarity with the Caribbean will say, *I thought everyone there was black.*

On our islands you will find descendants of the Carib and Arawak tribes, Europeans, Venezuelans, Chinese, Syrians, French, Portuguese, and Lebanese, but of them all, the two largest groups by far are East Indians and Africans. Centuries before Trinidad became a British colony, before Sir Walter Raleigh discovered the natural Pitch Lake that gleamed the blackest blue along spools of water on Trinidad's knee, before Columbus spotted the island, Amerindians called it home. They called it *Ieri*— Land of the Hummingbird. But when Columbus sailed upon them, these people were captured, enslaved, and littered along the coasts of other Caribbean islands, forced to work for Spain.

Our island changed hands, and when the British captured it from Spain, they brought African slaves to work the leafy grounds of the sugar plantations. This was the only group of people to exist on the island as slaves, and when slavery was abolished in England, the wealthy landowners in Trinidad then brought indentured laborers from India to replace the Africans on the plantations.

At least we geh pay, the Indians now say, *dem niggas an dem come as slave.* They know the history but continue to etch in these lines drawn for them. They perpetuate a war, the East Indians and Africans, one group thinking they are better than the other, East Indian children rhyming in the schoolyard, *Nigga nigga come foh roti, all de roti done, when de coolie raise e gun, all de nigga run.* And Africans taunting, *Eenie meenie miney mo, ketch ah coolie by e toe, when e ready let im go, eenie meenie miney mo.*

And so this enmity between Africans and Indians led them, and others, to maintain the perceived purity of their bloodlines, further carving hatred into our islands' history. Interracial couples and their multiracial children are still shunned as they were in my mother's childhood and my grandmother's. The blended are labeled mulatto, dougla, cocopanyol. These words are hissed and spat at my family: my grandmother is mixed, my Indian grandfather is not.

The shorelines of the islands are still unmarred by cement skyscrapers, but throngs of tourists trample lands natives can no longer afford, and boardwalks, chlorinated pools, and lobbies adorned with plastic plants have been cropping up with the image of paradise being sold.

But the republic of Trinidad and Tobago is where coconut trees rise out of the land, their backs braced against the breezes, spines curved into C's all along the shores, and coconut husks ripped from their mother trees dot the sand on every coast.

Our stories are rooted in the Caribbean, our histories woven into its bougainvillea trellises with their paper-thin petals; the lone road winding round and round the mountain like a serpent strangling a tree, coiling up and down again to the virgin beaches untouched by hotels and tourists, crowds, and money; the foliage so dense and green it's a prismatic shade of malachite, almost as though the vegetation itself is choking the life out of the island. This is a place where the intoxicating aroma of curry drapes itself around you in layers; where bake and shark sandwiches are fried on the beach; where the main ingredient for every dish is the heady bandanya, our word for culantro—no, not cilantro, it is much stronger than that. Here, people devour every part of every animal from the eyeballs to the guts and lick their fingers and pat their bellies when they are through.

The island can be traversed in a day, less than that if you know what you're doing. A mere ten degrees north of the equator, it is a place of heat so intense it can drive a person insane, and yet the waves curling against the seashore deep in the valleys between mountains and the luminous rivers that seem to fall from the sky itself can quench that same person's soul for eternity.

Trinidad is our fears and our loves. There we discovered our beings, we dug deep and planted our roots assuming we would never leave, sucking on the armored cascadura with its silver-plaited shell, devouring the sweet flesh beneath, the only fish the legend says ties you to the land forevermore, smacking our lips when we were done. We never thought we would have to leave this place, since our mothers and fathers planted our placentas beneath mango and plum, pomegranate and coconut trees.

But in the end we choose to flee.

We leave. We do. With no intention of turning back, we embrace America for everything Trinidad was not.

BEGINNING

2006

FALL SWEEPS THROUGH NEW JERSEY wrathfully this November, turning the vibrant green leaves the color of rust. Everything and everyone is curved to the earth as though hastening their descent to ash, to be blown about and sting the eyes of the living.

My grandmother finds my grandfather splayed out on the cold, hard floor, the left side of his head oddly flat against the tiles, his neck twisted grotesquely, his face pressed into the darkness between the hem of the couch and the floor. Rebecca discovers Shiva this way on returning to their senior citizen apartment complex in Jersey from a matinee and lunch with friends. Finding him like this, she pauses in the living space they've bifurcated—half the bedroom his, the other hers; half the living room his, the other hers.

She pauses.

Rebecca places her handbag on the dining table, her keys next to it, and takes out her phone. Her actions are measured. Who should she call?

Her husband, my mother's father, my grandfather, Shiva Singh, lies at her feet, possibly dead, and Rebecca contemplates whose number to dial.

When I first heard this story, I felt the heat of anger consume me—but it quickly zapped away, to be replaced by an intense curiosity. *She pauses.* Why would my grandmother not hysterically dial 9-1-1 and scream at the operator on the phone to get someone there as swiftly as possible? Why the calm? The calculated movements?

Rebecca calls my mother, and then it's my mother who makes the emergency call; she does so frantically, in the way we would all expect my grandmother to have reacted.

Later, my grandmother confided in me, *It was right dey een front ah meh, Krys. So. Easy.*

Here is what I now believe is the truth: I think she calls my mother in hopes she will find an ally who will say to her, *Let im go.* But in searching for permission to let him die, Rebecca is shot down by her child. She will be denied her freedom over and over again by her children in the coming years.

Arya screams through the phone for her mother to get into the ambulance, and Rebecca, numb, follows the instructions. Rebecca melts into the bustle of machines beeping and people barking. Once there, she waits for her children to arrive, striking up a conversation with someone nearby. This is how they find her: laughing.

Her girls prod and push her into Shiva's hospital room. As she enters, Shiva's hand falls from my mother's grasp. It hits the bed with a thud. Lifeless. Two nurses buzz around him arranging a bowl of water, a sponge, a pair of scissors, and an electric razor. Then they wait with fingers poised while my grandmother is handed the paperwork. He has a cerebral hemorrhage and is diagnosed with a hematoma. While doctors advise surgery on the pooled mass of blood as the best course of action, it's a choice, and only Rebecca, his wife, can make it.

Three of their seven children are able to rush to the hospital when they hear the news—Arya, Gita, and Pooja. Their three voices rise before my grandmother is given time to think or read what's been placed before her. *Mammy, sign it now. E goh dead widdout it. Sign it now!*

There is another moment of hesitation, the second my mother is privy to, and it is in this space where my curiosity and compassion bloom—as a wife to this man for the past fifty-three years, does she not want to sign anything to help him survive?

I watch as Rebecca's daughters shove her into a chair and swarm her. My grandmother wears her hair in a military-style haircut, so when she presses her fingers to her eyes and bows her head away from her daughters, she reveals rolls of fat pleated at the base of her neck. Her buzzed hair is a motley of home-dyed browns each as unsuccessful as the last at covering her lustrous silver.

Yuh wahn im dead eh? one of them accuses her. *Sign de damn papahwerk. Yuh eh see everybody waitin on yuh? Yuh is de onliest one eh realize we hah toh save e life awah?*

From her seated position, Rebecca is forced to look up at everyone from behind gold spectacles, half-moon magnifiers obscuring the cinnamon hue of her eyes. Her face is peppered with skin tags and moles she gave up on trying to remove years ago. A dusting of face powder a shade too light quivers on the whiskers sprouting from her chin. Bangles jingle on her wrists, and gems glow on her thick fingers, her nails filed to points. Draped on her body is a cream and blue pantsuit with gold trimmings. Her legs seem to just fall from her, akin to sturdy tree trunks planted in soil long ago. Though she tries to hide her legs with stockings when the hem of her pants rides up past the ankles, her varicose veins bloom beneath her thinning skin, a latticework of greens and purples imprinting history on her very self. My grandmother remains a robust woman but one whose body has now succumbed to age and the erosion of farm work.

In front of everyone, they bully her into signing the papers. *Is yuh who goh keel im if yuh eh sign dat papahwerk right dey.*

Her daughters give her no time to breathe in between accusations. The papers shiver in Rebecca's grasp as she lowers them to her lap.

We should read it, my grandmother mumbles.

Read wah? Read wah, eh Ma? How long yuh wantah read? Like yuh eh get it awah? E go DEAD! Listen toh wah dem doctahs tellin yuh. Sign it. Here, look de friggin pen.

The second Rebecca signs, the razor buzzes against Shiva's head, and I feel raw all over. They shave his head haphazardly and leave behind a lane of silvered hair on his left side. This deflated man, a ventilator pumping air into his lungs and a catheter snaking down to a urine bag, is not the grandfather whose broad muscled chest rippled when he hacked down trees or battled snakes.

The Shiva Singh I knew was a tall man with skin the color of a sapphire sky, sweat beading his arms like gold dust. He used to snap pomegranates from their branches just for me, crack them in half, and let ruby petals flutter to the emerald grass. He gnashed at the bloody insides of the fruit, sucking the arils dry, and spitting them where the chickens would peck at them later. I would stand at his side, one hand tucked comfortably into his, and as I gazed up at him, he seemed to pulse with the intensity of a twilight sky. My grandfather passed me one aril at a time, making sure I spat out each seed, afraid I might choke. He rustled my hair and kissed the top of my scalp.

Finished, he let go of my hand and walked past the barrels of water to a stone sink at the back of the half-concrete, half-wooden house. Burgundy droplets spilled down his face and dripped off the point of his chin. The stillness of the water's surface was broken, imbuing the water with the rich color of cabernet wine. He scrubbed his neck, back, and chest, a light breeze cooling his wet skin. Reaching for a towel draped next to him, he dried himself and looped it on his shoulders. The strands of his hair were atramentous, the depths of its blackness fathomless. He kept it oiled and combed, parted neatly off to one side, the fragrant sweetness of coconut lingering on him. His skin was the darkest shade of cacao, the powdery smoothness of chocolate pulled taut over supple muscles, his features devoid of wrinkles and time.

I followed a few steps behind him as he slipped his hand into his pocket to extract another pomegranate. He twisted it in two. The halves filled the crescents of his hands as he stood on the edge of his property overlooking the steep drop to the well, the chicken pens, and the winding road leading past rivers and trails to the cocoa plantations, orange groves, and banana fields. The house cast a shadow over his frame as the sun followed its path overhead, its warmth never reaching him. The sky was clear, wispy hairlines of clouds swirling past the horizon of bergamot and rose.

That landscape was familiar to us, and as I took my place beside him, I felt the overwhelming emotion of reverence grip me when we took our ritualistic gaze over our view: a sloping gravel road following the gentle curve of each hill, a lazing river in the distance; galvanized metal against plush elephantine grass; collapsed trees as bridges over rivers; and bunches of figs where serpents wove and hid. My grandfather and I often foraged together, filling burlap sacks with oranges and bananas, and though we wandered deep into the heart of the forests, I knew this man, my protector, would always keep me safe.

A nurse brushes past me as they take him away, the squeaking of those rusted wheels a haunting sound echoing in our heads as we flutter to his side to say our goodbyes. My grandmother sits the furthest away on one of those plastic bucket chairs, no whispered words of prayer falling from her lips.

We mark his surgeries throughout November in weeks.

Week one, surgery one: seizures start. Unsuccessful.

Week two, surgery two: my grandfather's body writhes on the bed like a struck snake. His hands have been secured to the railing to keep his wires in. Muted howls emanate from him through his oxygen mask.

Week three, surgery three: I've often heard people talk about the eyes when they see someone close to death. They say the eyes of the dead are hollow, that the emptiness they see is fathomless, that if you are captured too long then you too will follow. In his eyes I see all of this, and I am terrified. He chokes and splutters at my mother, and she looks at him far too long, absorbing his pain.

With each procedure, my uncles and aunts force Rebecca's hand to produce a signature of approval. My grandfather becomes more unresponsive with each passing surgery and I think to myself he will never come home. Never again will we sit and watch a Bollywood movie together on a Sunday afternoon when he would ask me to read him the subtitles because his eyesight failed him; never again would he slip a crisp bill into my hand and then act as though nothing had transpired between us; I would no longer have a grandfather.

My mother's behavior borders on the subservient—bathing him, changing his sheets and clothes, swapping out his bed pans. Yet I begin to see: Arya wants him dead just as much as Rebecca.

But.

There is tradition to hold to. He is her father, and no matter what he's done—what has he done?—the hold he has over her is firmer than my grandmother's pain. She can't cut herself loose from this man. I realize my mother knows *why* my grandmother is indifferent to my grandfather's death. I struggle to understand what has happened among them but can't know without asking them.

I fitfully attend school, sleep, and work. I gain temporary respite by turning away to conjure images of when he'd toss me over his shoulder, run up the stairs, and tuck me in next to him to watch a show or for a nap. We'd leave behind everyone else— parents, grandmother, cousins, aunts, uncles—and he'd ask me to tell him everything since I'd seen him the weekend before.

Each time he is in the operating theater, I think of how we used to be. For as long as I can remember, my grandfather took me with him to the banana fields. He strapped me into his jeep, and while I prattled on, he dug around in his pocket for my favorite mint candy with a chocolate encased inside. We bounced and leapt over hills and potholes until we got to one of the many rivers. Here he tied burlap sacks around his waist and clipped cutlasses and sickles to his back. We had to cross an overturned tree to get to the other side of the river. With some gentle coaxing, I walked in front of him, both hands held over my head, each of his calloused palms wrapped around one of mine. *Doh look dung*, he whispered, but I couldn't help myself. In the muddy water swirling beneath us, I saw alligator eyes and snakes, all of the things my mother warned me existed in these waters. She would know, having followed these paths through all shades of the day as a child. I faltered. My grandfather dropped and held me around my waist. *Poh yuh hand forward and creep creep creep till yuh reach de end. Doh worry, ah right behind yuh. Just creep slow.* There was an urgency in his commands and actions that rattled me, but the assurance of his hands stabilizing and guiding me forward kept me calm.

When we got to the leafy banana plants, I collapsed in the shade of their sprouting leaves and drank some water from an enamel cup he presented to me. Bunch by bunch, he cut the fruits down, tumbling them into sacks. He cracked one from the main stem and peeled it for me. I let the warm sweetness melt in my mouth. After I was done, I jumped up, but my grandfather hissed, *Geh dung, geh dung! Lie dung on yuh belly, Krystal, now!* I just dropped. He pulled his cutlass off his bag like a sword and hurtled forward. I rolled over and looked up to see him slice off a snake's head in one swift motion. I walked toward the head but he shoved me back and said, *No! Dey does still bite doh mind de head cut off. Yuh hah to mash it up good.*

The snake's head was face down in the grass, its underbelly wet. My grandfather placed the flat blade over it and stomped, then ground his boot into the blade, ensuring the head was obliterated. I looked up at the tree I took refuge under only to find the snake's fat body, the same color as the branches, woven round and round the trunk and leaves. I looked up at my grandfather in awe, this killer of serpents, gatherer of food, this man who'd saved my life.

In the hospital I sit with my head in my palms and I squeeze tears out of my eyes; I try to preserve this image of him but it cannot be sustained; I need to know him.

I WAIT FOR MY MOTHER to come home. When she pushes through the entrance of our third-floor apartment in Jersey City—New Jersey's second-most-populated city, sandwiched by the black waters of the Hudson and Hackensack Rivers, as well as the Newark and Upper New York Bays—I've prepared myself to ask her everything.

An aura of cold clings to her jacketed frame. Her lioness's mane of barrel curls shimmers with melting snowflakes. Winter's grip is tightening, and it is an unaccustomed cold that tortures our bodies even though seven years have passed since we left the islands.

This climate is a far cry from the tropics of coral and blue ixora hedges bordering our front garden in the shade of palm fronds. The scrimp of a backyard we have now is covered in dirt. Tufts of grass struggle to grow here, paling in comparison to the lush backyard of our vast house in Trinidad. There, our evening ritual was to suck grapefruit pulp straight from a hole sculpted at the top of the rind, sugar stuffed into the golden globe, or to scoop jelly out of coconut gourds, hairy spoons hacked from slivers of the husk. It is the space we crave, room to live and breathe as we once did instead of cramped together in apartments with barely room to move and nowhere to nurture flowers or fruits and vegetables.

The black number five tacked to our yellowed front door in Jersey City swings past as my mother turns the lock into place. Salsa music from the floor below swells into the room. She and I sigh together, sick of the noise and tight space. The way she tosses her sneakers and gym bag into a corner, instead of shucking them at the door in their designated spots, tells me just how tired she is tonight. The snowflakes that twinkled in her hair have melted and, soaked now, her bouncy curls lie flat and greasy against her scalp.

I sit at the kitchen table. I must probe gently. Weariness shrouds her. To relax and escape the pressure of the hospital where she visits and cares for my grandfather daily, she tells me about the hours she spends on the elliptical machine, the weights she lifts, and the swimming lessons she takes on and off at the Y. The two hours she fits in after work each day help her relieve stress. *Oh Gawd Krys, toh hah all dis ghadderin inside meh eh easy nah. Is ah good ting ah hah meh dawtah toh come hwome and tawk toh.* She lifts her tee and rips off the sweat belt binding her waist before she collapses on the chair opposite mine.

My mother babysits in an affluent suburb of Westchester. She works with a family, babysitting four little girls, from six in the morning to six at night, drives to the hospital, where she spends a couple of hours caring for my grandfather, goes to the gym for an hour or two, and then comes home to cook a meal.

Whey Colette? she asks. I point to the bedroom. My sister, as always, has chosen to remain alone in the sanctuary of our room from the time she returned from school. My mother and I go through what has become our routine. She asks me about my day at university, and I revert to the comfort of my home language and answer, in what I notice is our idiosyncratic thrice, *Good-good-good. Yuh know, de youge-wal—school, werk, and hwome. You?*

Her days have a tiresome uniformity. Mondays through Fridays, the privileged white children she babysits, with their undisciplined ways and spoiled attitudes, drag her around their house like a rag doll. And when their parents are home—and many times they are, making her job even more stressful—the children are free to do as they please, stomping around, treating my mother as more of a servant than a nanny. When my sister and I were younger, before my father joined us in America, and sometimes after, we would occasionally go to work with our mother to escape the suffocation of our apartment. But eventually we stopped, disgusted by the children's uncorrected behavior. Above all, we could no longer bear to watch our mother subjected to the whims of toddlers. *Arya!* the little children hollered. *Arya.* Perhaps because I grew up in a country where people older than I were called auntie and uncle, my mother's name screamed from children's lips never ceased to grate my nerves. *Arya,* they yelled, *I'm done with my toys, clean up my mess. Arya!*

If they couldn't have their way they kicked and punched, slapped and spat at my mother's face, her legs, her arms. Though the parents sometimes chastised their children, it was never with any severity and always ended with them laughing it off. *Oh you know, they're kids. I don't know where they learn these things.*

We sit for a few minutes at our wood-trimmed ceramic kitchen table—one my mother purchased at an estate sale, the way we acquired almost all of our furniture. I prop my head in the cradle of my right palm and listen. I listen because my father will not. She unloads her day's tribulations. I wait for an opportunity to interrupt but only after she's at ease.

Audience laughter tumbles from the living room. My father rocks back and forth on the recliner enjoying George Lopez's half-hour sitcom. My mother raises her voice so I can hear her; my father turns up the television. If either of us complains about the volume, he'll *steups*—suck his teeth in the characteristic Trinidadian defiance, the meaning of *kiss meh ass* drawn out with the long sucking—and make it even louder. My mother, to keep the peace, leans in, says a quick *Hi hon,* and without waiting for a response pulls the door shut. Starved for adult conversation, particularly in a language that makes her comfortable, my mother continues her tirade.

The top half of my mother's body disappears behind the door of our refrigerator as she burrows for the fresh chicken she chopped the previous evening, then rubbed with homemade green seasoning. Although it is already nine p.m., my mother insists on bustling around our narrow kitchen to whip together a "quick" meal. I tell her I've already eaten. *Oh yeah? Wah yuh eat?* When I tell her it was pizza or pasta from my waitressing job at a local restaurant, she laughs. *Dah eh no food, chile, ahgo make yuh someting toh satisfy yuh belly.* She extracts a large basin from the fridge. Plastic clings to the chopped chicken piled high in the bowl. It is tinged a bright chartreuse green. She's rubbed curry powder into the meat and left it to marinate with the seasoning. With a flourish she unveils the chicken, passes it under my nose, and says, *Sniff dat. Even meh raw meat does smell good.*

She dices tomatoes and onions before tossing the juicy reds and crispy whites into the sticky meat. With one hand she sparks a burner, and with the other she fills two pots with lukewarm water. She pours rice grains into one and golden split peas into another. I know if I offer my help she'll accept it reluctantly—I only slow her down.

Her eyes never shift to the clock; her fingers never set a timer; her hands never grasp the handle of a measuring spoon nor cup. She pours, stops, considers, pours again.

She sets a pot on a burner and adds olive oil. While one hand extracts a bowl from a cupboard, another stirs the split peas. She flicks saffron into the peas, and it cascades in a shower of gold; she adds only a pinch of masala. Black specks mottle the brightness of the dhal, turning it a darker hue of yellow.

To a bowl of water she adds Trini curry powder and two halved cloves of garlic. *Trinis hah de bess curry,* she says. While waiting for the oil to heat up, she busies her hands washing some of the dishes and tidying up the mess she's created while in the process of dicing and chopping. When the oil is hot, she slides the sparse curry mixture from the bowl and into the pot with her right hand and covers the pot with her left. Her movements are as fluid as waves. Water and oil hiss and steam. The pungent scent of seared herbs and peppers tickles my throat; my belly rumbles. Rich green curry crackles; teeming brown bubbles spit. After she toasts the curry powder till it is on the verge of burning, she adds the chicken. Rice and dhal continue to boil in their respective pots.

She strains the rice in the sink. Billowing white clouds of steam rise and quickly dissipate around her head. On a fourth burner, in a steel ladle, she browns two cloves of garlic in oil. The garlic somersaults among bubbles until golden brown. She pours the torrid, garlic-infused oil into the dhal; it whistles and pops. My mother grabs the star-shaped dhal ghotni and swizzles the softened split peas until they turn a creamy yellow dotted with masala.

She achieves each step of the cooking process with finesse. She twirls around the kitchen. With a final sweep of her elegant arms, one we both laugh over, she signals to me that dinner is done—fluffy rice, chunkayed saffron dhal, and curried chicken.

The sting of habanero saturates the air. My mother spoons a mountainous amount of food onto two plates. She sits across from me with fork in hand and opens her mouth to call to my father and my sister, but I speak before before she can.

Ma, why Gramma wahn Grampa dead?

She drops her fork. It clatters to the ceramic countertop.

Oh Gawd Krys, dem memories and dem eatin meh up inside evah since e gone in dat hospital. Meh only wakin up so in de middle ah de night toh see e two eye burnin on meh so like fyah.

She starts to tell me about a beating that has haunted her for thirty-six years. The ease with which she slides into the telling of this story shows me she was bursting to tell it as much as I wanted to ask. With my grandfather struck lifeless in the hospital, she's finally safe.

Our steaming plates of food are pushed to the side. They grow cold. Runny dhal pools in the middle of the rice; it clumps. The glistening curried chicken loses its shine.

Veins in her neck pulsate as she speaks. Her eyes dance and dilate, nostrils flare, cheeks pucker, and palms slam the table. The fluorescent bulbs burning down on us seem to dim, and she glows amber in the darkness slithering around us.

We start at the beginning. We go back to the haunting, to the cycle, to the deafening roar of silence from women echoing off the coasts of the islands. I learn that my mother and my grandmother do want to tell us. All we must do is ask. Then listen.

They reach deep into the gullet of Trinidad's history to extract stories women carry, stories men like my grandfather have striven to squelch. Their voices are thread thin and low— slow and rhythmic musical notes from the side pockets of a steelpan. Their words crescendo like the pulsation of island music. I close my eyes and listen to their textured words layered with Trinidadian Creole. They will spend a lifetime trying to escape the islands and these memories, to unclasp the shackles around each wrist. The cadence of their language is mature and differs from the shrill intonations of the children they once were. Their words are incantatory, a chant I cannot, will not forget. I feel it like blood pumping in my veins.

These two women pour themselves into me, and for four years it is difficult to pull apart our separate lives. What I learn of our islands, our people, and their buried collective history torments me before it shifts to something else entirely. My family's history attacks me in waves as notorious as those that clobber the Caribbean shores.

My grandmother, my mother, and I: we enter this world together, collaborators.

ARYA

1972–1986

WITNESS

～～

SILKEN STRANDS OF MIST lingered over the galvanized metal rooftops, rising out of the valley in peaks. Hordes of chickens stampeded from one end of their pen to another, dredging up the stale scent of bagasse and excrement. Up the hill, closer to the house, dewdrops slid off glossy avocado leaves and around the orbs of grapefruits and pomegranates. The heat of the sun sliced through the night chill.

Arya crouched at the side of the half-wooden, half-concrete house. Hewn logs of the kitchen walls shielded her. She curled and snapped her bony, brown toes; she tightened her burning thigh muscles. The ominous thump of footsteps against the kitchen floorboards squelched her attempt to draw a fresh breath of air. To relieve the tension from her folded legs, she rocked back onto her haunches, wrapped her arms around her knees, and locked each hand around an elbow. Her hands were calloused from the hours of farm work she and her six siblings performed each day during the twilight hours of the morning. At eight years old, Arya was an expert at slaughtering, defeathering, and roasting chickens, milking cows, churning butter, leading goats to fresh pastures each day, feeding the chickens and then collecting their eggs, and carrying bunches of figs on her head while going at breakneck speed.

—*Krys gyul,* my mother tells me, *we din hah electricity oh nutten yet so we wake up wid de cock crowin four een de bleddy mawnin, and ah hah to feed chicken and duck, milk cow, tie up goat, and cut grass befoh ah even tink bout school. And den, meh hah toh walk ah mile an ah half toh reach dey.*

That morning, instead of threading her arms through the hoops of her backpack after the hours of work in the chicken pens, fields, and orchards, she disobeyed her father's rule that ordered them straight to school. As Arya hiked from the valley of chicken coops with her brothers and sisters up the gravel-covered hillock, to the outskirts of their lopsided house, the dramatic drop and pop in her stomach started again. She knew she would be lunging her way to the latrine soon. Her siblings shed sickles and cutlasses to equip themselves with pens and pencils, notebooks and rulers. The brothers tossed a sack of ripe oranges plucked from the groves at the kitchen door; their mother had to squeeze and strain them one by one to serve to their father with his meals. *Ma,* they said with a thump on the door, *we gone.* Arya dropped the rope used to tether the goats and donkeys to the grass-carpeted earth.

Arya, come nah gyul, her brother Amrit beckoned to her. *E goh ketch yuh if yuh stay hwome and is nah only you dah goh get lix mahn is all ah we.* They all paused at this, but Arya shook her head, craving the comfort of her mother's attention while ill, the concern, the fleshy warmth of her embrace. She stepped back and motioned for them to continue on without her. It was almost eight; the farm and field hands would be here soon, and they still had a mile and a half to walk to school.

—*Ah know dey goh geh een trouble if e ketch meh, eh Krys,* my mother tells me, *boh ah was sick and we was ahready late. Dere was dis teachah who din like Grampa, and e used toh soak ah leddah belt een watah toh beat meh wid foh no reason. Ah couldn't handle dat today.*

She watched the backs of her siblings recede in the distance as they scurried to school barefoot, casting apprehensive glances her way, refusing to draw attention to themselves or her. They carried their lunches, tins of roti stuffed with channa and aloo clanking on dented wire handles. Their individual frames bled into one as they followed the path that snaked its way through the estate before stopping abruptly at the paved main road. Eventually trees and mountainous terrain obscured them from view. Though they would race to be punctual, none of them ever were. Their morning's work was, and would always be, too much.

In the shade of the cocoa house where the beans were raked and dried after the weeklong fermentation process, Arya unlatched the hutch and released her favorite of the rabbits—a soft ball of alabaster fur with glassy red marbles for eyes. The earthy scent of drying beans lingered in the air. The rabbit nuzzled her neck. The fettered donkey nudged her face with his wet nose and nibbled at the rabbit's bottom. The latch creaked as she locked the rabbit back inside before trekking back down the hilly landscape to a well just off the path not far from the vicinity of the house. It should be safe now, she thought, to return to the house and tell her mother she wasn't feeling well. It was late enough in the morning for her to assume her father had left to tend to the business of another farm and would not catch her.

Shiva had inherited over one hundred acres of land in Trinidad from his mother—pastures, forests, groves, and fields that rolled and dipped well into the horizon. And because his disabled sister, Nollie, lived with him after his mother died, he acquired her share too. His mother, before parceling out land among her children, owned much more. Distrustful of Trinidad's corrupt banking system, she secreted away the money she made from her estate into an iron chest she kept at their house. Among the crops her estate produced, cocoa, coffee, orange, banana, and ground provisions were the most profitable. Eventually Shiva's mother became a local moneylender, essentially a bank of her own. She lent money to businessmen, drawing up paperwork that stated they would pay her back within a certain time frame and with interest. But Shiva didn't follow his mother's example after she passed. He learned from her mistakes, knowing there were too many times she didn't get her money back. He chose to place his money with the banks, but not all of it—the iron chest remained in the house, and in it a large sum of money always stayed. The key he carried with him at all times.

Shiva employed hundreds of laborers but was suspicious of them, as he was of everyone else, and so he sent his children in to work before they came, charting how much produce he expected his children to bring back and how many chores they were to complete within the given time frame. The workers were then expected to do the same, oftentimes more. He usually came home for lunch and a nap before he was off again in his truck to oversee another estate.

At prearranged times, the Citrus Growers Association would pull up in trucks, workers with burlap sacks tied round their waists and slung over their shoulders hopping out. Shiva was always present to oversee them. They'd enter the orange groves and pick their supplies to make orange juice for the island; he trusted no one else to be in his place for this task.

Rebecca would likely be furious with Arya for appearing at home when she ought to be in school, risking them both a beating from her father. He never cared if she or one of her siblings was ill, only that they all obeyed his rule of always attending school after completing the farm work on time. Children here were bred to work. A child was your free labor opportunity, and while that was true throughout the island, Arya's father took particular advantage. Many others of Shiva's class paid helpers, cooks, and cleaners, and Arya envied their families. What did they do, Arya wondered, with all their free time? Sleep, she decided, sweet, sweet slumber. Very few students in her class had to wake up as early as she and her siblings did. Only the poor ones who lived well off dirt roads, high in the mountains where the clouds lingered thick. But her father had money; he just never liked using it.

Arya was prepared to deal with Rebecca's temporary anger at her because she knew in the end her mother would send her to collect some lime buds. She would boil them to make a tea, which she would swirl with milk and hand her in an enamel cup. Young lime leaves were what many people on the island believed helped to settle an upset stomach. Her mother would help to hide her from her father for the rest of the day. All she had to do was stay out of his way and be quiet.

As Arya trod the familiar path she and her siblings had carved from the well to the house, she wound elephant grass around her wrists in layers until it resembled shackles. Approaching the kitchen door with tentative footsteps, she heard her father's voice draw out not Rebecca's real name, which he found difficult to pronounce, but the name he decided to call her: *Ruuubyyy!* Arya ran from the doorway and around the wall to the side of the house. It was much too early for him to be back home. He must have never left.

She crouched, afraid. The air pulsated. She recognized the savage rage in his voice, having faced it before. But when he was like this, it was Rebecca he wanted, and having witnessed him beating her mother, she desperately wanted them both to escape.

—*Some people used toh say it was een e blood,* my mother tells me, *dat kinda angah dat used to consume im so, ha toh be een e head and coursin troo e veins foh dat kinda imbalance gyul. E was rootless.*

A cramp pulsed in her right thigh until it became a frozen mass of knots. Tears seared her eyes. She massaged her leg and prayed for the cramp to dissipate. She tried to hug her knees again, teetered, tipped over. She straightened her arm to stop her fall, and her left hand thumped the weather-beaten boards. Her father's prowling on the other side of the wooden barrier halted. A bubble of breath caught in her throat. She tried to swallow, but fear lodged air more firmly in her chest. Her abdominal muscles contracted. Arya flattened herself against the side of the house beneath the kitchen window. Shutting her eyes, she hoped the wood had no holes to give away her hiding place. She couldn't hear anything, but she pictured her father's black, knee-high rubber boots pulled carefully over his khaki pants and his white shirt tucked neatly into his belted waistline.

His rubber soles thudded against the floorboards. Footsteps stopped at the kitchen sink in front of the window. Eyes still closed, she pictured him leaning over the sink, his sweaty forehead smudging the clear glass. She knew he was peering outside in search of the mysterious thump. She knew he was hoping he'd discover her mother and knew that if he found her, his fourth child, he would beat her bloody.

Her father strode across the kitchen and walked through the side door. *Whey yuh dey Ruuubyyy?* His saccharine voice twisted her mother's name over and over again. Arya gathered her oversized tee in one hand and cringed at her father's voice. Frozen against the side of the house, she prayed her father wouldn't find her. She scrabbled into an alcove beneath the kitchen, a hole animals must have gouged out to hide from predators at night. Mud clung to her elbows and knees. In the narrow strip between board and cement she followed the pattern of her father's footsteps.

He was between her and the stairs adjacent to the kitchen. Arya mapped how she could get to the door of her room, shut it behind her, and silently slide the brass latch and lock into place. But with the top half of the door to the kitchen always opened, she couldn't make that escape route undetected. There was the option of running away from the house, but she couldn't just leave her mother.

—*Ah wanted toh, Krys,* my mother confides in me, *boh ah couldn't leave Mammy. Ah had toh make sure she was ahright.*

Something had triggered her father's rage; she felt his anger rising. There had been times Rebecca was attacked for failing to return a cable, a spray can, or a rope to its proper place on the farm. Other times his anger was provoked instead by a farm hand who'd broken a tool or forgotten to round up some animals; Shiva would return to the house and take it out on Rebecca.

Scurrying footsteps. Pounding footfalls. The kitchen's uneven floorboards groaned overhead. Arya retreated from the hole under the house. She peeked between the chinks of boards of the wall. Her father was holding her mother by her neck; he threw her into the kitchen. Her mother scrambled among tin pots and pans, grabbed a lid, and wedged the silvery shield between her and her husband.

The stained bottom of her mother's printed dress faced her. The material was scrunched against the plastic tablecloth. Arya watched as her father glided closer to her mother. Her mother groped the table behind her, fumbling to find a weapon. His charcoal eyes smoldered against his oily black skin; those eyes that mirrored the deadly still in the midst of a hurricane.

He loomed over her. *Who use meh spray kyan, eh Ruby?* She

trembled, admitted it was her. His hand cut through the air; her mother's head reeled back, her body slouched against the table. Pot covers rolled and rang on the floor. As her eyes and brows twitched in pain, blood trickled from the right corner of her mouth.

Arya watched the toughened skin of her mother's hands. The fingers fluttered to life before they stumbled over another pot handle. She yanked it. Tangy mango takarie cooked with crushed garlic, peppers, and masala spilled onto the tablecloth. Forest green leaves and vines snaked along the white of the plastic connecting crescents of apples and oranges.

He sneered, *Wah yuh goan do wid dat? Hit meh?* He backhanded her. He taunted, *Hit meh nah, hit meh.* Then he laughed a voracious laughter, one that emanated from deep within him and enveloped them, swallowed them whole, a laughter as eerie as the unnatural stillness of the air surrounding them.

The half-filled pot of food hung from Rebecca's hand as she loosened her grip on the handle. Her skin was the color of almonds, the back of her hands and the heels of her feet ingrained with the same ridges as the nut. Her coarse hair was chopped close to the sides and back of her head, a plush pile on top, a fountain of it stopping right before her sparse eyebrows. Muscles undulated along her forearms and legs as she slumped backward, releasing the pot from her grasp. Arya searched her mother's umber eyes for a flash of retaliation, but there was nothing but the thump of the pot as it hit the tabletop.

He backhanded her mother again.

—*Blood juss fall on de table like raindrop,* my mother says.

Arya turned her back, leaned on the wall, and slid down. Her legs and buttocks settled on stones embedded in fowl-shit dirt. Arya tried to concentrate on something else. She screwed up her face in an effort to grasp at anything but winced with each thump and thrash behind her. She focused on the manure her legs were sticking to and wondered where the yard chickens had gone. She dug her jagged fingernails into her scalp. Knuckles clenched, she pulled her soft curls, a gesture she found comfort in when distressed.

Doh hit meh, please doh hit meh, her mother's voice begged. He heaved her out of the kitchen and catapulted her onto the uneven concrete right outside the kitchen door. Arya slid on her belly, still watching around the wooden stakes underneath the house.

In khaki pants—already shit-splattered and mud-stained from his morning work in the chicken pens and coffee fields—he stomped around her mother. Up-down, up-down, up-down. He ground his heels around her fallen figure; he sneered, and then dared her to get up. *Git up nah. Wah appen, Ruby? Git up nah.* He wiped sweat dangling from his nose with the back of his hand.

Her mother folded her left leg underneath her body and gradually eased her weight onto the ball of her right foot. She pushed off the ground with her right hand. As she looked up, her neck arced gracefully. Blood droplets rolled down her cheeks, around her chin, and caressed her neck like tears.

Every hit, every kick was deliberately delivered, slow and heavy. His boot was a pendulum. It swung back and forth. Shitty mud. Black rubber boots. Her mother did nothing to defend herself. Her body bucked with each lash.

When her mother fell, Arya shut her eyes, opened them, watched what she didn't want to see. She reached out for daydreams in the far corners of her mind. Sometimes these thoughts preoccupied her while she was in school, took her away from life on a farm, and into the civilized streets of Trinidad, where she ran a house that hadn't been pieced together with wood and cement over the years, a house with running water and a toilet inside. There, instead of enamel dishes, she'd have actual china and silverware, a bathroom for showers, and on the sink a real tube of toothpaste, not sticks from a mint bush her brothers and sisters scrubbed their teeth with while slinging sacks over their backs every morning. What would it be like to envelop herself in a hammock under her own home, to relax and not be scared? Wherever she escaped to, there would be no more confinement and seclusion, and there, she'd scrub at the bitter scent of cocoa that'd saturated into her very skin, scrub it all away, and flit away from these lonely villages in Sangre Grande on to a town where neighbors could see and talk to one another, where conversations were likely to happen without the constant anxiety of the next beating. In one of these towns, she'd have a life and, in it, children who weren't terrified of their parents but who frolicked and played with other children in their quiet neighborhood, where she'd make her own cloistered childhood a thing of the past. But today, these thoughts wouldn't come.

—*Krys chile,* my mother says, *foh as long as ah could remembah, ah dreamin bout leavin dat place. Where ah could go, whey ahgo end up, wit who. Juss fah fah fah ahwey from dey. All ah know is no mattah what meh kyant stay dey. Dat place wudda keel meh.*

Her mother lay curled up with her arms crossed over her chest and her hands protecting her head. From the curve of her torso, fat rolls pleated and flanked her waist.

He strode away from them and disappeared among a cluster of barrels filled with collected rainwater at the far corner of the compound. Her mother remained motionless. Arya strained her eyes trying to locate her father, without moving, without alerting him to her presence. Everything was still. No chirping birds, no wind weaving between tree trunks and emerald leaves, no dripping faucet, no barking dogs, no pecking hens. An imaginary watch counted the seconds in her head. Tick. Tick. Tick.

—It was so quiet, eh Krys, my mother tells me, *dat anyting ah hearin juss soundin so loud.*

The rustle of thin paper drew Arya's eyes away from the barrels. Her mother got up slowly; her palms slapped the blackened cement, leaving behind bloody handprints. Her face was bruised; the swelling along her hairline formed mountains and valleys. She dragged her right foot behind her as she headed toward the stairs.

Arya rolled over and was getting to her knees to run to her mother when she heard her father's return and scuttled back into the space under the house. Fear fanned wings of ice around her heart, clenching the fluttering organ in its raw grasp. *E eh see meh, e eh see meh, e eh see meh,* she chanted to herself, her eyes squeezed shut.

Her father was holding a wet rope. It hung limp within his hands. Thick, taut knots ran the length of it. The dizzying smell of petrol reached her nose. Soaked in oil, the natural white strands of rope were now a dense yellow. The slapping, cuffing, kicking, spitting: Arya had seen them all before, even the rope, but not the gasoline-slicked rope.

—E use to threaten toh bun she alive, Krys, says my mother, *tawk she troo how e goh do it—wet de rope een oil, tie she up, light de matches, and drop it. E use toh laugh when e say it. Boh we nevah see im do it. Ah was sure e was goan bun she alive dis time.*

Rebecca tried to run, but her leg slowed her down. She limped while her pointy nails clawed empty air. Shiva swung the rope over his shoulder. Flecks of fuel stained his white shirt and black forearms. Grease seeped into his shirt. Overcoming her momentary immobility, her mother bolted. He lassoed the knotted line and struck her across the head. She dropped. He loomed over her.

The sickening thud and slap of sodden rope on her skin was

dull and monotonous. Her cries of *Please doh hit meh, oh Gawd please doh hit meh* ceased.

—*E juss din stop, Krys,* my mother says, *e juss keep goin, lashin she like ah animal, spit flyin everywhey.*

His inky lips parted to bare ivory teeth.

—*And,* my mother continues, *e juss makin dis noise inside im, dis rheal horrible sound.*

He tossed aside his snake whip. Ribbons of rope coiled at his feet. Satisfied, he turned. Arya's tears now streamed freely down her cheeks. Before her father walked away she noticed that his pencil-thin lips were curved upward in a smile.

Turgid air pressed her body flat. She fought against it and pushed up hard and slow. The weight of urine dragged her panties down. The golden liquid trickled down her legs, streamed past her calf and in between her toes, before it mingled with the fowl-shit dirt. Convinced he would reappear again but this time with a lit match, she was too afraid to make that step forward. A horror replayed in her head: her father knotting the gasoline-soaked rope around her mother's wrists and ankles, then the grate of a match on the side of a box followed by the sharp smell of sulfur. Arya found herself whispering, *Oh Gawd please doh leh dat appen. Please, oh Gawd please no.*

Then the Box Cortina's engine sputtered to life and reversed from the ground floor with a screech. Gravel clinked and spat beneath the car as he raced off. The bellow of the engine died to a hum. Her mother did not stir.

With him gone, Arya wanted to run to her mother, but her legs were uncooperative. She eventually wobbled over, the rope coiled at her feet. She kicked it aside. Her mother's face was bashed and bruised. Blood trickled from her ears, mouth, and nose. Both legs bubbled with welts. She touched the cotton covering her mother's shoulder. She tugged it. She grasped each shoulder and shook. Her mother's eyes remained shut. A solitary coldness spread throughout Arya's torso and limbs. She felt her frozen image splitting, cracking a webbed pattern over her. She fell like shards of ice and glass sprinkling, twinkling, and shattering like diamond rain upon her mother.

Rebecca opened her eyes. A look of puzzlement creased her brows. She shook it off by looking around and getting up. Arya tried to help; her mother cast her off like unwanted clothing, eyes sliding right over her. She stumbled up the stairs, through the two connecting bedrooms that all seven siblings shared, and into the third that she occupied with her husband. Arya, in the shadow of her mother, followed. Rebecca gathered together a dress, a pair of worn-out shoes, a tube of beige lipstick, and stuffed them into a wrinkled paper bag.

Arya yearned to reach out to her mother, feel her welted forearms hot from blows, kiss her scalded skin with cool lips, and plead, *Ma, please doh goh. Doh leave we again.* This time she stopped herself from doing what she'd done in the past after these beatings. Every time she'd drop to the floor, tears coursing down her cheeks, and twist her mother's dress in her hands, screaming, *Ma, wah we goh do widout yuh? Ma, please doh leave. E goh beat we ma, please doh goh.* She'd learned her pleading would go unanswered. Instead, she stood in a corner, restrained. Her mother's eyes, resigned, defeated, glossed over her again as she rolled up the bag she'd packed and tucked it into her armpit. She hung her head and walked past Arya, through the doorway, into the gallery, and down the front steps.

Arya momentarily crumpled to the floor before flying down the back steps and around the house. Her mother took the lone, winding path leading off the property; already she was a dot in the distance. Arya pursued a different route, plunging through snarls of bushes and branches. She raced the mile and a half to her brothers and sisters in school. Her pleated uniform filled and fell with billowing bursts of breezes. Urine dried on her legs. She didn't stop or slow down until she saw the sign for Cunaripo Presbyterian School.

Teachers protested when she disrupted their class. They threatened her with guava whips freshly cut for the day's disciplining. Arya bypassed them. When they smelled the stench of urine and fowl feces clinging to her, they were startled, and she saw her siblings turn to face her. Wheezing, she told them, *Mammy gone again cau Pappy beat she so bhad.* Their faces transformed from embarrassment at the filthy appearance of their sister to defeated acceptance.

From eldest to youngest—Gita, Rahul, Reeya, Arya, Amrit, Pooja, Chandini—they walked in a conquered line, feet caked with dust, gravel wedged between their toes. At home they would prepare the meal their mother had abandoned.

BETRAYAL

*—On one hand e use toh rheal take care ah we, and on de nex e use
toh rheally mistreat Mammy,* my mother tells me as she simmers
coconut milk, garlic, and taro leaves for callaloo on the stove-
top. *Not juss de beatin and ting. Mentally too, yuh know? It was juss
confusin foh meh, Krys, how toh feel bout him. And look at im now
movin from hospital toh hospital so we could try and fix im up. E goh
nevah be de same again. E like a vegetable now.*

Arya was beginning to see the many forms betrayal could
take, how it complicates relationships and reduces people to
an animal viciousness. Arya sometimes yearned to be numb
to the images of her mother being thrashed, left behind for
dead, but then, she didn't want to forget. Was she destined for
the same fate as her mother? Like the many other women on
the island who did everything the "right" way—who acted
demure, obeyed their parents, wed when they were deemed
ready to whoever was chosen for them—and were still rou-
tinely beaten by their husbands? Or worse, those who got pregnant out of wedlock and were shunned? For Arya, accepting
either would be defeat, and there was so much fight left in her.
Yet when she realized that even her father, a man who stood for
honor and tradition, could break what he believed, then rules
began to crumble.

—*E was a man who was well respected, eh Krys,* my mother tells me, *because e was de owna ah dis big estate and could gih people jobs*—*to cutlass and clear rung de bottom ah de orange and cocoa tree an dem. An e use toh make sure all ah we fass foh Divali every year, and every year we havin we lil puja, we Indian prayers an everyting een Hindi, de pundit tawkin een Hindi and e playin music een Hindi while me eh undahstand ah damn ting.*

Shiva was a devout Hindu and often went to the temple to pray. Every year for Divali he had his entire family abstain from meat for one month before inviting a pundit into his home to perform a prayer service where the fine strains of the sitar and the delicate drumming of the tabla crescendoed over the calling of the kisskadee birds.

Shiva also thought the most important thing was for his children to attend school and get an education. Unlike their parents, his children would be literate.

—*Ah propah education is wah e use toh say toh we, Krys,* my mother tells me. *Allyuh children goan toh school and geh yuhself ah propah education. Nah like me.*

Since there were no Hindu schools in Cunaripo where they lived, the Singh children all attended the only establishment in their village—Cunaripo Presbyterian School. Every morning they recited the Lord's Prayer and Psalm 23 before starting school.

—*Here is whey ah was confuse, eh Krys,* says my mother to me. *We was Hindus goin toh Presbyterian school, so when Divali time roll ahrung and time come toh pray een Hindi meh eh know a werd, so while some ah dem prayin een de Hindi hwome, I secretly prayin toh Jesus Christ, sayin our faddah who art een heaven and de lord is our shepherd.*

One day after school Arya heard Jagger calling out to her, Avinash at his side, *Aye gyul.* Jagger, ten, was one year older than

Arya, and his brother Avinash one year younger, so together they were in three successive standard levels in school. Their primary school was small—just one room stretching like a train car from one end to the other—so they were familiar with one another, Arya more so with Avinash, who visited their house every couple of weeks.

Aye gyul, Jagger said again, *dah is yuh bruddah, yuh eh know dat awah?*

Arya didn't know what to do or how to act. She had never thought about why Avinash came to their house every other weekend or why he spent the day with them. Jagger wanted her to realize who they were to one another, and also what her father had done. Now everyone else knew too, teachers and students alike.

—*It was a stigma, Krys,* my mother tells me, *yuh faddah cheat and hah ah outside chile. Now people know tings bout yuh family. On top ah dat e is dis mahn dat command respek from everybody, who does do e prayers an follow e religion, leh e chilren go to school to lun bettah, and is dese kinda low tings like beatin e wife, chilren, sista, and now fadderin ah nex oman chile dat gettin to be known by de public?*

Arya ran home, where she found Rebecca toting a cluster of bananas at the base of her neck from down by the well.

Yuh know all dem bleddy orange and them roll dung de hill, Arya, her mother said to her, *wastin all dis time runnin up and dung. Whey de ress ah dem chilren? Goan an clean up dat mess.*

Reaching for the sack tied around her mother's waist, she asked her mother about Avinash. The darkness that rose from her mother was one she associated with her father only. Her mother's face fell, and she told her what she had already told her elder siblings many times before. *Dah is e son, not mine. E eh nutten toh yuh. Hit im when e come. Bite im. Beat im up.*

When Avinash came to them that weekend, Arya observed her siblings' reactions to him, and for the first time seemed to register what they did. Arya would usually be in the kitchen, helping their mother or strolling through the forest for a half an hour while their father was gone, but now she watched them until they heard their father's truck pull up to the house. They scattered until Avinash was deposited on the front stoop. Shiva walked off to check on some of the animals, and the siblings scooped handfuls of gravel into the front of their T-shirts or dresses. The stones weighed the cotton down into the curve of a bowl. Avinash stood with his hands stuffed into his pockets, and as his oversized pants sank lower on his waist, he tugged them at the belt loops to readjust. A trio of her elder brothers and sisters made their way around the wall and flung gravel into his face. Avinash rubbed at his eyes, beat at his face, spluttered; they laughed and did it again. When they heard their father coming, they scattered.

When Shiva came back and patted his son on his head, he didn't notice the settled dust that plumed upward from his touch. Her older brothers and sisters only saw what their mother felt; they had sworn loyalty to their mother and couldn't turn away now. Arya saw something that prevented her from kicking and spitting at him the way the others did: the way Avinash adhered to Shiva's side when he was around them, casting his gaze downward so Arya couldn't even recall what his eyes looked like; the way his body was always tense as though he needed to protect himself from everyone at all times and at all costs. The paralyzing fear that enshrouded him like a stench kept others coming back to taunt him, and it was this same shawl Arya walked with, the very same fear she saw in Avinash's eyes when he recoiled at the lightest touch of her fingers grazing the dip in his back. Arya and Avinash were the same.

Soon he began to trust her, able to see she was never the one to cause him harm. The kindness she extended to him—applying a warm washcloth to his wounds after they'd beaten him up and warning him of their plans for him when he came to visit them—drew them closer together.

One day Arya was in the kitchen helping Rebecca concoct remedies for her older sister Gita, who was sick from diarrhea and fever. Arya was busy rinsing the freshly plucked lemongrass to boil and make into a tea to help break Gita's fever while her mother wrung juice from the salmon-colored bulb of the cashew fruit to mix with warm water to help with binding. As Arya turned to drop the stalks into the pot, she caught sight of her brother Amrit standing just inside the kitchen door, a grin plastered on his face, sweat from hacking and sawing at a tree trunk dripping off his forehead.

Am—she started to say, but he cut her off with a furrow of his brows and an index finger shoved into his lips.

Amrit, muscles dancing in a frenzy beneath the tautness of his black skin, kicked and punched the kitchen door open with all his might. There was the unforgettable sound of human skin and bone meeting with the force of that door.

Mammy, is Avinash, Amrit said, *ah get im rheal good.*

Son awaited mother's approval and received it in the form of a smile. Once it was given he opened the door to reveal Avinash covering his bloodied and broken face just outside the kitchen. Amrit shoved past him, stomping down on his feet with the heel of his boot. Avinash doubled over, blood dripping from his hands.

Despite her mother's hatred for Avinash and her desire to pass that on to her children, Arya ran out to help him through that day and many more. Amrit did not stop, couldn't seem to stop hurting Avinash whenever he came around the chicken pens or fields, dropping wooden buckets on his head or burying him with bags of feed, always backing off, palms up, saying, *Is ah mistake, meh din see yuh dey.*

—*Ah tink Amrit feel Avinash mighta geh someting from Pappy,* my mother says to me, *take someting from we toh gih im. Ah juss kyant believe e was juss bein cruel. And Avinash was fraid foh e own self. When dem accident and dem staht to excalate so, is rheal damage Amrit doin im.*

Even though they all carried fear in their eyes, Arya's brothers and sisters did not pause to truly look at Avinash, but she did, and the terror she found lurking there each time was all too familiar to her.

This gnarled coupling of fright and friendship followed them both well into their adult lives. As they grew from little boys and girls racing through savannahs to get home on time to tend to their chores, the Singh clan's behavior toward Avinash became less cruel, more muted. Avinash, no longer a little boy, chose when to visit the house, so there were fewer opportunities to antagonize him.

—*E use toh still come eh Krys,* my mother tells me, *boh it was rheally only toh tawk to me and nobody else.*

One year, sitting in class with his half-siblings and other local kids, Avinash fell for a certain Indian girl. Avinash told Arya about this girl he liked, described to her the black hair laced with satin ribbons and how she twisted those colorful ribbons into a bow just at the curve of her buttocks. Arya listened to him and began to spin her own dreams during the day, wondering if she could ever find someone to feel this way about her. Avinash also told his half-sister Pooja since she was more outspoken than Arya and knew the girl. Together, the three of them hatched a plan to help him win her.

But Pooja was deceptive. She walked out with them one day, pointing at the girl beneath the dazzling sunlight. *Dat one?* And Avinash nodded just ever so slightly as his straight hair, the same onyx color and texture as Shiva's, fell across his face. Arya thought she was pretty too, with two braids falling past her shoulders and white ribbons entwined in the blue-black strands of her hair. She was prancing around a friend, and they were sharing a laugh. Her teeth flashed bright and even; her nose was petite, her lips the color of coral set into the deep brown of her smooth skin.

Both Arya and Pooja could see why Avinash liked her, but there was a cutting look to Pooja's gaze that surprised Arya. It was the same look that nagged her later that night when Pooja laughed in their communal bedroom to the remaining audience of the Singh clan about the girl Avinash was smitten with. *Allyuh eh know how Avinash tabanka for a gyul, she rheal tie up e head, mahn, and she doh even know e exist.* Then she went on, spluttering with laughter, about how she told the girl, *We know im rheal good and e hah rheal stink mout. Like ah latrine gyul. Kyant go anywhey near im. Bess yuh stay ahwey.*

When Arya told Avinash he shouldn't trust Pooja, his trust in Arya deepened and his attachment to her became fiercer than ever. But though they were close, Arya harbored her secrets from him, never telling him she'd seen his mother.

—*Ah know who she was,* my mother tells me. *E muddah was somebuddy rheal close, and we din even realize.*

She found out exactly who Avinash's mother was one day, in the most peculiar way, at the market, as she frolicked around shoppers, stealing a mango, chennet, or pommerac here and there to suck while she waited out the boredom of her mother's ritual grocery run. Caught in the throng of people surging forward to haggle for mounds of mangoes or globes of breadfruit, Arya drifted to and fro, keeping an eye on her mother, who selected a block of burfi unsure of whether or not she should buy it. Arya had rarely had such an Indian sweet treat, but her mouth watered from having once tasted the richness of the milk mingled with the comforting flavors of ginger and cardamom.

Suddenly Rebecca went rigid, staring at something far off in the distance. With people swaying and weaving among and around them, Arya couldn't make out what her mother was looking at. Rebecca yanked her daughter's arm, and they began cleaving their way out of the market. Thyme and dasheen leaves grazed her on their way out, leaving the familiar smells of a kitchen caught mid-cook gliding over her torso. Avinash's mother had a stall, but Rebecca had never run into her before.

—*She wanted toh tell meh everyting, Krys,* my mother says. *All ah di hah toh do was ax.*

In the middle of the marketplace, people spilling around them, shoving them this way and that, calling for a pound of sugar or flour, eyeing the scale with eyes pointed like diamonds, Arya found out the woman her father had slept with was there at that very moment.

—*It geh woss, Krys,* my mother says to me. *De betrayal run deep.*

Avinash's mother wasn't only a marketplace seller, she was a regular picker at their farm. She worked Shiva's estates day in and day out filling baskets of cocoa and coffee, the same work Rebecca did once upon a time when she met Shiva. Arya began to understand her mother's anger better—that woman having his child, seeing *her* husband, a man Rebecca had fought to obtain and keep.

Go and see she, Rebecca said to Arya. *She does sell breadfruit and yam and dasheen on ah stall. When yuh pass whey make sure yuh kick and trow down she provision and ting.*

Arya went in search of this woman, but not to follow her mother's orders. She wanted to see Avinash's mother, to see this woman who lured her father away from their family, this woman who helped disgrace their family in the eyes of the Trinidadian people. As much as she didn't want to, Arya did resent Avinash a little that day, because his existence proved to people they were not what they appeared to be. Try as she might, Arya was a product of Trinidad, and upholding a family's honor and image was of the utmost importance to her then.

When she found this woman standing at her stall, rags tucked into the string around the apron at her waist, a kerchief tied around her head, Arya froze. Her hair pruned close to her head, her nutty complexion, the shapeliness of her breasts and hips through heavy market clothes, everything...

—*Krys, ah coulda drop dead,* my mother says. *She was de spittin image ah Rebecca. E leff Rebecca foh Rebecca. De mahn hah ah type. E know wah kinda oman e like boh is shame e shame foh likin mix up oman who nah Indian.*

BEATEN

—*AVINASH*... my mother says his name with profound sadness as her hands are elbow deep in marinating chicken feet in cold water, onions, cucumbers, salt, habaneros, garlic, limes, watercress, culantro, and onions for a pickled dish we call souse. *It eh make no sense tellin im anyting bout wah appenin wid Pappy now nah. Foh wah? E kyant do nutten. Ah does tink about im often eh. Juss growin up sometimes e was meh only friend, Krys, de only one.* My grandfather is still in the hospital. We are unsure of his future. The only thing that seems to calm my mother's mind is cooking.

Most days, Avinash and Arya parted ways on the way home from school. Arya's younger siblings—Amrit, Pooja, and Chandini—would either be not far behind or just in front of her along the curves of the road home. Every so often Arya checked to see if she'd have company on her walk back, but once she was halfway home she gave up on that, assuming they'd all trespassed onto someone's property to suck the meaty inside of a sapodilla freshly purloined on a new route home. Her brother Amrit loved to scale trees and pluck fruit for them, often bouncing fruits into the skirts of their uniforms while they sat at the bottom of the trees. But Arya, who despised stealing and was terrified of getting caught, stopped joining them when they walked through different farms and forests, and so eventually they stopped inviting her.

Arya bounded up the curving gravel pathway, a verdant hillside lush with banana and fig trees plunging into valleys on either side. Elongated leaves slapped and flapped like freshly laundered clothes hung out to dry. She heard traces of magic being whispered from the depths of the valley. The trees spoke a language only she could understand, spun her dreams and promised her a reality. They told her she would leave this place someday, abandon this forested world for the city and dwell within the stone walls of a house of her choosing; she'd never have to look back; scorpions, snakes, alligators would be of the past, memory obliterated, replaced by the faces of a handsome man and chubby brown children. Maybe she could even leave the islands, travel the world. Oh, how she dreamed as she walked that snaking pathway to her board house each day, chain-link fence squeaking in the wind, hunting dogs howling on the ground floor.

She spotted her father unloading something from the back of his mud-splattered jeep. It caught the light of the sun and beamed in her eyes. She rubbed at them and tried to figure out what he was doing and whether or not she could circumnavigate him, maybe skulk around the pomegranate tree and slip in through the kitchen, where her mother was no doubt clanging pots and pans together in preparation for dinner. *Arya,* he called to her, his back still turned. She froze for a moment, not sure if she should sprint or answer. *Yeah, Pappy?* she answered.

Is yes. Nevah anyting else, yuh hear meh? She nodded at him and walked closer with hesitant steps, afraid he'd slap her round the head for not answering him the way he expected her to.

Look wah ah geh foh yuh. He held a bicycle by its shiny new handlebars. The silver gleamed in the sunlight. *Foh yuh toh go toh de new school.*

There had been rumors about Cunaripo Presbyterian having too many failures in the past couple of years, but with Guaico Presbyterian three times further away, Arya didn't think she had a chance of going to a better school.

—*Ah doh know how e geh we een dah school, Krys,* my mother tells me. *Avinash too eh. Yuh see it like up here een America how everyting is accordin toh distrik, is de same way it was back den— yuh hah toh go toh school een yuh own village, and Guaico was de nex one ovah.*

Education, as well as status, was important to Shiva, and he would not tolerate having his children attend a failing school.

—*Yuh see, Krys,* my mother tells me, *meh di hah to walk toh school bout ah mile and ah half ahready, plenty time ah walkin barefoot, so toh make it to Guaico ah needed something like dis.*

Arya's fingers reached up into her curls and twirled a spiral along her index finger. *Foh me, Pappy?* Never before had she owned something new. Being the fourth child of seven, things were always passed down no matter the gender.

Yuh wahn it oh not? Meh goan return it if yeh eh wahn it! She dodged forward and snatched it from his grasp, darting backward just as fast with the bike, not wanting to stay within reach of him in case he felt like clouting her across the head for her previous lapse.

—*Krys,* my mother says, *ah din know if ah was dreamin . . .*

They stood together for a few seconds, a thank you pregnant between them but neither knowing how to deal with it until he said in his gruff voice, *Goan an make yuhself useful. Clean up dem chicken pen.* Arya teetered her schoolbooks on the bike seat and steadied them with her hand. She wheeled it into the ground floor, ignoring their vicious hunting dogs as she passed by.

He continued to clank around in the back of his jeep. As soon as she was out of sight, she stopped, dropped her books, and ran her hands along the body of her new bike. This one item would instigate jealousy in her siblings. The metal was smooth and cool. Already she wanted to spray the hose on the tires to wash off the dirt it had collected in the ridges while she wheeled it from the front to the back of the house—that urge to keep something prized new for as long as she could.

Her mother was rolling and pinching dough in the sweltering kitchen. *Mammy ah hwome,* Arya hollered as she parked her bike just outside the kitchen door. *Who dey chile?* Rebecca stuck her head outside. *Oh Arya chile, is you, come come come and help meh quick toh chunkay de tomahto choka.* Arya showed off her bike. *Wah is dat? Whey yuh geh dat from?* Rebecca asked. *Pappy buy it foh meh. E say is foh de new school ah startin tomorrow. Me eh hah toh walk no moh. Is ah bettah school yuh know, Mammy.*

Huh! Her mother huffed and disappeared into the kitchen, leaving behind a puff of flour. *Chile, fohget bi sick-cle and come help meh wid de food. Yuh done ten yeahs and still kyant make ah propah tomahto choka. How yuh goan find ah husband me eh know.* Arya trudged behind her mother, reluctant to leave her bike behind unguarded. *Me know how toh cook, Ma. Since six yuh teachin meh. Ah go find ah husband juss fine,* Arya said but thought to herself that whoever she decided to marry would have to haul ass and get her out of this godforsaken bush. The thought of escape was so sweet it felt like fresh cream in her mouth.

Arya went through the motions of the afternoon, helping her mother cook, cleaning the chicken pens, tying the goats, toting sacks of oranges up and down the hill, collecting water from the well; she did these things with the image of her shiny bike printed behind her eyelids and closed her eyes often, lingering in the darkness of that picture she preserved, the anxiety of using it tomorrow building within her.

Without the watchful eyes of their father boring into them, the siblings all piled around the bike, caressing it with their dirty hands. *Why* **you** *geh dis foh?* was the resounding question among them. Arya, too scared to say anything to them, especially her elders, waited for them to disperse before wiping it down with a rag. They walked away cutting her evil looks while she smiled inside because of this extravagant gift that none of them received. She kept asking the same question herself and found it hard to believe too.

At the end of the day, they were exhausted. Their books remained untouched, the pages never ruffled. Instead the wooden boards of the house absorbed the snores of their tired bodies exhaling for the night. School was a place where only privileged, pampered children succeeded, for they did not have to tend a farm.

In the morning, Arya dashed downstairs to wipe down the bike again. Everyone was only just stirring from the cock's crow, and sunlight had just begun spilling its sticky heat onto the world. She tried to swing herself up onto the seat but, having never ridden one before, it proved trickier than she imagined. Several tries later, with no luck at even getting her thigh over the seat, she realized this thing was much too big for her. She leaned it against the wall and stepped back. The bars and seat ran almost the same height—above her waist.

—*Krys gyul,* my mother says, laughing, *yuh grandfaddah geh meh a rheal big bike, so big ah couldn't ride de ting, boh if ah din take it toh school dat day e sure take it from meh and gih it toh somebody else.*

Arya waited for her siblings to scamper on ahead of her after their morning duties were completed; she couldn't bear the thought of their jeering if they realized she couldn't ride the bike. Once on the main road, the house and path a speck in the distance, no cars careening around the bend, Arya hoisted herself over the seat. She crashed both left and right, landing hard on her knees, gravel embedding itself in her skin. Determined to learn, she tottered from side to side, her schoolbooks getting banged up in the process. With school now over three miles away, she arrived decorated with cuts and scrapes but having learned to stay on a couple of seconds at a time.

After winding the metal chain around her bike, she snapped the lock into place and tugged hard to test its security, ensuring it wouldn't budge, lest someone attempt to steal it while she was in class. Patting the key into the pocket sewn into her uniform blouse, she smiled and shook dust out of her hair before heading to the morning lineup. Arya tucked her chin shyly into her chest, trying not to make eye contact with anyone else.

This one-floor school looked the same as her last. Each classroom was separated from the next by a wall, the patterned cement blocks permitting breezes to ruffle the pages of their copybooks throughout the day, cooling the thin film of sweat on their brown bodies.

The teacher to whose class she was assigned had three items on his desk: a leather belt soaked in water, an old-school grater, and a guava branch he stripped and wielded as a whip.

E does try and use at lease one ah dem everyday, a girl with an opulent plait leaned over and informed Arya when she noticed her fixated on the grater. Arya just looked at the girl's black braid dangling at her waist and said nothing. Because of her constant tardiness, she'd been subjected to each of these punishments before, and while they were all painful, kneeling on punctured steel was the worst of the three.

Several times throughout the day—lunch, recess, and quite a few bathroom breaks—Arya hustled to the back of the school compound to check on her most prized possession. Her heart rested when she saw the red, black, and silver bicycle, lumped with a handful of others, pristine, against the rusty chain fence.

During her last class of the day, giggles erupted around her, passing like a stringed explosion from one person to the next. Students put their heads down on their desks to gaze at their laps, and when they looked up, they gave one another knowing grins. Arya glanced at the teacher, and her eyes shifted from his moving lips to his three weapons. As more laughter punctuated the silence their teacher demanded when he spoke, Arya hoped that whatever was happening didn't end up on her. Because of her ragged appearance in tattered seconds too large or too small, her mud-splattered legs, and the chicken feathers waving from her curls, she'd often been chosen by the wealthy groups of girls in class as their scapegoat. They thought her a joke, and often jeered at those who worked on farms before coming to school: *Why allyuh even bodderin comin toh school? Is on de fahm yuh goh end up anyway.* Arya longed for uniforms like theirs, pleated and pressed, made by the hands of an expert seamstress, not shoddily slapped together like hers. Their hair smelled of citrus and coconut; their braids were looped behind their earlobes and fastened with silk ribbons.

Rising from his desk, their teacher cleared his throat, giving them all fair warning that he knew something was going on and intended to figure out what it was. His eyes scanned their desks and faces, searching for a culprit. The girl with the thick hair next to Arya slid a book in her direction. Without thinking Arya reached for it and gasped as she looked down. Before her was a pornographic magazine. On the cover was a picture of a nude woman with her legs wide open, her fingers dangling non-chalantly before her privates. Her breasts appeared engorged, her nipples flat and round like fried bake. Never had Arya seen anything like this. Uncomfortable with even her own body, she never lingered on her womanly parts but showered and changed as fast as she could, covering these bits she thought offensive.

The flurry of movement and sound from her direction drew the teacher's attention to her, and he started walking down her aisle. Not knowing what to do, Arya slipped the magazine into her textbook, folded her trembling hands in her lap, and looked down.

Singh? he said, to which she had to answer, *Yes suh?* But he said nothing else, sweeping her desk for a telltale sign. All the giggles had gone now as he rapped the edge of his ruler on her desk. He tapped her book, then slid the ruler between the pages and flipped it open to the magazine. Arya shut her eyes and felt her neck and face flush heat. No amount of saying it was not hers would convince him, she was sure of this.

He slid his ruler beneath her chin and forced her to look at him. In his face, she found a look of puzzlement. It told her that of all the things he expected, this was not it. There was a chance he'd believe her. No words passed between them as he tucked the magazine into his armpit and carried on class for the rest of the allotted time. Never had this happened. Corporal punishment was freely doled out for students talking too much. For this he could flog her in front of the whole school and everyone, including her parents, would pat him on the back and tell him he did the right thing.

Someone rang the brass bell with exaggerated arm flaps. Last bell of the day. *Singh?* Arya looked up as she was beckoned by her last name. Everyone else scurried out of the room; no one looked at her. The teacher rapped her report book with a ruler.

KRYSTAL A. SITAL

Arya's attention strayed to the courtyard. Through the lattice-work of cement blocks, Arya looked for her chained bike. If she was to endure punishment, then at least she had something to look forward to.

Make sure yuh muddah sign hyah and hyah, the teacher said. *Okay, Miss Singh? Singh? Yuh hah someting bettah toh do dan listen toh meh?* Arya shook her head. He said nothing of the magazine. Mundane words about parental signatures and her marks and that was all. There was more talking, but she couldn't concentrate on the words her teacher was forming with his lips. To everything she replied, *Yessuh, yessuh,* and when he was done, she slipped the thin report book into her hands and dashed out the door.

—*Krys gyul,* my mother says, laughing, *e eh say nutten and me eh say nutten eiddah. Who know, maybe e keep de book for hisself.*

In the ten minutes or so it took to listen to her teacher, almost the entire school had dispersed, save a few troublemakers, the same factions everyone tried to avoid. Arya unwound the chain lock, lifting and threading gingerly, but it clanged against the metal poles. She hopped on the bike and tried to kick off but ended up wobbling away, the wheel bucking under her like a donkey. They looked up at her, but no one budged.

A steady trickle echoed from the ravine alongside her. About a quarter of a mile down the road Arya felt someone's presence. A tall Creole boy was lumbering behind her, the look of malice bursting like stardust from his eyes. By the span of his shoulders and his height, Arya could tell he was easily four or five years her elder. She'd seen him around before, knew of him even though she was a village over.

—*E din go toh school anymoh, Krys,* says my mother. *E di fail e Common Entrance exam too many times, and e family was poor, dut poor so plenty times we see him beggin all ovah de place.*

54

Arya hopped off her bicycle and jogged beside it, the spinning of the wheels click-clicking next to her. His footsteps quickened behind her, thumped the pitch. Then everything went black and she heard the ringing in her head before she felt the pain. Her right temple throbbed where he'd punched her in the head. No words came from him, just his thick fingers snapping around the handlebars and yanking the bike from her.

No! Arya screamed, pulling it right back, her bookbag swinging from the front of the bike. Grunting, the boy shoved her back with both arms, and Arya toppled over, the bike crashing down on top of her.

—*Krys, yuh muss be mad foh me toh leggo and run,* my mother says. *And let Mistah Shiva ketch meh comin hwome widdout dat bike? E go keel meh foh sure if e see dat. Wah ah take from dat boi eh nutten toh what e goh gimmeh if I reach hwome widdout dat bike.*

He stood on top of the bike forcing the pedal into Arya's stomach. She screamed and retched but never let go. Stooping down next to her, he unhooked her backpack from around the handlebars and flung it across a ravine as thin as a serpent's tongue next to them. She watched it sail across the strip, landing with a soft thud. Thinking she'd scamper after it, he pulled the bike up, bringing Arya standing with it, her hands still fastened around her gift. The boy sneered and growled in her face, *Fockin leh it go.* Arya butted her head into his. He slapped her across the face before walloping her on the back, hoping to break her enough to make her release her hold. But she never did.

After thrashing her and then yanking at the bike until he was spent, the boy gave up and sauntered away. Her body ached with each step, blood matted to her head, bruises forming along her arms and legs.

—*Ah cuss dat boi all de way hwome Krys,* my mother tells me.

*Boh ah wasn't lettin go. Is hit foh hit whenevah ah could leggo one
een e ass.*

Her body throbbed and burned in different areas, but a feeling of triumph surged her forward as she trudged the rest of the
way home, that bicycle still in her grip. By the time she crawled
through the bushes at the side of the house and scoped out the
front to make sure there was no one around, she'd incurred more
cuts and scratches in crosshatches along her face, back, and arms.
Uncovering one of the barrels of rainwater at the side of the
house, she scooped water out with a bucket and doused the burning all over her body. For a few seconds coolness prevailed before
her injuries screamed out again.

Red padded Velcro parts protecting the bike were ruined.
They'd been shredded and pounded into the dirt. She ripped
them off and stuffed them into a bag to add to their heap of garbage. Now it was all a garish silver, the only other color the black
rubber tires that she'd cleaned for the second day in a row. She
stashed it away and limped down the hill to catch up on her work
for the day.

Her siblings noticed her wounds, but they each had their own
scuffles to deal with, and the only way they could help was to
hasten their duties to help her finish hers.

—*Dey di jealous meh foh gettin dat bike, eh Krys,* my mother
tells me, *boh if one ah we slack off like dat den all ah we geh lix, so is
help dey helpin meh foh dey own skin.*

Just for a moment Arya considered telling Avinash. They'd
grown incredibly close over the years, closer than she was to
her own siblings, and she wondered if he and his brother Jagger
would retaliate for her. But she knew Avinash would be jealous of
the bike too, and rather than risk all they'd cultivated, Arya let it
go, leaving her to wonder if this boy would attack her again.

Then, with genuine concern, her elder brother Rahul reached across the abyss between herself and her siblings and asked ever so tenderly, *Arya gyul yuh ahright, wah appen?* And Arya, broken and exhausted, told him everything.

And ah leff de bookbag right dey, Rahul. It still dey, she said. *Meh eh know wah Pappy go do if ah go back tomorrow an it gone. All meh school books and supplies.*

The softness his features had taken on transformed before her. His eyes grew stony, and his brows knitted together as one. *Whey im now, Arya? Whey de bookbag. Come wid meh, lewwe go.*

Now? Wah bout Pappy?

Dey go covah foh we, he said, gesturing at the rest of their tribe, but she was doubtful they could get everything done before their father returned. Rahul dragged her back toward the school, but on the way he veered off the path to ask one of his friends for a ride.

Oh Gawd Rahul boy, his friend said, *ah kyant wait foh yuh toh geh yuh own cah cah de way yuh does ordah meh ahrung, "Drive meh hyah, drive meh dey nah boi."*

Mahn, dis eh no time foh foul speech, said Rahul. *Some mud-dahcunt done gone and beat up meh sistah. Lewwe go.*

Driving, the trip was painless, and they reached their destination in minutes. The boy was there with a few cronies digging through Arya's school bag.

Woi, Rahul hailed him, leaping out of the car before it came to a stop. *Ah see yuh rung hyah, ah know who yuh is. Yuh feel yuh could beat up meh sistah and git away wid it?*

Rahul's strides were long and matched the rhythm of his upper body, his shoulders taut and square. The boy's friends all scattered, leaving the contents of Arya's bag in the dust.

You! Rahul said, grabbing him by his collar, lifting him up, and ramming his back into the tree. The boy did nothing, didn't even squirm or fight back. Rahul was taller, broader, and stronger by far; to anger him would only make things worse. Her brother's grasp was tight enough that the boy's shirt began to rip, and even though he'd just beaten her up Arya felt sorry for him. The whipping her brother wanted to give this boy could prevent him from walking for days.

Rahul, Arya interrupted, *is ahright leff im nah. Look all meh tings hyah.* Arya stooped down and scooped everything back into her backpack, dust and all.

—*Ah doh know why, eh Krys gyul,* my mother says to me, *ah juss watch de way he watchin Rahul like he so use toh gettin beat up and ah juss din wahn Rahul toh beat im up anymoh. Ah lil ruffin up was good but no lash oh nutten.*

The boy looked Rahul in the eye, but what he revealed was utter sadness. Rahul seemed unable to hit him despite his arm being cocked for a punch. Instead, he shoved the boy's back into the tree over and over again threatening, *If yuh evah mess wid meh sistah again ahgo keel yuh, yuh hear me? Ahgo trow yuh ass een dat ravine and nobody go find yuh. Now goan from here. Goan yuh muddahass yuh.*

Rahul didn't look at her as they all clambered back into his friend's car. They returned home shortly before their father and rushed to help everyone finish up. Arya searched for something in her brother's face, in his actions, that united them through this experience. No one had ever cared enough to defend her before, and she yearned for a more profound connection with one of her siblings. But Rahul didn't give that to her. By the next day all was forgotten, and the gallant brother she witnessed returned to the brother who ignored her, too busy with his older friends, cars, and beer.

To prevent her bike from being vandalized, Arya rode past the school and chained it up close to Avinash's house just on the outskirts of Sangre Grande, in a village much less remote than hers. It was her chance to glimpse a different village, so when Arya collected her bike at the end of the day she desperately wanted to explore more. She had no time, though, and was too afraid of getting into trouble. Whenever her father sent them all into town for market trips he always ordered through clenched teeth, *Straight dey an back.* And she listened.

—*E live closah to de school,* my mother says to me, *boh whey e live it hah moh people and cahs and everyting. Rheal diffrant from whey we livin up een de bush. It juss look and sound like ah brightah place. Ah juss wanted toh be closuh toh glimpse it, yuh know? Stick up een de bush all de time.*

EXAMS

～

—Ah juss want toh get outtah dey, Krys, my mother tells me over dinner one night, *and de only whey ah di see ah doin dat was troo school. And so meh daydreamin, Krys, dreamin dreamin dreamin because ah ahl de tings dat mahn used toh make we do.*

Arya escaped her life by daydreaming, often strolling through the forests that cupped their home. Once, when she was sixteen, an infection broke out among their chickens, killing off their birds by the hundreds. Arya and Amrit were charged with ridding the farm of the dead birds, so they tossed them along the banks of the closest river to the house. In the heat of the dry season, the muddy water sank low, and the bodies eventually clogged the water flow.

When their father found out, he made them pick up the birds one by one. Hundreds of decomposed carcasses littered the banks. Flies and buzzards swarmed them. Blood and guts, sticky and putrid, were strewn everywhere.

—Meh stomach wanted to come troo meh mout, Krys, my mother says to me, *ah di trow up so much. Ah di hate im so much foh makin we do dat.*

The heat pressing around them pulled the bodies apart, the outsides going in a different direction from the insides. Maggots sprayed a fine mist over them, and Arya and Amrit dusted them off frantically.

With nowhere else to turn, Arya swept her mind to day-dreams while picking up the chicken parts, her arms and clothes smeared red, worms teeming all around. Lost in her own head, she didn't hear Amrit as he spoke to her, keeping up a steady stream to cope. Side by side, they continued till the job was done.

—*School was de dream foh awhile, eh Krys,* my mother says to me, *until ah realize it juss dey toh keep we een we place, Krys. We wasn't suppose to bettah weself atall. But ah wasn't goan leh dat stop meh.*

Arya repeated standard five at Guaico Presbyterian School when she failed her Common Entrance exam the first time. When her second chance rolled around, Arya ensconced herself in a corner of the chicken pen and studied when she should have been cleaning the pens and feeding the hens. Instead of taking the goats further out to fresh pastures, she hurried them out of sight of the house and crouched under a tree to practice her math and dissect her language arts. All Arya knew was, she wanted nothing to do with farming, and getting an education was her only escape from her father's estate.

—*Gramma di fail she Common Entrance exam ovah an ovah again Krys,* my mother tells me, *an ah din wantah end up like she.*

The second exam day rolled around, and Arya sat on sweaty palms. She was so nervous, she needed to pee. The students had been instructed not to break the seals of their booklets, so she didn't allow her fingers to stray anywhere near hers, lest there be some commotion. At fifteen minutes to start time, the air crack-led around them, fraught with anxiety and pressure. A boy raised his hand. Arya recognized him from another class. He was the ringleader of the most popular boys at school, handsome, his Indian features prominent, his skin the color of ground nutmeg, his head topped with abundant black hair combed back with coconut oil.

Suh? Excuse meh, suh? the boy said. The proctor halted his marching up and down the aisles of the room and turned on his heel.

Yes?

I forgot my pencil, suh, would you happen to have ah spare? the boy said in his most proper English.

Ah spare? Ah spare?

Everyone was ready for an explosion. No one forgot their pencil and asked a proctor to supply one for them. This boy would have had a better chance whispering to someone close by and praying he didn't get kicked out of the room. Now he was sure to fail the exam before it even began.

But then the examiner took a closer look at the boy.

Wah is yuh name? the proctor asked.

Rudallsingh, suh, the boy said, puffing out his chest a bit.

*As in **Doctor** Rudallsingh?*

E is my faddah, suh.

The tension dissipated. He was a golden boy.

A A ah din recognize yuh foh ah second, boi. Come come come, ah hah ah extra one right hyah.

People watched him with envy as he was invited to the front of the class and instructed to choose what he wanted from the desk drawer. Then as the Rudallsingh boy walked back to his desk he gave his friends a smile and a wink, mouthing, *Ah get away wid it.*

Deciding she'd rather use the washroom now than wait till after, Arya slowly put one arm in the air, calculating that this was the best time to interrupt since their proctor had a smile on his face.

What? Yuh wantah pencil too? Yuh tink ah is ah pencil faktry awah? Puh dung yuh hand one time, he said.

Arya sat the exam, and while her second time was a success, she didn't perform as well as she'd hoped, her scores qualifying her only for Sangre Grande Junior Secondary School, a bottom-tier facility where most people flunked or dropped out. On the day results were posted, Arya watched her fellow classmates hug one another and either whisper or scream which schools they passed for. The daughters of all the doctors, lawyers, and businessmen qualified for the top colleges—St. Augustine Girls High School and Lakshmi Girls Hindu College. Arya knew the uniforms of each school well: the red, black, and blue plaid sleeveless dress of SAGHS, pleated to the knees, a belt looped low at the hip bones, a stark white shirt tucked neatly underneath, and the bright blue pleated skirt of LGHC, with a matching tie knotted around the stiff collar of a crisp white button-down shirt. They were both seven-year schools designed for eleven-to-seventeen-year-olds. Both schools accepted nothing less than excellence, and Arya, a year older than her peers after being left back, would never have been accepted to one of them, no matter how hard she tried.

Though she was disappointed with her results, Arya had no choice. She opted to attend the junior secondary school, along with other children from neighboring farms. She donned a dull blue skirt that turned grayer the more she ironed it, black sneakers, a striped tie, and a white shirt, untucked, since no one cared to correct them as in the prestigious schools, where they measured the length of girls' skirts with a ruler.

—*Ah still geh furduh dan Gramma, so dat keep meh goin, eh Krys,* my mother says to me.

Sangre Grande Junior Secondary School, unlike more

prestigious high schools and colleges, was split into morning and evening sessions. Students went to school Monday through Friday, for only half of the day.

—*When yuh goh dey,* says my mother, *dey doh expek yuh toh amount toh anyting cause once we done foh de day is back toh wokin on de fahm. Dis halfaday schoolin is someting dey juss gih yuh toh hol.*

Arya attended school diligently and worked toward taking another exam that would allow her to pursue her studies at another college. She was determined to climb the ladder of schools, desperate to escape the bottom rung she was dangling off of, where there would only be donkeys, chickens, and cows in her future.

At sixteen Arya was eligible to take the transfer exam, which she did, and passed. She entered Northeastern College, a full-time, seven-year school located in the heart of Sangre Grande. All-day school was a luxury for Arya; she could finally leave the rural part of her life in the past. For two years she could attend Northeastern and be a full-time student, be taken seriously, choose areas of study she found interesting and pursue whatever she desired.

But her first day on that campus proved to be a rude awakening, showing her just how determined she would have to be to escape her father and his farm. Arya wasn't allowed to choose her courses when she arrived at school. Of all the programs she imagined—industrial arts, home economics, mathematics, English, chemistry, biology, physics—she was placed in the agricultural science program.

—*Dey **gih** me dat, yuh know? Wah ahgo end up doin wid agriculture?* my mother asks me. *Become ah farmer, dah is wah. And foh two yeahs ah hah to take dese damn classes, dese subjexs meh eh wan no part ah.*

Along with the others transferring from a junior secondary school, Arya was grouped into areas no one wanted. Despite having a natural affinity for mathematics and enjoying English and history, she would never get a choice. Her natural abilities would never be recognized because the system—the country—needed farmers, and this was how they kept lower classes in those roles. Arya was in contention with a system she didn't yet understand.

That first day, after she found out what the next two years would hold for her, Arya walked out of school with slumped shoulders, her bookbag straps slipping until she dropped it on the ground and kicked it against a tree. Guttural sounds escaped her lips, but did nothing to abate her frustration. From the pocket of her skirt, Arya counted out her money for the bus ride home. Dragging her bag behind her, she headed to the washroom building to relieve herself before traveling.

As she approached the bathrooms, Arya recognized a trio of menacing black girls harassing a lone Indian girl. They lived in a small place, so even though they'd never been to school together, Arya knew these girls from the area. They were troublemakers, and Arya had had run-ins with them before. The racial tension between blacks and Indians was charged, often ending in brawls. Arya, friendless, was conscious of this and tried hard to avoid such scuffles.

The Indian girl's books were strewn across the courtyard, the ribbons in her hair undone; the three bullies tugged her skirt and blouse, rubbing the material distastefully between their fingers. The only available exit now was past the washrooms, and to get to it Arya had to pass them. In tears, the girl gave them her money, no doubt her allowance for the week. There were no teachers to help, and unless she was well connected to someone at the school, no one would have stepped in anyway. Arya knew better than to get involved, so, as quietly as she could manage, she slipped around the building and tried to slink past the gate. If she ran and they saw her, it would only excite them more.

The girls' hisses and sneers stopped. They were upon her. *Ay ya yaaai, look who dey,* the ringleader squealed, *is one ah dem Singh snakes from up een de bush.* Bullies often used their last name in conjunction with a snake to belittle them. *Too much snake Singh-in up een dey,* the ringleader continued. *We juss hah toh help geh rid ah dem. Cut off dey head. One. By. One.* Footsteps thumped past them; the other girl ran away, leaving behind her scattered belongings, blue ribbons flapping at the ends of her two long braids. Arya was tempted to point out that the girl they had been terrorizing had gotten away, but figured that would only intensify their interest in her.

Look who dey, said one, *meh din know yuh comin toh dis school now.*

Lil miss ting, said two, *ah remembah she wid she bicycle.*

T-T-T, said the third, *whey yuh tink yuh goin eh?*

—*Krys gyul,* my mother says to me, *dat is what dey use toh call meh when ah was youngah. Triple T, T-T-T. Foh tin, tall, and terrible nah. When ah tell yuh meh hate dat name. Meh hate it. Meh hate it so much. Is cause ah was tall tall tall, tallah dan everybody.*

Even before Arya was a teenager, she'd done what Trinis would describe as *shoot up like a bamboo*. Her legs and arms unfurled from her body in the same way the mass of curls atop her head tumbled down around her shoulders. It was the kind of growth spurt that caused immediate awkwardness. Unsure of what to do with her limbs, she stumbled around for a while, tripping over her feet, knocking things over with her arms, making her the butt of jokes both at home and at school. And once something like that happened it became a haunt till long after it passed, people remembering plagues and never allowing them to disappear, holding on to days and memories long gone, preserving some things that should never be preserved.

By then, Arya had grown into her limbs but still towered over all of her classmates. This paired with her shyness made her slump and draw her shoulders inward, giving her the mark of defeat; it was this that bullies preyed on. She'd always escaped minor scuffles with nothing more than a torn uniform and a thumping heartbeat, using those long limbs to kick dust behind her or to pull herself into branches overhead so she could hide. She almost never had anything that anyone coveted before. But miles from home they knew she'd have money for travel, and this was the first time she'd been in the girls' reach with no witnesses.

Arya ran. They followed her until she was tired. The four of them traced the meandering roadside beneath the pulsing Caribbean sun. The trio stopped only to fill their uniform skirts with pebbles. They flung them at her, whipped her bare arms and legs, her unprotected head. Arya hunched over, ground her teeth, and walked faster, pumping her legs, feeling the burn spiral her inner thighs. She could have tried outrunning them if she hadn't already felt so tired, so defeated.

Wah appen, yuh nasty lil snake? one said, the same annoying play on her last name, Singh. *We ent see yuh long time.*

Yeah gyul, whey yuh hidin from we? Yuh tink yuh bettah dan we eh, said another.

All allyuh Indian de same, said the third. *Come hyah lemmeh set yuh straight.*

—*Tings between Indians and Africans back den was bhad, Krys,* my mother says. *Dem Indians an dem eh backward nah, dey*

*targetin innocent black gyuls and dem and beatin dem up de same
way, tawntin dem, tellin dem dey skin dutty and hair hard.*

They ran up to her; two yanked both her arms while the third
tried to pry open her fingers that held the money. Arya refused to
open her hands, and the third girl pummeled her. Still she refused
to let go.

No! Arya screamed. Her defiance infuriated them further. Their cuffing intensified. They scratched her face, tore out
her hair. She blinked away blood pouring down her face as she
rammed them with her shoulders.

—*Ah feel de root and dem come out een clump Krys,* my mother
tells me. *Meh fraid toh watch de blood dat come out meh head. Black
an Indian, di hate we hah foh each uddah on de island run deep.
Always fightin, nevah mixin. Every time African geh into ah fight wid
Indian is de hair and skin dey goin foh. And de Indians and dem eh
no backward nah, prancin arung sayin dey hair soff soff soff and dey
complexion light. Meh eh know why dese gyuls and dem targettin
meh so. Meh eh do dem nutten. Only ting meh could tink of is cause
ah was quiet and scared-y. Ah di always keep toh mehself, no friend
or nutten like dat.*

Arya rolled herself into a ball trying to protect her body. They
kicked, slapped, and bit. One of the girls pummeled her face, and
for a second she lifted her thumb away from her clenched fist and
it grazed Arya's mouth. Instinctively Arya chomped down. The
girl bucked and screamed, tried to pull her hand away, slapped at
Arya's head with her other hand.

—*Ah wasn't lettin go foh nutten,* my mother tells me. *Ah geh
dat blasted ting in meh mout so ah hol on strong. Gimmeh de chance
an ah wuddah bite off de whole ting.*

The other two girls reacted to the screams of *Meh fingah!
De bitch bitin meh fingah. Dis muddahcunt bitin meh fingah!* by

dropping blows on her jaw, but Arya flung her head side to side like a rabid beast. When they did force the girl's thumb out, blood sprayed from around the base of it.

Yuh nasty lil coolie, the girls screamed, *yuh muddahcunt yuh! Yuh goan get it now, yuh tink we playin? And we go take all yuh money.* They encircled her again. They spat on her. Arya felt their fingers and nails sinking into her. She kept her head down and her eyes closed, her hands and arms latched around herself. She was certain they would kill her. They pushed and shoved, but she didn't budge. Her eyes remained closed. She had no sense of where she was on her route home. If someone could only pass by and distract them long enough so she could escape.

Suddenly they lifted her. There was no ground beneath her feet and then her back landed flat. Warm sewage enveloped her. But those hands remained ever fast around her money. She looked up at the three of them standing above her. They took turns spitting on her. Over and over.

But they didn't venture down into the drain after her. Instead, after some time, they turned around and left. Arya wanted to anger them by screaming, *Wah happen toh allyuh niggahs? Yuh give up? Yuh done loss? Meh money right hyah.* And she imagined herself holding her money up triumphantly, but she said no such thing, terrified they'd attack her again.

The girl whose finger Arya had bitten turned around one last time, narrowed her eyes, and ran her index finger across her neck in a slicing motion while mouthing *Ahgo get yuh* before she wrapped her thumb in the skirt of her uniform and continued on with the others. They cackled as they ambled away.

Arya clambered out of the ditch and wiped the stringy black sewage off as best as she could. She rolled around in the grass rubbing off chunks, not letting her mind wander as to what they might be. Her body throbbed and burned, but a feeling of triumph swelled within her as she stood slowly to trudge the rest of the way home, her footfalls squelching with each step but with her travel money still in her grip. She avoided main roads and even side routes, choosing instead to hoist herself over fallen trees and through thorny brambles. The putrid smell rising from her only worsened as the waste dried in a thick layer over her clothes and body.

At the bus stop people said, *Wah kinda nastiness is dis?* or *Chile, go from hyah, dis kinda bush people ting we doh wahn dung here so.* Arya ignored them all and kept her chin up. When it was time to board the bus she saw the bus driver struggling with whether or not to let her on. Passengers yelled at him, *Doh leh she on hyah nah. Dat is high class nastiness. Is report ahgo report yuh if you leh she on **dis** bus.*

Arya faltered and tears sprang to her eyes as she stood on the steps holding the money out to the bus driver, the money she fought so hard to hold on to because it was her passage home.

If yuh doh lemmeh on, Arya said hoarsely to the driver, *den meh eh goh reach hwome tonight.*

Whey yuh goin toh, chile? he asked her.

Her destination was far, and so he told her to sit right behind him. People *steups*ed in true Trinidadian anger as she sat down. They threw words at her back the entire way home. *E shoulda nevah leh yuh siddung on dis kissmehass bus.* Arya closed her eyes; they burned from fatigue.

Once home, she drenched herself in rainwater from the barrels. Her brothers and sisters had seen her as they milled about the house tending to their own workload, but there was no time to stop and find out what had happened. Their father was already home. Shiva was in the kitchen threatening their mother, and this distracted from Arya's appearance.

—*Yuh know if Pappy di see meh so, Krys,* my mother says to me,

is beat e wuddah beat meh on top ah dat? Ah know it. Poor Mammy
dealin wid im een de kitchen so ah get awhey from im dat day.

Their mother cowered by the sink, Shiva's fist hovering above
her head. Today Arya was lost among her siblings. She hustled to
the fields to pick up on anything that hadn't been tended to for
the day, one brother or sister calling over her shoulder telling her
what they'd already done and what still needed attention.

Recalling when Rahul stood up for her when she was younger,
Arya wondered if he would do it again. But she couldn't get him
in one place, and he seemed uninterested in her, her bumps and
cuts unnoticed. Arya dreamt up a world for herself where her
brothers would pull those girls aside, grip their slender throats
in a farmhand hold, the callused skin alone doing some damage,
then growl at them never to touch her ever again. And even her
sisters would get involved, banding together to slap the trio into
their place, letting everyone know the Singh clan was not to be
messed with. But in the end Arya had to let go of her fantasy, leaving room for those three girls to target her again.

The ferocity with which she protected herself seemed to have
marked her, and though she was never physically attacked by
them again, they and others continued to terrorize her, calling
her a *Singh snake* and *T-T-T.* They'd harass her by commenting on
her clothes, tugging on her hair, and embarrassing her in class.

—*Dey use toh say look look look hyah de Singh-in snake slidin*
out from de bush, my mother tells me. *Boh lemmeh tell yuh some-*
ting, eh Krys, ah geh beat up and taken advantage of meh whole life.
No way meh lettin dat happen toh meh chilren.

MONDAY THROUGH FRIDAY, Arya traveled to and from Northeastern College without any detours. Her father would time her,

so there remained no room for friends or escapades. Her brothers and sisters would tempt fate and return late every once in a while, going off to places Arya had never been, sampling beer and rum, kissing sweethearts. They would get caught and pummeled, but afterward said it was worth it. Arya wasn't so sure that was true.

Shiva bought his eldest son, Rahul, a car. It was a delicate blue, powdery under the luminous sun. They all fawned over it. The inside was beige, and Arya inhaled the crisp scent deep into her lungs, knowing her father would never bestow a gift like this on one of his girls. Their father gifted only the best to his eldest son, the one, as tradition would have it, who would inherit what he owned.

—*It was ah rheal beauty, Krys,* my mother says, *only een meh dreams ah couldah imagine drivin ah cah. We couldn't believe Pappy buy dat foh im.*

Rahul pranced around like a king, sharing the car with his friends. When Shiva wasn't around, they took frequent trips to the beaches and rivers on and off Trinidad's coast, drinking and belting out calypso songs along the way. Arya wanted to warn her brother to be careful, he couldn't go on like this, but her timorousness stopped her. Rahul would lash out at her, tell her she was too young, to mind her own business and let him have some fun. Who was she to deny him this? They all had too little of it on the farm anyway.

—*Yuh know, Krys,* says my mother, *e oldah dan me so e eh goh listen anyway. And when Pappy ketch im is rheal lix een e ass, yuh know.*

One day, Rahul, much too bold, disappeared with a friend all day long. They drove up to Balandra, a beach in northeast Trinidad about half an hour from Galera Point Lighthouse in Toco. They drank and snacked without a care in the world. Her brother, much too drunk to be driving, spun out of control and crashed the car into an embankment on the brink of a roaring river.

—*We din know if dem was ahright oh anyting, Krys,* my mother tells me. *E juss din come hwome.*

Rebecca and Shiva paced in separate rooms; the siblings gathered together on the floor of another. The air surrounding them was congested with heat so thick not even a fan could give them the slightest relief. The silence was filled with the raucous croaking of frogs, crickets clamoring in a defeaning cacophony, an owl's intermittent hooting. Rooted in their ways, their parents lit oil lamps out of habit despite the recent addition of electricity on the farm. Evening's darkness began to form pockets around them all, growing tentacles until they heard a spray of gravel in front of the house.

Shiva stormed outside. They didn't hear their mother move. Arya was the first to jump up and run to a window. Rahul stood next to the car. Even in the dusky light, the crumpled outline of what had been a pristine Ford Escort was jarring.

—*Ah couldn't tell yuh how Rahul climb outtah dat alive,* my mother says, *an bot e an e friend come outtah dat, barely ah scratch on dem so, eh Krys.*

Their surroundings darkened by the second. Rahul and Shiva stood staring at each other, night threatening to swallow them.

Pa, Rahul said, scratching the back of his neck as he approached his father, but Shiva produced something from behind his back. Arya squinted in the darkness unsure of what it was.

Wah is dat Pappy carryin? Amrit asked her, and Arya jumped, unaware the rest of her siblings had joined her.

Ah wantah help im, Arya said.

Nah Arya gyul, we kyant help im now, Amrit said, putting his hands around her shoulders as though to hold her there.

Without hesitation, Rahul turned around and fled, leaving behind his crumpled car, the tow truck, and the driver. Shiva disappeared under the house. They heard the sputter of the engine before the jeep roared to a start. A new hunt began. But evening tides had rolled in, and the smoky hues of periwinkle were replaced by a rich blanket of sunset blues.

E gone, said Arya.

Is bess, said Rebecca behind them, and they all jumped. *Dat mahn wuddah keel im dis time.*

They turned back to the window as the tow truck driver was yelling to get Shiva's attention. Their father's wrath was pointed in the direction Rahul escaped, but they all knew their brother must have dived into the thicket of trees by now. Shiva's only chance of finding his son would be to patrol the main road in the hope Rahul would emerge to hitch a ride into town, and even then the chances of Shiva discovering him at the right time would be very low.

Allyuh chilren goan toh bed now, Rebecca ordered. They pecked their mother a good-night kiss on her cheek and piled into their room.

Arya fell into a shallow pool of dreams but woke and dozed, woke and dozed, a cycle of sleeping and jumping until she heard her father's return. Her siblings' sleep was sound, their bodies and minds resting for the days to come.

There was no noise or commotion upon his entrance, just the shuffing of his feet as he removed his shoes, the creaking of the floorboards as he made his way to the bedroom, and the rustling of cloth as he changed.

—*Ah so happy, Krys,* says my mother, *dat e din ketch Rahul. Is bess e out dey dan e ketch im because de madness dat possess im when e din see Rahul come hwome dat day was someting else.*

When Arya and her siblings rose to the cock's crow in the morning, twilight still clung to the periphery of the world, but that didn't stop them from clambering over one another to race downstairs and see the car. It didn't escape them that their father had already left; they expected him to be up and in search of their brother again. Arya hoped to find out from one of his friends where Rahul was hiding. They'd all give him updates on their father's moods and let him know when was the best time to return home.

The car sat right where the tow truck had dropped it the evening before. The beautiful car was now a warped mess of spiked metal. Tree branches jutted out from the broken windows, and one of the doors hung despondently off its hinges. Jagged glass and steel protruded from every angle, making the car difficult to approach, impossible to touch. Where they once caressed it with their hands at the end of the day, now they all stood back, horrified. How Rahul managed to survive this crash unscathed was something they'd never understand.

—*Foh weeks Rahul hah toh hide from one place toh de nex, Krys chile,* my mother tells me, *from one family membah house toh ah friend, whoevah goh take im een foh ah lil while. Dey all know how Grampa does get when e like dat, it wasn't rheally no secret, juss someting we prefer not to tawk about.*

On their return home from school that day, the shattered glass glittered in the same place. Amrit insisted on asking Shiva if he wanted them to move the car for him.

Come nah, Arya gyul. Ahgo teach yuh how toh drive.

No, watch we goh geh lix foh juss axin.

Ahright, ah go ax im mehself and if e say is ahright, yuh wantah lun? We goh hah rheal fun.

How yuh know how to drive boi?

So dah is ah yes? Amrit said, throwing his head back and laughing, his bulbous Adam's apple dancing in silhouette. *Mahn, doh worry how ah lun, long time now ah know and is time yuh know too. Come nah gyul, yuh done sixteen almoss seventeen ahready.*

Arya stopped and considered. She desperately wanted to drive. She'd always dreamt of owning a car one day, wiping it down to keep it shiny, hanging an air freshener around the rear-view mirror so the inside would smell like wild cherries. Amrit extending this offer was such a gift, but she was afraid to breathe life into this dream, one her father could rip from within her grasp and throw a beating on top of.

Ah eh wahn yuh toh geh no beatin by yuhself foh helpin meh, said Arya. *Ahgo go wid yuh toh ax im boh not today, is rheally too soon. Lewwe at leass gih im ah week nah? Ah eh wantah find out wah e goh do today.*

A week unfolded before them. They knew now where Rahul was, information obtained from the same friend who was in the accident with him. But their father didn't. Shiva never asked them and they never told.

Amrit was galloping home next to Arya. They'd been lucky their father hadn't taken out his anger on them.

Yuh ready, Arya gyul? Yuh ready? We goan have ah rheall good time.

Amrit, wah make yuh tink it goh goh we way? Firss, yuh kyant ack so happy happy when we goan toh ax im.

Ahright nah gyul, doh worry.

But Arya was worried. Her father's wrath followed a pattern—first he exploded, and that was usually followed by a period of seclusion where he tucked himself away from the rest of the family; it was during this time she was terrified of disturbing him. They found him behind the cocoa house cooking something for himself over an open fire. Arya hung back, allowing Amrit to handle the situation. Her brother's demeanor changed when they were within their father's sight. His effervescent body language stiffened to somber, and his happy face drew downward.

Pa? Amrit said as he stepped toward him. *We notice de cah still right whey de mahn leff it and we was wondering if yuh wahn we toh move it dung de hill foh yuh. Me and Arya kyan do it.*

Leff it right dey, Shiva said. *De insurance people hah toh come and assess de damage. Doh lay ah fingah on it till dey reach.*

The infectious lightness that had taken flight inside Arya while she and Amrit pranced home that day evaporated when their father growled those words at them. Amrit deflated.

Ahright, Pappy, said Amrit.

Arya shot forward to grab her brother's hand so they could retreat to the house. *Come lewwe go fass nah, mahn,* she whispered.

ONLY A FEW DAYS LATER someone from the insurance company came. Arya and Amrit happened to be next to the house collecting eggs from the hens.

Come close nah, Arya gyul, said Amrit, *so we could hear bettah.*

Boi, me eh wantah geh no closah foh Pappy toh lick whey meh ass foh macoin, said Arya. *Yuh know how e hate when e feel people mindin e business.*

Amrit moved closer under the pretense of examining a calabash on the tree. It took everything for them both not to jump and hug one another when the man proclaimed the car junk. Their father looked pleased, and though they were confused, they hurried away from the duo standing by the car. They trembled with excitement as they placed the eggs in crates to take into the house.

Amrit, Shiva called.

They both froze mid-bend.

Yuh see wah ah mean? Arya hissed. *Doh stay bend so, goan and see what e wahn befoh it geh woss.*

Amrit placed the almost full egg crate at Arya's feet and jogged over to their father.

Take dis cah from hyah, ordered Shiva, *is junk. Dey goh come geh it when dey ready.* And their father climbed into his jeep and left.

Arya made two trips to put the eggs inside, then came out to find Amrit standing on the puckered hood. *Careful,* she warned him as she walked around the car herself, wondering how they could get in. Amrit bounced up and down trying to pop a portion of the hood back into place, but the serrated metal was rigid. His footsteps stuttered a bit as he tried to regain his balance, and a sliver of metal sliced into his skin. Blood dripped from above his ankle. Arya was alarmed.

Doh worry, gyul. Relax nah, he said as he ripped off a piece of his shirt and knotted it around his leg. *Come, ahgo show yuh how we goh geh in dey.*

Amrit leapt off the hood with the agility of a monkey and landed lightly on the ground. He wrenched at the door, which hung from its hinges, pulling and twisting until it gave way in his hands. He crawled through the back and folded himself into the crumpled front seat. *It eh too bhad,* he said, but Arya was doubt- ful. *A A gyul, we rheal lucky, de key een here ahready. Ah tawt we wouldah hah to hotwire de ting.*

The engine hacked to life as her brother turned the key, and for a second she was certain it wouldn't start. When it did, a happiness washed over her that made her tremble. She was so excited she started bouncing around.

Whey we takin it? she asked.

Dung de hill. Hop on de hood, lewwe go foh ah ride. Dis front seat eh een no shape foh yuh toh climb een.

But Arya declined this invitation, telling her brother to drive down, she'd be right behind him. Amrit drove down the hill on the other side of the house, past the well, past the chicken pens, and stopped at a razed piece of land.

—*Grampa di gettin ready foh anuddah chicken pen, Krys gyul,* my mother tells me, *so dere was dis nice piece ah open land just dey foh we toh use. Puhfek foh drivin.*

Their father had been preparing this plot for the erection of another chicken pen, bringing even more money to the farm. The once dense forest had been shorn of trees and grass, its expanse simultaneously breathtaking and overwhelming. Greens and yellows blurred before them under the sun. Amrit stopped the car at the edge of the field and climbed out, signaling for Arya to make her way in.

Trembling, she climbed into the backseat of the car, then through to the front. Her hands shook so badly, she was afraid she'd start crying. Never had Arya sat behind the wheel of a car, though it was something she'd fantasized about.

Her brother perched on the front fender and leaned toward the cracked glass to tell her what to do. He explained to her how she had to shift the gears so it didn't grind and get stuck. His directions came too fast for her—*Push de clutch, leh de clutch out slow, doh dungshiff!*—and she was confused, the loud sound emanating from the gearbox frightening her. The car bucked and reared like a horse, even throwing Amrit off a few times. But her brother knew just how nervous and anxious his sister could become, and he helped to calm her before they started again.

They passed the next couple of weeks this way. From the minute they woke up, they worked toward this time they shared together. It was their secret, and they didn't tell their other siblings, wanting to preserve the little gold they'd found.

Arya, though frustrated, was determined to learn to drive and started to understand what she had to do after a week. Together, they forgot how this car came to them; they forgot their eldest brother was no longer at home, but was still hiding and depending on the kindness of others to shelter him.

—*One munt di pass, yuh know, Krys,* my mother says to me. *One munt,* she says again shaking her head. *Rahul di gone foh dat long and who knows, Pappy was probably tryin toh find im de whole time, boh is was bess e din.*

Rahul sent messages with his friends, begging to know if he could come home. The generosity of people was running thin, and he had nowhere else to go. Arya was never sure of her father's frame of mind and therefore didn't voice her opinion, while her siblings told Rahul enough time had passed and nothing had happened in his absence.

Rahul came back to the farm jubilant to see the familiar faces of his family. He returned when his father was away and joined Arya and Amrit in scrubbing the concrete floors just outside the house. They had every intention of racing down the hill to continue Arya's driving lessons, but exchanged a look of understanding that said they couldn't with Rahul in tow. They had no idea how he would react to them taking advantage of his misfortune, or if he'd try to take the car on another joyride once he found out it was still running.

Anxious to be away from their older brother, they both fabricated chores and took separate paths to the field, where Amrit hopped on the roof and whistled for Arya to start. Now Arya barely needed guidance as she navigated uprooted tree stumps and grass-covered holes. When they were done that day, Amrit and Arya scurried through the rest of their routine and dove into their room with the others. They were afraid of how their father would react when he discovered Rahul had returned. Time passed, and their silence was filled with the familiar sounds of night.

Nothing happened.

—*We couldn't believe it, Krys chile,* says my mother, *de boi come back and nutten, nutten from Mistah Shiva. Wasn't like im nah, boh we take it when we get it.*

YET BITTERNESS DESCENDED all around them as the relationship between Shiva and his eldest son quickly hardened. The accident wasn't the only thing to blame, but they couldn't seem to recover from this point. In the weeks after his return, neither one moved toward ameliorating their relationship, and so Rahul started looking for a way to leave.

—*Tings di geh rheal bhad between dem, Krys,* my mother tells me, *everyting is ah beatin now, and e beatin ah big mahn so? Grampa din know how to communicate so e end up losin e chilren one by one.*

Gita, the eldest of them all, ran away with a man two decades her senior. Soon after, she left Trinidad for Bermuda, trading one island for another. Rahul reached out to her, telling her he wanted to go to America. Gita explained to him it would be easier to get to America from Bermuda and advised him to join her before applying for a visa to enter the States.

Rahul was hellbent on leaving, focusing all his energy and time on plotting his escape. Arya saw this and was scared for her brother, but mingled with that fright was envy. She wanted to be able to leave the farm behind the way he could, but the rules throughout the islands were different for women. Right now, under the protection of her father, she was safe. Out in the open she didn't know what could happen, and that scared her more than anything.

Stories of other girls leaving their homes reached their ears. Some, like Arya, left out of a thirst to explore but, without the support of family and someone to vouch for them, couldn't find jobs and had to return home. Parents were shamed for not being able to control their girl children, so when they returned, the acceptable societal reaction was to ostracize them. Other times girls came back pregnant, the story of the father refusing to marry her a common tale. The families then tried to raise the child as their own or give the baby away to someone else. But that daughter was now spoiled goods, couldn't be respectfully given away either. A flagrant mark burned on her the rest of her life.

—*Dah is how oman and dem treated on de island, Krys,* says my mother, *and dah is also why ah kyant juss pick up and leave like Rahul. Pappy ahready hah to hang e head een shame cause Gita juss pick up and leff and everybody find out. E din geh ah chance toh gih she ahwey de way e was suppose toh.*

Within two months of the accident, Rahul left. And within days of his departure, a brand-new Ford Escort was delivered to the property; a tow truck took the old one away. It was the same shade of blue as the last one, and for Arya, after having driven a broken car for so long, its sleekness was disconcerting. They realized now why their father had looked so pleased with the insurance assessment.

Since the elder siblings—Gita, Rahul, and Reeya—had already dispersed in one unpleasant way or another, that left Arya, Amrit, Pooja, and Chandini still at home. Arya, now the oldest, was taken aback and almost dropped the keys when her father handed them to her, telling her she could use the car to go to school.

—Krys gyul, says my mother, *it was de bicycle all ovah again. Ah couldn't ack nohow. Ah hah toh hol mehself togeddah and eh ack nohow.*

As soon as Shiva turned his back, Arya grabbed Amrit and jumped into the car. They took a spin along the main road and back. Their squeals filled the air as they rolled the windows down. Arya's curls streamed in the warm breeze. A smile played on her lips, growing to a grin. She glanced at her brother, and they both screamed out together.

NASTY LIL SINGH-IN SNAKE, they hissed at her, *slippery snake, yuh nasty lil cunt of a snake.*

As one of only a handful of students who owned cars, Arya had become a magnet for envy. Most of her classmates had seen at least one of the Singh brood grow up, and they'd grown accustomed to seeing their clothes riddled with holes, no shoes on their feet, mud smeared on their arms, the foul scent of animals clinging to them. Seeing Arya in a car while most of them walked or took taxis seemed to threaten their belief system.

—Ah wasn't no backward wid dis eiddah, eh Krys, my mother tells me, *cause is kickin off an kickin off een meh cah, sprayin up duss and everyting, makin ah rheal show foh people toh watch. Finally, ah hah someting. Dem juss couldn't handle it.*

Arya drove her car to Northeastern College for the rest of that term, anxious about her end-of-year exams. In January, she turned eighteen, a year older than everyone else since failing her Common Entrance exam in standard five.

—Ah hah toh pass six oh seven subjex toh move up, Krys, says my mother, *an considerin ah din like nutten dey gih meh, it was rheal hard.*

The week of testing dawned, and Arya wrote one subject after another, phrases starting to blend together as she was sucked into the vortex of exams. She emerged feeling lightheaded, the world around her a brighter place.

The next step was the University of the West Indies. Though Arya had never visited the campus, she dreamt of what it was like and how it would feel to walk down its corridors, the weight of textbooks in her arms. She imagined it to be a dignified building, the red, white, and black flag of Trinidad flapping in the courtyard, large windows encasing each floor. Arya wanted to be there, for she knew education was the best way off the farm. How fortunate her father would support her every step of the way.

But Arya only passed three of her subjects. Unable to move on to the advanced levels, she began to flail, unsure of what to do.

—*Yuh see, Krys,* my mother explains to me, *dere was no room foh mistakes. Eiddah yuh pass oh yuh fail at dis point. Dere was nutten foh me toh do.*

Her dream of attending university was disintegrating before her. Those hallways she envisioned started to shake and shift, replaced with images of Arya plucking fruits from trees for the rest of her life, her fingertips grayed and fuzzy from the stickiness of fresh produce. Informing her father she failed would only drive her further into the land. He would think she wasn't made for school and should stay at home with him, so Arya desperately searched for another way.

Had Arya passed her exams, she would have been able to continue to her advanced levels, her education a free ride. All other options now required her to pay. She had to choose between applying for jobs or trying for another school. She found one facility in Arima that allowed students in her situation to try to pursue their education. Because she had no other choice, Arya threw herself into this option. When she told Shiva she didn't qualify with her subjects, she also mapped out her other choice, detailing the cost for the semester, what route she would take, and the times she would be back on the farm.

Pa, she explained, *ahgo be able toh continue on. Plenty students like me does goh dey.*

Arya didn't know anything for sure; most of the information on the school she'd procured from hearsay. When her father grunted his approval and paid for the semester in full, Arya counted her blessings and worked hard in the two months' interim before starting.

Her elder sisters had all found some form of escape under the pretense of study. Gita went to San Juan, and Reeya to Tunapuna. Agreements between Shiva and members of his family in those areas were formulated so his girls could live with them, for a fee, while attending school nearby. Part of the agreement was that they'd all come home on the weekends, no excuses. His first two girls fled the farm for the same reason—they yearned to be closer to the vibrant life of the city.

When her sisters visited on the weekends, Arya wanted to live vicariously through them until she could attain the same for herself, but they were parsimonious with what they shared. Living in another world, they lorded it over her. They all marked Arya as the timid one. So far she'd been the only one who chose to stay, and they expected it to remain that way.

But then Arya saw what happened with her sisters over the years, and while she struggled between staying and leaving, she knew she didn't want to end up like them. Gita ran away and eventually ended up in America, but with six children all before the age of twenty-six; Reeya also eventually ended up in America, where she became pregnant with twin girls, flourishing a bouquet of flowers in front of her swelling belly at her wedding. If ever they needed to come back, they couldn't.

—*Not dat dey goh wantah,* says my mother, *boh dere was ah way toh do tings een Trinidad and dat wasn't de way.*

The morning dawned for Arya's fresh start at yet another school, and she was as determined as she'd always been. After she joined her siblings and parents in farm chores, she took some time to freshen up. She pressed some baby powder into her armpits and bosom; she inhaled the sweet smell. Fluffing her hair out with her fingers, she sprayed it into place. She would make a good impression this time.

Arya knew only that the school was about twenty minutes away in Arima. Never having seen it before, she drove slowly through the town, absorbing the colorful buildings along the way. Arya's driving slowed to a crawl as she stared at large houses with open galleries on the second floor, quite unlike the lopsided farms slapped together with boards and sometimes exposed brick. Stone balusters ringed the verandahs, lending a grand air. Horns honked behind her, and she was forced to pick up her pace. A man with coconuts hanging off his shoulders rapped on her window, but Arya shook her head and sped off.

In the heart of Arima, she pulled over, unsure of where to go. She popped her head out of the window and asked for directions to the school. Several people told her it was on the outskirts of town, and complimented her car. Arya wrinkled her upper lip, wondering what kind of school was so far away from the town's center. Parking in the shade of a mango tree, she trotted toward the place where people had guided her.

Before her was what appeared to be an abandoned cow shed. The doors had been ripped off their hinges, allowing wind that carried the rank scent of manure to sweep through the barn.

Dis kyant be it, Arya muttered to herself, checking her watch. She had another ten minutes or so before classes convened. Soon other girls and boys her age began filtering in. That was when Arya noticed crudely contructed benches placed throughout the shed. Groups of three or four people sat alongside one another, putting their books down at their sides. Arya stood just outside the doorway, reluctant to accept this was the school she'd signed up for.

—*Dat wasn't no school nah,* says my mother. *It was ah cow shed and de place smell like shit.*

Arya stared, disbelieving, from face to face as they all settled down to wait for an instructor to arrive. How could they stand the smell? How could they call this a school? It took everything in her being to sit down and look to the front. There was no floor beneath her shoes, only hardened dirt that had been trampled by many feet. Birds squawked and flew through their classroom, sometimes lingering to drop a dollop of feces.

Their teacher strolled in late. He was a large man with broad shoulders and calloused hands. His roughened neck resembled leather. When he boomed a welcome to them all, Arya knew this was a man who knew farm work. She wondered what he would be able to teach her concerning the delicate subjects of literature and history. The answer was nothing. He was there to help them even more with agriculture. Stewing in her seat, Arya hunkered down and waited for it all to be over.

In her car, she shook with rage and disappointment. The semester had been paid for in full; how could she now tell her father this was not what she wanted to do? Without a backup plan, something solid, Shiva wouldn't allow it. A thought entered her mind, but Arya pushed it to the side, hoping something else would come to her.

For one week Arya perched on a bench closest to the window in that cow shed. She listened as this man started with the forestry of Trinidad and Tobago. Already familiar with everything he said, Arya was sure she could teach this class herself, as could many of the pupils there. Agriculture for them was their only way of life. While some of the students seemed especially interested when the class discussed various species of fish, nothing could tempt Arya to stay here and finish.

And when nothing else revealed itself to her, Arya resigned herself to leaving school behind. All those who failed their exams at Northeastern in June were informed that the University of the West Indies offered six-month internships in different departments. If you did well, they kept you on. Arya wasn't ready to start working yet, but her only choices left were a job or the farm.

—*When ah say ah wasn't ready toh wok, Krys,* my mother explains, *ah wasn't ready toh give up on meh studyin as yet. Ah wanted so badly toh go toh school and den geh ah good job. If ah juss gone so toh geh ah job den is rheally low jobs yuh qualify foh, and ah wanted moh dan dat. So ah tell Grampa me eh goin back dey. De final backup foh me was de government job.*

THE UNIVERSITY WAS IN THE TOWN of St. Augustine, an hour's drive from Cunaripo and less than a half hour's drive from the capital city, Port-of-Spain. When Arya discovered where she'd be and how close it was to the city, an ache spread through her. All her life she'd wanted to be a part of the city scene, but she also thought being a university student was in her future.

Arya borrowed an outfit from one of her sisters and used a curling iron on her hair for the first time. Daubing some powder on her face, she spread it around, added a touch of rouge and matching lipstick, then took a step back to look at herself. Her transformation from a greasy farm girl to a primped interviewee astounded her. She was careful to avoid her father, slipping away while he was busy doing other things. In a bag she'd borrowed from a sister was a pair of hand-me-down pumps she'd never had an excuse to use before and her letter from the school detailing the date, time, and location of her appointment.

As she followed the signs to St. Augustine, the narrow roads opened up and grew spacious and curvaceous, Arya turning the steering wheel from left to right with delight. Being this far away from home for an unknown amount of time thrilled her. Signs for the university began long before she reached the town. Large savannahs fanned out on either side of the road, and Arya reveled in their avocado hues.

The roadway leading to the school was flanked by immaculate lawns. It was an impressive stretch that intimidated Arya. She had always thought that the day she stepped foot here would be when she was a university student. With a deep breath, Arya nudged the car forward and pulled into the closest parking lot. The Trinidadian flag flapped above her at the entrance to the building. Students milled about in starched uniforms, books held against their chest or slung over their shoulder in a backpack. They moved with purpose and vigor, their eyes bright with knowledge and understanding. Tears burned in Arya's eyes as she hustled into the cool interior.

Someone said her name softly, and Arya looked up. Striding toward her was a girl she knew from her early days in school. Neesha had sprouted into a tall young woman, almost taller than Arya herself. Her hair was pulled back into a thick ponytail that flipped out on her shoulders. Her amber-colored eyes were large and welcoming.

Ah eh see yuh so long, gyul. How yuh doin? Ah din know yuh goin here too. She flung her bookbag down between her sneakers and went in for a hug. Arya, not sure how to respond, stepped back. She never wanted to cross paths with anyone she knew. Knowing others were able to attend school was enough. Seeing them here was just too much.

Ah not hyah, Neesh, Arya stammered, *ah, ah juss here toh apply foh ah job.*

Their exchange following that was awkward. Arya created more and more distance between them, and Neesha seemed almost happy for it, really in search of an ally on campus. Neesha pointed her in the direction of the office she was looking for, and there Arya found a man behind a desk who took a distracted glance at her letter and said, *We only hah postal jobs available at de moment.*

Her mind raced. She didn't want to deliver mail, foreseeing how that job could be as tedious and mindnumbing as farmwork, but she didn't want to offend this man and end up jobless either.

Am, sorry mistah, boh is dere anyting else available? I don't rheally tink ah wahn dat, said Arya.

The man shoved together the papers he'd been shuffling around and stared at her over the counter.

Whey yuh from? he asked.

Sangre Grande.

Whey een Grande?

Arya hesitated. When she told him exactly where, he'd know for sure she was some farm girl looking to escape the country. He wouldn't help her then. But she couldn't come up with the name of another place fast enough, afraid he'd question her even more and realize she was lying.

Cunaripo.

And what kinda job yuh lookin foh, Miss Cunaripo?

Ah wantah wok een ah office, said Arya.

Oho! Een ah office yuh say. He seemed tickled by her. *Okay, hyah's de ting, chile, ah could set yuh up wid de Census Bureau, boh dat is de bess ah could do foh now. Stay dey an do ah good job and yuh could move up. Undahstood?*

Arya nodded, not sure what she was getting herself into. The man walked around the room, yanking sheets of paper from one drawer or another. Finally he stapled them together and handed them to her.

Fill dat out and come back nex week Monday, he told her in more of a whisper. *Meh name is Jo. Joseph. Yuh ax foh meh hyah and meh alone. Yuh will hah toh take some classes, boh yuh look like ah bright gyul.*

As he continued talking, Joseph filled the small office with his booming voice. There were a few other workers clacking away at their desks, but they didn't seem to mind him, and Arya wondered if he was in charge. Without a thank you, she stumbled backward and headed out the door. At the last second she looked back. *Mistah Joseph, tank yuh, tank yuh.* He waved her away, a smile stamped on his pleasant face.

Outside the door, students walked past her, but she was no longer looking at them; instead she studied the sheaf of papers in her hand. The first half required all her personal information, and the second detailed her job as a census official. Relieved to have a job, Arya leaned against the cool stone wall and closed her eyes. Noise seemed amplified, as though her hearing had suddenly been turned on. The light coming through the windows seemed brighter, sharp almost.

—*Ah geh ah job, Krys,* my mother says, *ah job! Foh de fuss time een meh life ah could acktually see mehself off dat fahm.*

Arya dashed out of the building, the electricity sparking through her barely contained. A man with a snow cone cart was parked close by. He fanned himself with a folded newspaper beneath an umbrella. His black skin gleamed from the glare.

Kyan I hah one ah dooze? An how much?

He scraped crushed ice from around his box and scooped it into the bottom of a white foam cup, pumped red syrup on top, drizzled a generous amount of condensed milk, and then repeated all three layers again. Arya's mouth watered, already tasting the sweetness. When she sucked on the straw, chunks of ice blended with milk, brown sugar, nutmeg, and cinnamon took over her senses. She thanked the man so profusely he had a bemused look on his face as she sauntered away.

When her official workweek arrived, Arya rolled in on a cloud of pure glee. She wasn't even dismayed when she realized she would be in the field for the Census Bureau. The training classes she attended for a week focused on how to best approach people and cajole them into answering personal questions about their household. Arya barely paid attention to any of the tactics, looking forward to escaping the room they were in to roam the streets of the city for an hour or so before heading home.

Because they knew Arya owned a car, they placed her within her district. She scrolled through the addresses in Cunaripo, Cumuto, Guaico, Tamana, even some more popular parts of Sangre Grande. Displeased she'd mostly be working within the rural areas, Arya decided to start in Sangre Grande first.

—*Grande was de tung toh be een, Krys,* my mother tells me. *It was de closess toh we, and every chance ah geh now, if meh kyant be een Port-ah-Spain den is Grande meh gone. Ah use toh juss like toh watch people sometimes. Watch dem buy clodes, watch dem drive dey cah. An just imagine and dream.*

Most families in Sangre Grande sympathized with Arya driving from house to house in the dusty heat just to fill out questionnaires. They invited her into their galleries to sit on their wicker chairs and offered her bottles of soda or glasses of homemade sorrel to sip on. While their glasses sweated along with their bodies in the heat, they patiently answered pages of questions until Arya reached the last batch, which covered personal income. Hospitality soured, and Arya was promptly escorted back to her car. Arya braced herself each time, feeling the air change around them as people bristled at the question about their annual household income, but try as she might, nothing she said could assuage their apprehension.

Why yuh need toh know dat foh? We doh know yuh. Who yuh goan an gih dis infohmation toh? Nah, goan from here now, chile, yuh done take up too much ah meh precious time.

Most of these people still kept their money away from banks, locked in iron chests beneath their homes, tucked into sofas, or filed away in the pages of books. Her father was the same, paranoid whenever people asked him questions about his business, so Arya understood them.

—Boh ah couldn't finish de questionnaire, Krys, my mother says. *Widdout dem answerin dem lass set ah questions it considah incomplete.*

Joseph's words echoed in her head, *Stay dey an do ah good job and yuh could move up.* But Arya was failing miserably. The farm families were the worst. They trusted no one, not even kin, so when she approached their houses with her broad smile and sheaf of papers, their suspicions grew with each question.

Yuh tink we hah time foh dis? they hollered. *Yuh eh see we hah wok toh do?* And if they knew her and her family, *Chile, wah de hell wrong wid yuh? Yuh eh come from ah fahm yuhself? Yuh tink ah hah time toh siddung so ansahrin question aftah question? Look, goh from hyah.* These were the ones who let her introduce herself and explain why she was there. Most of them tucked into the countryside didn't even let her in.

Arya returned to the Census Bureau's office with her unfinished questionnaires and ran through one excuse or another, hoping they would offer her another job, but she saw on their faces that they'd heard it all before.

Four months had passed. All she needed to do was hang on for another two more before she could switch departments.

If they let her.

—*Yuh see dere was still no assurance,* says my mother, *no mattah whey ah go, so ah know ah lucky toh be dey, but aftah ah while it eh feel so lucky no moh nah.*

On one of her days out, Arya came to a house that sat high on a steep hill. Her car threatened to roll back down the slope several times on the way up. She'd been to this house before, but no one had ever answered her call at the gate. That day she parked outside and honked her horn incessantly. She was as fed up with everyone as they were with her. Only for a few seconds at a time did she let up until someone rapped on the passenger side of her car. She jumped, a scream catching in her throat.

Aye gyul, said an Indian man in his thirties. *You is de one who does come rung here axin one set ah questions?*

Arya nodded.

Well lemmeh tell yuh someting eh, he continued, bending down further to be eye level with her. *Dat mahn up dey is ah rheal crazy mahn.* He pointed up to the house with a key while the rest jingled from a bunch. *Ah wouldn't mess wid e nah.*

In Trinidad, when someone issued a warning like that, you listened. Arya thanked him and kicked off in her little Escort. The next day she stormed into the Census Bureau ready to demand another position. She couldn't put herself in danger like that any-more, she planned to say to them; who knew what that man was capable of?

Arya stood before everyone in the office and told them of her close brush with a madman. She detailed how he drove her off his property, brandishing a cutlass in his hands, his hair wild and crazed about him.

—*Ah di ketch up een meh own lie,* my mother tells me. *Ah juss didn't wantah do dis job anymoh so ah tawt ah had to make it ah rheal performance, yuh know Krys?*

When she was done, she was out of breath from her perfor-mance and sure they would be on her side. When no one said anything, Arya added, *We should definitely mahk dat address so people know not toh goh dey.*

They let her go. *No more jobs available,* they muttered, and Arya suspected they sniggered behind her back after she left.

—*Meh only regret is ah din leave dat godforsaken job long befoh dat, Krys,* my mother tells me. *Huh! Four monts and nutten toh show foh it.*

IT TOOK ALL of Arya's courage to approach her father again for yet another opportunity. She realized how comfortable he'd gotten having her full-time on the farm again. Arya wanted none of it. Slowly, she was being sucked into the very life she'd been struggling to escape. When someone mentioned job openings from the Ministry of Labor, she wanted to be one of the first to show up. Surprisingly there was little resistance when she informed her father of her plan.

Arya pulled out a small box of clothes hidden under her bed, in the room she shared with her siblings. In it was some make-up, new clothes, and several pairs of heels she'd bought herself in Grande while working for the Census Bureau. Arya selected an airy blouse and checkered pants that adhered to her long legs. To complete the ensemble, she chose open-toed black stilettos. She wrapped the outfit up in a sheet and put it at the head of her bed.

Just as she did before, Arya waited for her father to leave before getting ready. She didn't know how long the application process would take, but Arya had every intention of lying to her father. This was her chance to explore the city, and she was going to revel in every second of it.

The Ministry of Labor was in the capital, Port-of-Spain, the heart of Trinidad. To get there took close to an hour and a half, and that included a walk, a taxi to Sangre Grande, and another taxi from there to the capital. Her driving was limited to rural areas, small towns, and villages, so this was the best way for her to get there. Used to traveling by now, she was just thrilled to get as far away from the farm as possible.

Arya had more than enough money for the trip wrapped in paper and stuffed into her brassiere. Her father had been unusually generous, and she wondered if he was testing her.

The dense wall of trees on either side of the taxi melted away to buildings taller than Arya had ever seen. Her face was plastered to the window as she watched people strolling along the sidewalk. At a stop was a couple with their arms linked at the elbows; they crossed the street. The man was dressed in a tailored gray suit, white collar standing at attention around his neck. The lady beside him was wearing a hibiscus red dress that clung to her curves. She wore lace gloves and held a matching lace umbrella over her head. Together they sashayed across the road as though aware they were the center of attention. Their brown skin was smooth and lustrous against the elegant fabrics covering their bodies.

Yuh eh see how dem wawkin hoity toity so, someone beside her said. *People like dem dey feel dey bettah dan we.*

Arya nodded to avoid confrontation, and though she hid the yearning on her face, it burned deep inside her. She wanted to be like that woman strolling the streets of Port-of-Spain.

All the passengers were eager to disembark after a long, hot ride, but none more so than Arya. This was her first time in the city, and she wanted to walk through this place she'd dreamed of so many times while cutlassing grass in Cunaripo.

Arya stopped to buy a snow cone from a peddler. Shops lined the streets on both sides. She licked the condensed milk off the top of her cone as she peered through the windows at women getting their hair done, their fingernails painted, their bodies measured. There were lights on in the middle of the day for ambiance, running water for convenience.

—*Krys gyul,* my mother says, *ah see wah de easy life was all about. People geh up een de mawin, de take ah showah, poh on some make-up, goh toh de mahket oh de shops, nobody toh ansah toh. Ah nevah hah dat.*

The freedom of eating what she chose, walking where she wanted without a time constraint, reignited her passion to leave home.

She walked past one financial building after another, their gray silence looming far above her. Eventually Arya came to the Red House. Statuesque palm trees stood in front, their fronds fluttering in the breeze. It was as beautiful as her textbooks promised. In school, she had learned it was constructed in 1844, many years before she came to exist. The building was painted red to celebrate sixty years of Queen Victoria's reign, parts of the structure made and finished in England before being shipped to and assembled in Trinidad. Since then it had been called the

Red House, though its color seemed burned, almost copper at midday. Two wings of the Red House fanned out before her, an archway connecting them together above the street. Domed windows and doors, columns running all around.

—*It look like ah castle, Krys,* says my mom. *Ah nevah see ah buildin like dat een meh whole life. Ah feel important juss bein dey and watchin it.*

Her stomach began to rumble, calling for food. Too anxious to be on her way that morning, Arya hadn't eaten anything since the day before. She looked around for a vendor and found someone selling Trinidad's most popular street food—doubles. She asked for one with just a touch of pepper. In seconds an open doubles lay in her palms. Curried chickpeas steamed in between two slices of fried split-pea buns. Two of those with a side of cream soda were her brunch that day.

The Ministry of Labor was located in a slender building. Within its walls was a flurry of paper and people clacking away at typewriters, yelling back and forth to each other. It wasn't the calm she imagined, nothing like the Census Bureau office at the university. The onslaught of activity took her by surprise, but she welcomed it. Anything to be in an office environment. Amid the activity, someone steered her through two sets of doors to a second, much quieter office where a lady sat talking on the phone, with several women behind her doing the same.

When one of them waved her over, Arya approached timidly. The woman's eyes roamed Arya's slim legs, the curves of her waist, the muscles in her flat stomach as the blouse rippled over it, her fluffed-out curls, only to land on Arya's carefully made-up face with contempt.

Wah yuh here foh? she snapped.

Arya explained she was there for a job, described her work

background, and expressed her desire to be in an office in the city. She even attempted to sweet-talk the lady by saying, *All ah allyuh look so happy hyah, if only ah could be bless like you and wok here too.*

Wah? Yuh wantah wok here? The lady laughed at her. *Wah kinda experience yuh hah toh be wokin een ah place like dis? Look,* she continued, looking at a sheet of paper before her, *we eh hah no opahnins hyah oh anywhey close toh hyah. De bess one foh yuh is een Grande. Close toh yuh house een de bush.* This last bit she said with a sneer.

They didn't need anything from her. There was no formal interview, and all Arya walked away with was a job description of clerical work in the Social Welfare office in Sangre Grande.

—*Little dat oman know wid she wide self,* my mother says, *is dat Grande was moh dan good enough foh meh as long as ah geh wok een tung.*

So scrumptious was the doubles before, Arya went back again before heading to the bus and bought an aloo pie—fried dough stuffed with potatoes, spices, and onions. This was one of the few times Arya had bought herself food, and the experience was powerful—consuming meals she hadn't prepared.

Arya spent the day strolling through the capital.

—*Remembah, Krys,* my mother says, *all meh life ah wasn't allowed toh go anywhey oh do anyting. Dis was meh chance.*

On the bus ride home, Arya used her training from the Census Bureau to come up with a lie that would allow her to wander Grande every day until her job began. She would tell her father she had to take a secretarial training course in the city before being stationed at the Sangre Grande office. And so day after day she returned to Port-of-Spain just to browse the shops and eat street food to her heart's content. She fell in love with

Kirpalani's, a small store that sold everything from food to clothing. Then she discovered the sleeker, more upscale Woolworth's department store. Here Arya touched satin blouses and cotton sheets softer than she'd ever imagined. Buried in between shelves she unearthed things she never heard of before—candle holders, vases, decorative bowls, delicate glasses with stems.

On her second-to-last day in the city, she had to drop off some paperwork at the Ministry of Labor, and she spotted the director emerging from the front of the building. As she approached, she saw him chatting with someone, a handsome young man with eyes the color of brown sugar. The young man was dressed in his police uniform, every piece of clothing on him ironed and starched to perfection. His hands were clasped behind him, lending an easy air to his walk. As they strolled past her, Arya noticed a police officer's cap dangling from the tip of his index finger. For someone so young and in such formidable company, he was quite comfortable. They stopped for a second as the director asked the young man if he'd like to get something to eat.

No, tank yuh, suh, said the young man. *Meh muddah pack ah nice dhalpouri roti and curry duck foh meh.* He patted his trim stomach.

Dat is wah ah like toh hear, said the director.

They moved out of earshot, but Arya continued looking in their direction, the young man shaking his pleasantly square head moving from left to right as he conversed and walked.

—It was yuh faddah, my mother tells me, laughing. *E was rheal goodlookin yuh know. Rheal Indian starboi material.*

WOOING

—*Krys, dem oman an dem eh play dey use toh swoon for yuh faddah nah,* my mother says as she drizzles rum and wine over a freshly prepared black cake. *E was charismatic, ahgo gih im dat, but oh lawd e eh play was obnoxious too nah.* My grandfather's situation in the hospital seems to melt away as my mother remembers herself as a teenager.

At eighteen, Arya was the youngest and by far the sexiest of the many secretaries in the Social Welfare office. When she signed in or out for the day, or for lunch, a shadow fell over the lines of the book—the young policeman she saw at the ministry was now temporarily stationed there.

As Arya finished the last flourish over the *H* of her last name, he leaned in closer. She placed her lacquered nails over her signature. *Oh Gawd tell meh yuh name nah dahlin,* he said. *Look how long now ah tryin toh find out de preety preety name toh match de preety preety face.* With the flick of a finger, she shut the book and sashayed away. By now, Arya had grown into her limbs and controlled every movement, from the shiver of her hair as she let it cascade down her back to the snap of her skirt as it moved with her legs.

Dharmendra leaned against one of the desks, arms folded, ankles crossed, and he gulped her in as she walked away—her stilettos clicking and clacking on the tiled floor, black fishnet stockings stopping mid-thigh where her skirt began, a skirt suctioned on tight enough it looked impossible to peel off, and the scalloped neckline of her blouse revealing just enough cleavage to drive a man insane. Her lips were painted the same shade of pink as her nails, and her hair was styled in bouncy curls, unfurling around her shoulders and down her back.

—*Krys,* my mother tells me, *e use toh walk ahrung wid e heavy boots makin dis noise 'tok-tok-tok' and dat use toh aggravate meh toh no end. And e was loud. Loud and obnoxious, callin toh every Tom, Dick, and Harry befoh e evan entah de buildin. And e always hah dem oman and dem swoonin. From de time dey hear e comin is ooooh dis and oooooh dat. Moh reason toh ignore im.*

Arya cleared her throat and sat at her desk, smoothing her hands over her skirt, dusting off her blouse, aware his eyes were still on her. He picked his way in and around the office, making his way to her station. Dharmendra hailed everyone, even those he didn't know.

—*Yuh faddah was boisterous,* my mother tells me, *no uddah way toh put it. Loud and obnoxious. Ah couldn't stand im. Ah just wanted im toh leave meh alone and foh so de more ah try toh geh rid ah im de more e followin meh.*

When he reached her desk he said, *How yuh doin today, doo doo dahlin?* Her response to this question was a fierce look in her liquid brown eyes and the whip of her curly mane over her shoulder. This did nothing to deter Dharmendra. He gave her a boyish grin, a stray lock of hair falling across his forehead. He swept it away, whipped out his police baton and twirled it in his hand. Arya turned away from him, positioned her fingers over the typewriter and hammered away. He didn't have to slink away in shame because she ignored him; someone was always ready to strike up a conversation with him, and before he moved away from her, he always said something to the effect of *Oh Gawd dahlin, yuh look even nice-ah when yuh vex.*

At the end of the day, all the secretaries organized their desks, scrawled reminders for the next workday, and gathered round one desk or another to make plans for the weekend. All except Arya.

—*Dey din like meh nah,* my mother confides. *Ah was de youngess one dey. Young and hot hot hot in meh miniskirt and tight pants. I din care what nobody tink. And dem hen an dem only peckin cause is always de Sital boi dis and de Sital boi dat. Oh, who goh geh im. Dey eh like it atall dat ah gettin all e attention now specially since ah was new nah.*

What these women didn't know was that Arya had gone almost all her life without friends. With constant work to do on the farm, she just didn't have any time. If she did get away, it was in secret with her sisters, and that was always more than enough— knowing they would all share the blame if they were caught.

Arya strode out the door without saying good day to anyone. They followed her out of the corners of their eyes and ignored her as she ignored them. No waves. No smiles. The brisk island wind tunneled around her.

At her car, she unlocked and opened the door to release the pent-up heat from the day's sun. The Escort still smelled brand-new. She breathed it in, still proud to be the only Singh child to have a vehicle. It didn't even matter that her father only gave it to her after giving it to Rahul first.

Arya ran her index finger on the dashboard. It needed another cleaning. Though she scrubbed the Escort down inside and out twice a week, she wanted to stay on top of the dust accumulation. Sweat beaded on her forehead, stuck her back to the seat. She rolled the window down and leaned forward, pressing her forehead on the steering wheel. It had been a busy, monotonous week of issuing monthly checks to pensioners and helping poor people fill out paperwork in hopes of getting checks of their own.

A sharp rap on the half-rolled window made her jump. Dharmendra filled the gap with a grin. He leaned his crossed arms against the windowpane, the black hairs on his light-complexioned arms pressed against the glass.

How yuh doin, dahlin? he asked.

He stuck his head into the car. Arya slapped her palm against his sweaty forehead and pushed him back out the window. After he stuck his head into the car again and started with *A A oman, wah wrong,* Arya rolled the window up, pumping her arm as fast as she could. His chin got caught, and she pinched it with the window. The grin on his face never faltered, not even as he massaged the red spot on his handsome face.

—*Krys chile, e di like how spicy ah was,* my mother tells me. *Ah wasn't like dem uddah oman an dem bowin dey head an playin de ass shy shy shy when e tawkin to dem, giggling like lil schoolchilren when e tell ah joke. Me? Ah wok on fahm land day een and day out no mattah wah kinda job meh hah durin de day. Ah coulda stand up like ah man and is so ah do.*

Dharmendra smiled at her as though he had her all figured out. He had a small mouth with small teeth and the straightest, most even smile she'd ever seen. Like most other Indian men on the island, he'd taken to chewing tobacco—she hoped it was just an interest an elderly family member had sparked that would soon die down. Though not quite yellow, his white teeth were already losing their shine. Everything else about him was trimmed and proper, from his daily clean-shaven face to his starched uniform and shined shoes, though she realized he couldn't bring himself to tame his full black hair. When he removed his hat and ran his fingers through his hair, she glimpsed the little jolt of pleasure it stirred in him. He had the head of an Indian movie star, and he knew it, with his high cheekbones and light complexion.

—*Ah di undahstand why dem oman and dem trippin ovah deyself foh im,* my mother says, *boh not me.*

Cocking his head, he knocked on the window again and motioned for Arya to roll it down. She did, but only a crack. Dharmendra wedged his thick fingers into the space, pressing the window down. *Aye gyul, yuh is someting else, yuh know.* Without air circulation, Arya started to sweat. Her breathing was ragged. She needed water.

Ah eh know wah yuh doin, Arya said. *Leave meh alone. Clearly meh eh interested, boh you eh know nutten about gettin de message.* She squeezed his fingers in the window. He winced but kept smiling. *Oh Gawd dahlin, roll it up ah lil moh nah, it eh hut meh nuff yet.* Arya laughed. Sensing he'd broken the barrier between them, he dove in. *So wah bout yuh name, dahlin? Ah eh looking foh nobuddy toh tell meh. Ah wahn yuh toh tell meh yuhself. Ah wantah hear it from dem sweet lips. And oh Gawd, what ah color yuh paint on dem lips. Wah is de name at dat color, eh doo doo dahlin? Burgundy? Rose petal?*

Meh name is Arya, Arya said.

Yuh look like an Indian star gyul. Preety juss like dem. Prettier evan.

Look boi, meh eh hah time foh dis nonsense. Ah hah tings toh do.

So wah people does call yuh? R foh short? Ya-ya?

Arya.

Yeah, is ah rheal nice Indian name.

Tank yuh, boh doh tell me wah ah ahready know.

Ayayai gyul, yuh eh easy nah. How bout one ah dese days we goan get some lunch rung hyah.

—*Yuh know, Krys,* my mother says, *Grampa di make sure all ah we di hah we raasi name, we Indian name. We doh choose dat, yuh know, de pundit does choose dat foh yuh. Big name ceremony and ting each time.*

She rolled the window down and deliberated a moment. An angry red line ran across the back of his hand where it had been trapped. He tried to fill the quiet between them, afraid she'd decline. *Oh Gawd gyul, is lunch meh axin foh. And watch meh hand nah, is trap yuh trap meh foh so long and is because ah de sweetness ah yuh voice meh eh feel no pain, boh if yuh say no now meh goh feel everyting.* Her face brightened at this obvious palaver but never before had she heard sweet-talking with such intensity, such sincerity. No one had ever told her over and over that she was beautiful. After the growth spurt that earned her the nickname *Tin, Tall, and Terrible,* her sisters would introduce her as *An deez Arya, she de ugly one.* Her outgoing sisters would enjoy themselves while Arya slunk to the back, feeling exactly as they described her—ugly. Only after a couple of them had abandoned home and she'd started working, spending more and more time away from the farm, had she started to buy pretty things with her own money—skirts, heels, stockings, blouses—but never did she let Mr. Shiva happen upon any of them.

Arya dipped her head in agreement.

Dah is ah yes, gyul? Is yes yuh sayin? Yuh kyant take it back now yuh know. Oh Lawd Gawd, is smile yuh smilin on meh today.

Ahright ahright ahright doh push yuhself now befoh ah change meh min. Lemmeh goan now. Is wok meh hah toh wok when meh reach hwome.

You goh head, doo doo dahlin sugah plum plum, reach hwome safe, and ah goh see yuh tomorrow foh lunch.

Arya shook her head as she pulled away, only smiling when he could no longer see her, inhaling the sweet names he'd called her like a heady fragrance. Somewhere on a deserted road, long before she reached home, she pulled over and changed into clothes her father would find more suitable to work in and wiped most of the make-up from her face.

They went out to lunch the next day and the day after that. It soon became an everyday affair. Arya told no one at home, afraid this would somehow be ripped away from her if she did.

—*Doh evah tell yuh faddah meh tellin yuh dis,* my mother warns, *boh ah was goin foh de food. And papa yo de places e use toh take meh, chile! Rheal nice. Doh mind e hah toh tawk toh Tom, Dick, and Harry everywhey we go, boh dem places was niiiice. Ah wasn't goan give dat up too easy nah. Yuh tink ah coulda afford places like dat? Ah guess somewhey along de way meh staht toh like im back, doh mind ah din wantah admit it because ah di hate e guts so much in the beginning.*

PROPOSE

DHARMENDRA DOTED ON ARYA. He took her out to the finest restaurants on their lunch breaks. They sipped wine from goblets and water from stemmed glasses. Arya unfolded linen napkins to place them on her lap and fingered multiple utensils as he told her what each was used for, though she never remembered. She listened as he told her of his travels throughout the Caribbean islands, South America, England, India, America, Canada. He traveled thanks to the money he saved but also because he had no responsibilities and could. At only nineteen, she was impressionable and marveled at the majesty of these places, having never even set foot in many parts of their own island. She wondered if she would travel half as much by the time she was twenty-seven like him.

Coming from a father who was a policeman, and being a policeman himself, Dharmendra had inherited many connections and fostered many more of his own. Through him, Arya met the elite of Trinidad—ministers and politicians, musicians and entertainers. They all greeted Dharmendra with an air of comfort and refinement. This was the life she craved, to be in the midst of a thriving city, to mill around and shop, have the power to bargain for items, dine out when she pleased, to mingle, to laugh; to remove herself from the toils of the farm. But Trinidad was but a speck on a map, *ah drop ah oil,* and there was only so far she could go.

—*Patience Krys,* my mother explains, *ah wait cause meh hah toh do everyting de right way, de traditional way.*

Posing as her brother's friend, Dharmendra started making regular visits to the farm. To support their ruse, Amrit sat and talked with Dharmendra. Shiva sometimes joined them.

Arya, Shiva called.

Yes, Pa? she asked, already running wet fingers through her curls, dabbing her face with a kitchen towel, and running her hands over clothes she would never wear off the farm.

Bring we some watah and metai.

She set the water glasses on a tin tray and arranged the Indian sweets around them to cover up the blackened parts where the silver was chipped. Shiva was never one to buy new things if the old things were still functional. Her sisters pointed and giggled at her. Dharmendra never seemed to notice her ragged appearance. Never once did he show displeasure with the difference between her home and office attire.

Everyone could see how enchanted Shiva was with Dharmendra. He was a young, light-skinned Indian boy who came from a prominent family, a perfect addition to his household. This boy would elevate his status in society. And Dharmendra didn't shy away from religion; he conversed for hours, openly talking about being a devout Hindu often delving into beautiful renditions of the stories of various gods and goddesses on the Hindu spectrum.

They talked about weather, farming, religion. But when Dharmendra brought up politics, Arya and Rebecca stiffened in the next room, for politics was divisive in Trinidad, and they were nervous that this topic would cause a rift between the men.

Inching closer to the door, mother and daughter together craned their necks to better hear, but Shiva said something much too soft for their ears. Then the silence was broken by a chortle from both men. Arya hadn't realized she'd been clutching at her heart and holding her breath. Right then she understood how much her father's complete approval of Dharmendra meant to her.

Ruby. Shiva beckoned his wife next. He ordered her to make them some cutters, and she retired to the kitchen to fry or chunkay something fresh—saltfish akra, sehena, pulorie. Rebecca fried the balls of fishcakes, dollops of spinach and dough, and ground split-pea patties to a golden brown and then blended and seasoned some mango chutney as a dipping sauce.

Arya, Pooja, and Chandini scrambled to the second floor to peer from the holes in the floorboards. Shiva and Dharmendra did not always agree on everything they talked about, but with Dharmendra's jovial manner, there was no antagonism. Amrit remained silent most of the time, staying only as long as necessary, for he had chores to do. Arya could see that her father was smitten by how he allowed Dharmendra to smoke his cigarettes downstairs while they talked. Her father threw his head back and practically unhinged his jaw when he laughed, which frightened her more than anything, having only seen him laugh a handful of times and only when spying.

—*E use toh go huntin every Sunday,* my mother tells me, *leave late Saturday and come back Sunday evenin. Wid some friends, just ah couple, and one ah e cousins. Dey use toh goh on de rivah and bade and ting. Dat was de only time ah evah rheally see im laugh. Wid dem.*

When Shiva was leaving, Arya circumvented her father by walking around the back of the house to get to Dharmendra. Her mother and her siblings kept an eye out for her. Plopping herself down on the seat her father had just vacated, she popped a fritter in her mouth and gulped water from one of the tumblers. *So,* Arya said, plucking one of the topics from the day's conversation and dangling it in front of Dharmendra, making fun of both him and her father. They kept their laughter low as they rocked back and forth on their chairs. They both cherished these short moments together, and in between meetings, Dharmendra sent handwritten love notes along with one of her sisters whenever he could.

Yuh faddah reach back, Rebecca's words bustled in before she did. *Come come come Dharmendra, goan home now, yuh goh see she tomorrow. Nuff foh today,* and she shooed him out the front to where his car was parked. Mother and daughter smiled as he drove away, Rebecca as smitten with him as her husband.

—*Yuh know yuh faddah was de only one toh do dis,* my mother reminds me. *None ah meh bruddahs and sistahs de hah courtship and ting. And Shiva dint wahn nobody comin rung de house like dat. No blessin and celebration. Not-ting like dat. Krys, yuh parents' blessin is everyting. Remembah dat.*

IN THAT WHIRL of expensive restaurants, bouquets of flowers, and boxes of chocolates, Arya and Dharmendra spent their free time eating, dancing, and drinking. Their special song was "Red Red Wine," and in true Caribbean spirit it was the rendition by Bob Marley and the Wailers. Who cared who originally sang it as long as theirs was a West Indian lilt they could jam to.

—*It was we favorite song because yuh faddah was always drunk,* my mother tells me. *Meh nevah know de mahn sobah.* And, depending on when she told the story, her tone shifted to *Krys, e use toh drink too much. Wasn't no joke why dat was e favorite song nah. Sometimes e couldn't even walk an ah hah toh pull e drunk ass een de cah juss toh reach hwome een time.*

After some time, Arya told Dharmendra they were not working out. There was no one reason, but his constant state of drunkenness didn't help. She also wanted to test him to see what he would do if she tried to leave.

Dharmendra professed his love to her on his hands and knees, flinging his arms wide.

—*Yuh know yuh faddah had ah ting foh Shakespeare,* my mother tells me, *so is rheal drama foh dis one. Ah never know if e know ah was testin im, yuh know.*

Arya pushed him away. Able to do it once, she did it again. His words followed her home. *Arya, if yuh leave meh ahgo keel mehself. Ahgo keel mehself, Arya!*

Later, deep in the Cunaripo bush, she heard word of Dharmendra being hospitalized. With Rebecca's help, Arya slipped out of the house undetected to go and check on him. When she got there, Dharmendra was unconscious, hooked up to an array of machines that bleeped and clacked. His mother was weeping over him. She held his shoulders and cried out, *Oh Bhagwan! Meh boi, meh Dharmendra boi, meh sweet sweet boi. Oh Bhagwan, why yuh do this?* His father, in his starched policeman's uniform, was sitting in a chair next to his son's bed.

—*When ah tell yuh, Krys,* my mother says, *rheal Indian movie ting gone on dey. Poor gyul, rich boi, muddah bawlin. Boh dem movie and dem always hah ah happy endin right?*

Dharmendra's father noticed Arya and stood. She sidled in. His mother looked up. Her face was splotchy. She said, *Come, meh know e go wahn yuh hyah.* Arya stood next to the bed, not sure what to do; she interlaced her fingers with his mother's and asked what happened.

Dharmendra's mother had found him in his room at dinner-time. She'd been calling for him, hollering about the roti being done. When the roti got stiff, she decided to go up and check on him herself. He was on his bed, a large empty pill bottle next to him. His mother knew the strength of the pills—they were hers. Her screams brought her husband up, and with his son draped over his shoulder, he raced to the hospital across the street. Dharmendra's father waited for no one.

The hospital staff was intimately associated with the Sital family from frequenting their store and rum shop, but also because Dharmendra himself worked there while on duty. The staff rushed to his side and crowded around, pushing the family back. They pumped his stomach.

Now dey juss replenshin de fluids een e body, his mother told Arya. *Why e gone and do someting like dis? E is ah happy boi, ah rheal happy boi.* Arya froze. She thought the questions were for her, but realized they weren't when she saw his mother looking to the heavens. Neither Arya nor Dharmendra offered any explanation to his parents after Dharmendra awoke, but they shared a new secret now, one that bound them ever more tightly together.

IN RESPONSE TO HER TEST, to Arya, his was the ultimate display of love—the willingness to sacrifice your life for the one you love. But it could also be a trap, designed to force someone to stay. Despite it all, Arya and Dharmendra's love story unfolded.

One morning they arrived at work at the same time, something that rarely happened. There were rumors that they were an item, but for the sake of a good woman's family name, Dharmendra was supposed to follow the correct protocol: fall madly in love with her without ever talking to her or taking her out, ask for her hand in marriage, and then whisk her away to live with him in his family's house. Even though they both knew this, and even though prying eyes would follow them, Dharmendra convinced Arya to walk around the back with him, delaying their entrance to the building where they would part ways again and start their day.

There was a vagrant blocking the rain-drenched walkway, someone they knew because this island was so tiny, even the beggars became friends. An acrid smell hung around him, his shredded clothing revealing more bone than flesh. He'd fallen asleep in the rain and was soaked through, mud melted away revealing a much younger man under the mask.

Dharmendra was pressed and shined from the collar of his uniform to the tip of his steel boots. His hat sat smack in the middle of his head, perfectly aligned with his symmetrical features. He walked cockily toward the man, twirling his baton.

Aye, Dharmendra said, *yuh know dis here eh propahty foh yuh toh be lyin on. Goan move out de way.* He gave the homeless man a stiff kick in the ribs, eliciting a deep groan that made Arya's insides crumble.

—*E was showin off, Krys,* my mother whispers, *juss showin off to show off, no uddah reason.*

She put her hands on his shoulders and pulled him back with a soft *Dharmendra,* but that riled him up even more.

Yuh doh see ah lady een yuh presence awah? Move nah yuh muddahcunt yuh. Is ah policeman yuh disobeyin, yuh know.

Dharmendra, once her reprieve from the anger and violence at home, now rose before her to embody all she strove to escape.

—*E beat dat mahn foh no reason, Krys,* my mother says, *beat im and kick im like a dawg.*

A few days later Arya overheard some gossip about a vagrant dying. It was the man Dharmendra had beaten.

—Ah doh tink e was de cause foh de mahn death, boh e din help, my mother says. *Ah see dis violence een im dat day. When e tun dat on meh, it shouldah be no surprise, boh undah de circumstances, ah nevah tawt e wuddah evah do anyting toh meh.*

Omens and warnings were luxuries Arya couldn't afford; she was following the only route available to her at the time, the only thing that could get her off that farm.

A FEW WEEKS PASSED, and the memory of the vagrant, though still present, began to fade. One day after work, Arya and Dharmendra stopped at his parents' shop. Arya knew the inside well. Whether she had the extra money or not, while trotting home from school as a little girl, she'd stop in to have a look. There was always a spread to choose from: digestive biscuits coated in chocolate and wrapped in shiny foil, coconut cakes, caramel layered wafers, currant rolls, fudge, pepper mango, cheese-flavored wheels, salted prunes, fried split peas, spicy cheese curls, plums and cherries preserved with peppers and lime, and sugared tamarind balls just the perfect balance of tart, sweet, and spicy.

But Arya always walked past the array of soda bottles boasting the richest flavors of lemon, lime, cream, sorrel, apple, banana, ginger beer, and pineapple—past the wire mesh separating owner from customer—and stopped in front of a ball machine, its glass case stocked high with rubber balls of every color. They were waxy and bright and bounced high and fast, and for a nickel, a ball of a random color would shoot through the open slot at the bottom. If you weren't careful, it would fly past your hands and ricochet off the glass counter and, if you were truly unfortunate, would bounce out onto the busy road, rolling into one of the stagnant drains and slowly sinking into black gunk.

Usually Dharmendra's youngest brother, Ram, was the one grudgingly stuck in charge for the day. He watched as Arya came in time after time, spun her nickel, caught the bullet, and frowned. A hot pink ball was the one on display and a hot pink ball was the one she wanted. Rebecca never dressed her daughter in pink and, deprived, Arya became obsessed with the color.

One day Ram, in a magnanimous mood, jumped off his perch, unlocked the door, and walked around the counter. *Look nah, juss tell meh which one yuh wahn,* he said. *Yuh always leavin hyah wid one sowah puss look on yuh face no mattah which one yuh geh.* She pointed to the one on display. When he handed it to her, she just stood there staring at the luminescent pink marbled with curlicues and spirals, rolling it around in her sweaty palms. It glistened with perspiration. Ram slammed the top of the machine shut; Arya jumped. She stuffed her hand in her pocket and extracted her nickel. *Nah, gyul, keep yuh money. Maybe now yuh goh buy someting since yuh geh yuh ball.* But she bought nothing.

When Arya arrived with Dharmendra that day, Ram wasn't there. Another of Dharmendra's younger siblings was working the counter downstairs.

Nobody upstairs, Arya. Come wid meh lemmeh grab one ting nah. Though Arya was nervous, she was curious to see their home. On the second floor there was the familiar scent of garlic browning in oil. She turned to leave. *We kyant go back dung now, it goh look bhad,* Dharmendra said.

In the kitchen, his mother turned to them, every inch of her dusted with flour, and said, *Hello, beti,* calling Arya the Hindi word for daughter. A warmth like fresh honey trickled inside her. *Hello,* Arya said, looking down at the floor.

Allyuh wahn someting to eat? To drink? Yuh now comin hwome from wok, beta? she said to her son. Dharmendra made his way to the fridge, searching for a bottle of Pepsi; finding none, he volunteered to go downstairs for more. *Gimmeh some mango takarie wid ah piece ah roti toh hold meh ovah till latah nah, Ma.*

His mother studied Arya. They'd only seen one another in passing a handful of times before, and Dharmendra was always at her side. Her scrutiny didn't make Arya uncomfortable; her own clothing did. She knew that, from his mother's perspective, she was not a good candidate for Dharmendra. His family, like all Indian families on the island, wanted a docile Indian girl who wore traditional clothing and jewelry, her long hair parted modestly in the middle and pulled to the back of her head in a ponytail or wrapped in a bun. Instead what his mother found in front of her was a young woman with tights suctioned to her long legs, and an even tighter top, towering over everyone in her high heels, with curls teased high above her head and lacquered nails that matched her handbag.

Ma, Dharmendra said upon strolling back into the kitchen. He slipped one arm around Arya's waist and gulped Pepsi with the other. *Yuh know dese de gyul meh goan propose to?* His mother didn't react with more than *A A yuh doh say? Four monts and yuh done know,* disbelieving her own son.

Arya replayed what he'd said in her mind. She didn't know how to react because she didn't know the meaning of the word *propose.* She said the line over and over again, hoping the meaning would reveal itself to her. She smiled ambiguously at both of them. The twinkling in Dharmendra's eyes and the way his mother responded gave the word heft. Arya continued to nod and smile knowingly. She couldn't ask because that would only anchor their opinion of her more firmly—*ah uneducated country bookie from de bush.*

The rest of the evening passed without another mention of

this word. The only thing on her mind was getting to the gilded *Webster's Unabridged Dictionary* back home that someone had given to her father as a gift.

Arya sped home in her blue Escort. She rolled the window down. Wind whipped her hair in between her lipsticked lips. Once home, she ran her index finger down the page.

Dharmendra intended to marry her.

A waterfall of emotions thundered down on her until it dissipated to the calm below the pounding water, in a pool where her thoughts rippled.

—*Krys chile,* my mother says, *meh eh hah no love foh dis mahn yet. Ah din evan know wah love was. Ah eh know nutten bout sex, me, dis innocent gyul from de bush, meh know how we society see we as uncivilize, so wah de ass dis mahn talking bout proposal aftah four monts only.*

Arya, aware of her attitudes and the restrictions of her culture, considered Dharmendra's propostion. This respectable man could become her husband. She would leave her parents' home the right way. This man from the city could take her away from a life of latrines and wells and kerosene lamps and cock's crows, and give her one with indoor plumbing and electricity. A simpler, more refined life than she or her mother could ever have dreamed of. After waiting, after courting, after doing everything right, she knew he was her only way out.

HOUSE

—AH WANTED TOH *get ahwhey from dey,* my mother tells me while mashing some food she would later box up and send for my grandmother to spoonfeed my grandfather, who could now eat food after the three surgeries were done. *Ah wahn ah house wid ah inside step goan upstairs, not dis oudside step we hah hwome dey. An ah dunno why, boh ah ahways see mehself married toh ah police-mahn, somebody een authority. Ah mahn een ah uniform.*

Her dreams didn't change much over time; the same things propelled her forward.

Not long after Dharmendra mentioned his impending proposal, he took Arya away from Sangre Grande under the pretense of work. He drove them through a city Arya didn't know, easing through the backroads, where it was quieter, to a neighborhood where the houses were spaced further apart. She watched as Dharmendra stopped to chitchat with one person after another.

—*E always hah ah way bout im, Krys,* says my mother. *Everywhey we goh, people like im and dey rheal like im. E could geh along wid anybody, anytime, rheal charismatic.*

Dharmendra eased their vehicle next to a house, and Arya recognized his older brother Prana and Prana's wife, Nissi, sitting on the verandah in the front. They waved to one another.

Ah come toh show she, Dharmendra said to Prana and Nissi. *We goh link up een a bit.*

Next to his brother's house was an enormous plot of land with an abundance of fruit trees and bamboo spanning far back to the horizon.

Dis is **we** *own,* Dharmendra said to her, slipping his hand around her and resting his palm on the soft concavity of her bellybutton. *Ah goan bill we ah house.*

Yet again he'd taken her by surprise, painting the map of their future in intricate patterns with permanent brushstrokes.

Meh faddah gimmeh dis piece, he continued, *and meh bruddah Prana geh dat own. E done bill up e house and we juss hah toh bill we own now. Ah done hah werkahs and dem line up toh come and staht de process while ah werkin an ting. It goh take some time, cuttin dung dese trees and dem een de front boh we goh do it. Right hyah is whey de house goh be and den—*

Ah wahn ah inside step, Arya interrupted, surprising herself with her own interjection, but she didn't stop, sensing a moment ripe for the juicing. *Ah inside step dat lead up toh de second floor. And ah front yard and ah backyard so de house shouldn't be too close toh de road. Save as much as dem trees as yuh could, we goh need dem fruits and vegetables.*

She added her own flourishes to their map.

Yes madam, Dharmendra said with that handsome grin of his, *anyting yuh wahn dahlin. Is yours. Dis is all yours.*

Me eh wahn no bush, Arya said.

Doh worry, when ah done, said Dharmendra, disentangling himself from her and spreading his arms, *dis goh be yuh palace.*

Only nineteen and she could see it before her. He talked and she listened, her mind moving faster than his words till she no longer heard him and all she saw was what she'd always wanted: a house nestled in a plush, manicured landscape, close to other houses but on land all their own, never having to live in a remote place again. These things signified their legacy: a man in a uniform who exuded power, money and security, and a car that no longer smelled of bush and was sleek as the city she would live in.

But Arya had learned from her mother's mistakes and wanted certain things settled immediately.

Ah doh wantah live wid yuh muddah, she said, interrupting both his chatter and her own dreams. This was Rebecca's mistake, but it wouldn't be hers.

Wah yuh mean?

When we geh married ah wantah move een hyah, Arya said, *not hwome wid yuh parents.*

Because they both had jobs, it would take years for this place to come to fruition, and they both knew this. Yet Dharmendra agreed, giving Arya the security and stability she'd been searching for.

As time peeled away around them, they continued to visit their future home together. They razored the trees level with the ground and burned the trunks and branches in a clearing. Because pathways and sidewalks were nonexistent, they replaced the wooden planks used for crossing over the open drains, and constructed a concrete bridge to get to their house.

—*Ah use toh run away any chance ah geh to come and see how de house progressin,* says my mother. *Ah suppose toh be werking and ting.*

When walls had been stacked and the cement floors poured, Arya and Dharmendra found themselves rolling around on the dusty ground. They explored the inside of one another's mouths, Arya giving herself to him in these parceled-out moments, kisses and nothing more.

During these visits, Arya met both Dharmendra's close friends and his workers. These were men he'd befriended from the neighborhood, his charming personality attracting others who were always willing to help. They flocked to the foundation of their home after work, making wells of cement, into which they poured water and stomped up and down to mix the mortar. They labored shirtless, their brown skin ranging from cinnamon to mahogany. Sweat flew from their bodies as they drew close together, arms and elbows interlocked, sometimes falling into one another. They paused in their work to share a meal, toasting with bottles of beer, mouths full of food sent by Dharmendra's mother. They refused compensation for their time and work, and were vexed if Dharmendra and Arya ever broached the subject. They helped them build this grand house that towered over their own meager dwellings in the poorer parts of the neighborhood.

Dharmendra said to her, *Doh worry, Arya, dey goh come up some day and we goh be dey toh help dem too.* It was here in the span of these moments and words, when he taught her about others and even about herself, that Arya appreciated Dharmendra the most, thinking some day she would undoubtedly fall madly in love with this man.

Arya unrolled the blueprints, and Dharmendra pinned them to a tabletop he'd constructed with two sawhorses. When he asked her opinion of their home, it was so earnest, she felt like she might cry.

—*Yuh tink somebody di ax meh opinion on tings before, Krys?* my mother asks me. *E wasn't only axin meh nah, is design ah was designin dah house from day one. Yuh faddah bill dat foh meh.*

ACCIDENT

—◁≈▷—

TODAY THE AIR FELT DIFFERENT, the load of their work lighter. Everywhere she turned Arya envisioned sequins and feathers, languorous in the evening breeze, brown bodies shedding glitter from gyration.

Aye Arya gyul, Chandini, the youngest, asked, *yuh tink Mammy goh lewwe goh?*

Pooja shook her head.

Meh eh know nah, said Arya. *Depend on Pappy. Lewwe finish up we wok quick quick quick and check on dem.* The trio bowed their heads under the sun, black curls gleaming, and resumed working.

—*Krys, it wasn't any ole Tuesday nah,* my mother says. *It was Carnival Tuesday, chile. Dis was still de beginnin foh meh and yuh faddah. Everybuddy di looking forward toh gettin on bhad. And is plenty people yuh meetin from abroad—England, Canada, and America. It hah some ah de locals too, yuh know, from Guyana, Dominica, Jamaica, and ting, boh is de white people jukin up dey waist, tryin toh dance toh we music dat di send we inna fit.*

Arya, Amrit, Pooja, and Chandini—twenty, nineteen, eighteen, and seventeen—were the last four of the Singh clan left at home. Amrit was deep in the orchards working for the day. Still under the tyranny of their father, they yearned to join in the festivities but knew better than to ask. In baggy work clothes rid-dled with holes and spattered with mud and feces, with tools held on their shoulders and slung across their backs, they trudged back up to the house to check on their parents. Right before they reached the clearing near the back door, they heard the familiar drone of the jeep's engine. They ran into the tall grass on the out-skirts of the house and placed their tools down, far enough away that there could be no accidental clanging. They watched.

Shiva drove up the hill. Dressed the same every day in a pressed white shirt with the sleeves rolled up his muscular fore-arms, black pants folded and pinned at the shins, rubber boots twanging at the base of his knees, he maneuvered around famil-iar dips and bends, pulling into the bottom of the house within inches of the gate. He was returning from the banana groves and citrus orchards, from the chicken coops and cow pastures. Cutlasses and sickles rattled as he moved them from the jeep and over the gravel hillocks behind the house.

From the moment Rebecca heard the familiar sounds of the jeep, she sped past their wandering hens and roosters to the stone sink. Clothes were still soaking, waiting to be scrubbed. She dumped them in a bucket, drained the water, rinsed the sink, and swapped the detergent for a bar of body soap. She scrambled back and forth between the barrels of rainwater and the sink, buckets of water sloshing as they swung back and forth on a rusty handle. The barrels had been warming in the sun as it crept over the house, its rays licking the sides of the hard plastic.

The three girls knew their mother should've had cool water from the well ready for their father before he reached home, and they watched with trapped breath, praying the scene that unfolded before them would be smooth. They were not far from the well and were familiar with the steep drop of land that fell behind the house before rolling gently to the mouth of the well. It was hard to both ascend and descend; loose earth often unraveled beneath their bare feet and sent them all skidding down the side, bucket and all. Often, if their father wasn't home, they'd all take their time walking around the house, over the soft rises and falls of cool grassy pathways rather than the strenuous hike up and down.

Rebecca retreated to the kitchen. Their mother had already finished her portion of the farm work and was clanging pots and pans together. Shiva rinsed his muddied blades in a tin pail. He plunged his arms into the tepid water. Arya chewed on her cuticles. He paused. Arya bit her finger. He splashed water on his face. Arya breathed. He scrubbed his head, back, and chest over the sink, a light breeze cooling his wet skin. He reached for the towel Rebecca never forgot to place for him next to the sink, dried himself, and hung it around his neck. Shiva stood on the edge of his property, which overlooked the steep drop to the well, the chicken pens, and the winding road leading past rivers and trails to the cocoa fields. Arya, Pooja, and Chandini flattened themselves in the grass. Their father looked up at the sky; Arya did too. It was a cloudless sky today, turquoise stretching in every direction. The grand landscape before her was one she could never truly appreciate, though she knew the land sloping past her feet more intimately than she'd ever known another being.

Rebecca removed his boots. He continued to stare at the sky. Arya knew her mother was doing it as quickly and quietly as she could, hoping he wouldn't turn his wrath upon her yet again.

—*E di stop hittin she by now,* my mother tells me, *boh dah eh stop de abuse. She was like ah cage animal, Krys, train toh do wah e say.*

Throughout their entire lives, the children all whispered

about their father's instability. If he had known they spoke of him disrespectfully, he would more than likely have beaten them close to death. Invisibility and silence: that was all that kept them safe.

Their mother washed their father's feet, dried them, then placed house slippers on them. As he was walking up the stairs they heard her say to him, *Ahgo bring it up right now.* In her hands she balanced a tray of roti hot off the tawa, tomato choka, yogurt, and a jug of water with an enamel cup.

A half hour later Rebecca descended the back steps, avoiding the creaky parts. The tray was empty. Her husband would fall asleep. For two hours after lunch each day, in the lulling heat of midday, he was dead to the world.

Ma, e reach hwome yet? Arya asked from the window, pretending they'd not just seen everything. Rebecca bustled over to her trio of daughters and nodded. *Wah take allyuh so long? E done eat and ting ahready. Goan wash up yuhself. Leave de shovel and ting by de back door. Ahgo wash it foh yuh when ah done hyah.* They each claimed a barrel and cleansed themselves with rainwater. Even though they'd had running water for years, their father insisted on collecting rainwater and utilizing it.

Arya and her two younger sisters stood at their lookout points. They had to make sure their father was as asleep as he could be today. Chandini, the youngest and smallest, was on the verandah that looked into the living room where their father was. She ducked behind a chair. Pooja was at the bottom of the stairs waiting for any signal from Chandini. Arya, still in work clothes and boots like her sisters, was on the ground floor, at a point where she could see Pooja. She gingerly set one of their metal chairs in the middle of the floor, right beneath the living room. Testing it with the weight of her foot, she determined it was safe before she climbed on, careful not to tilt it back and forth. They trembled to think of what would happen to them if they were caught.

From a space between the boards, Arya could peer into the living room. She steadied herself by pressing her fingertips against the ceiling. A white coverlet brushed the floor. Her father's black skin gleamed against the white of the sheet. His unclothed chest rose and fell in the rhythmic pace of sleep embraced.

In her excitement, Arya hopped off the chair and it toppled. She caught it and steadied it with trembling hands. But then a humming carried on the breeze around them and they all froze. It was a sound they were used to, a soothing one that wasn't usually this close to the house when their father was sleeping. Nollie, their father's sister, wandered into the room, right where Arya was standing. Her vacant eyes swept around, and as she was about to express excitement at seeing Arya there, Pooja clamped a hand over her mouth and dragged her away from the house. Arya wasn't sure how to react, torn between yelling at Pooja for treating her this way and not wanting to wake their father so they could escape for a little while. Chandini skittered down the stairs, and the three sisters convened under the shade of the cocoa house, where their voices would not carry to their father. Rebecca was hacking at sugar cane stalks.

—*Someting was wrong wid Nollie, Krys,* says my mother, *boh we din know what it was. Juss dat she couldn't evah be widdout adult supervision. All ah we figure it out early, rheal early on, and we use to protek she from Pappy. She was so sweet, eh Krys, so sweet.*

Three voices warbled in unison as Nollie sat close by, a smile painted across her face, *Mammy, please lewwe goh, Pappy sleepin, we check. We eh goh geh een trouble. We eh goh do nutten wrong and we promise we goh come home befoh e wake up.* Though at first she said no, in the end Rebecca conceded. *Boh make sure allyuh chilren backside right back hyah een ah hour an ah half.* None of them glanced back to see the yearning on their mother's face as they pranced away from her. She was left with a cutlass in one hand and Nollie's fingers entwined in the other.

—*Krys gyul,* my grandmother confides in me one day when my mother isn't there. My grandfather is asleep in the next room; we share a meal at her kitchen table. *Yuh muddah, all ah dem dey hah such energy and meh dere not evan ole, only forty someting cutlassin cane an all kinda ting.* These are words she would never say in the presence of her children, and I'm thankful I have her to ask questions of as well. *Ah coulda be out dey too enjoyin mehself, boh instead meh stick up dey on de fahm wid Mistah Shiva.*

The giddy trio discarded their work clothes and donned hot pants or beaded skirts, lacy tops, and stilettos. Halfway down the gravel pathway they slipped off their shoes to run the rest of the way to the main road barefoot. There, as promised, was Dharmendra, grinning behind the wheel of his sporty new jeep. Arya and Dharmendra shared an embrace and a quick kiss on the lips before taking off. What Arya felt then was the intensity of her sisters' jealousy. She chose to ignore it in hopes that it would fade when they each found someone to call their own.

—*Back een dem days, Krys,* my mother says, *it eh hah dat many cahs and dem on de island nah, and it done ahready so small we could goh anywhey we wahn fass fass fass.*

Collectively they decided to stay in Grande. Inland from Matura Bay and close enough to the capital, Sangre Grande beckoned partygoers to the Atlantic side of the island. In the middle of town, older people milled around the shops and bakeries, clearly not as hungry for excitement as they were. As their car crawled past, they turned their attention every now and then to an uproar, but their curiosity was dashed when they realized the hollering they longed to join was emanating from nearby rum shops. Old men clinked bottle necks over their heads and belted out ancient Hindi songs, a language the young had abandoned.

A mini parade crossed paths with them. Dharmendra halted the car, and they all scrambled out to join in the whistling. African headdresses constructed from plumes of feathers sprayed forth in resplendent colors—tangerines, turquoises, vermilions, magentas, and golds. They were paired with Indian sequins and glass beads that glittered brilliantly beneath the Caribbean sun. Arya and her sisters inserted themselves into the crowd. They screamed the words to the songs blaring from the stage, floating in the street along with them. The singers, dressed in sequined bras with lines of jewels that cascaded from the nipples and connected to their matching panties and boots, jumped and waved, urging the crowd on with them. Dharmendra wrapped his fingers around Arya's slender wrist. She turned to him and he pulled her close, her curls flying behind her. They embraced and stared into each other's eyes. Arya threw back her head as they danced, exposing the graceful arc of her long neck. He never took his eyes off her, nor did he remove his arms from her waist. Arya flung her body back and forth; she twirled, her arms arched above their heads. She was free to move and laugh. Away from the farm, away from her father, she became the person she longed to be.

One of the band's scantily clad women hollered to one of her friends, *Ayayayayai, check im out nah.* She pointed her chin to Dharmendra. *De mahn tabanka, dis gyul rheal tie up e head.* With that they plunged their fingers into the pouches that dangled from their belted waistlines and flicked glitter on the couple.

Arya ripped away from Dharmendra, trying to escape the shimmering flakes as they fell and clung to their sweaty skin.

He gave her a quizzical look. The women, drunk and in the mood to gallivant, moved on. Dharmendra tried to embrace her again, tossing his hips to and fro, then in fast, small circles to a hot chutney rhythm, anything to reclaim the magic they'd succumbed to just seconds ago. Before she was even close to him she said, *Nah! Yuh know how hahd it goh be toh geh shinin duss outtah meh hair? Off meh skin? If Pappy see it on we, e goh know foh sure we wasn't hwome.* Comprehension dawned on his face. She flounced away in search of her younger sisters. Dharmendra consulted his watch.

—*Krys,* my mother says, *we di done stay too long ahready. Boh once everyboddy havin ah good time so we din wantah goh. Toh tink wah dat mahn goh do toh we skin if e wake up an we eh dey, de cutass we wuddah geh . . .*

Through the triangles of space framed by elbows held akimbo, she spied her sisters sandwiched between half-naked Indian men, borrowed headdresses tilting precariously as they bucked their hips to and fro. Glitter sparkled on Pooja's fair skin, the lightest of all the Singhs, and twinkled on Chandini's chocolate tones, she the darkest. Chandini pushed one of the men forward and balanced herself by placing her hands on his thighs. She bent over seductively, pressing her behind harder, rougher against his crotch.

Furious, Arya jumped over drunken bodies squirming on the ground, beer bottles miraculously still held upright in their hands. She yanked her sisters from between the men. They stumbled forward, and the men, their brown abs gleaming and their long black hair dripping, tripped and fell into one another. They laughed and clapped one another on the back, the two girls forgotten as they moved on in search of more.

The partygoers surged forward, leaving a gap between the foursome and the fete. A few stragglers stumbled and recovered. *Whey allyuh goin?* Dharmendra queried. A handful of men shouted back, *Arima, mahn.* Arya shook her head at her sisters; they frowned. A woman added, *Is whey de fete is, come nah mahn,* and winked at Dharmendra, the feathers atop her head flouncing flirtatiously.

They'd managed to bump and grind their way to nearly half a mile away from where their vehicle was parked. They trotted back and hopped in, breathless beneath the beating sun. Arya chewed the inside of her cheek while staring at her watch. Already, an hour had elapsed. The ninety minutes their mother gave them were drawing to a close. Dharmendra swerved onto Wallerfield Highway, the pathway to Arima, to the promised fete. The road curved along like a buxom woman, and he attacked those sensuous rounds with the awkwardness of a virgin. The wheel spun in his hands, his aggressiveness frightening, no longer sexy.

Ah tink we should goh back hwome, Arya said. *No sense in movin fah fah fah from de house. We goh done geh weself een trouble.*

Dharmendra said nothing, only pressed down on the gas.

Oh Gawd Arya, lewwe goh nah, we eh goh geh ah chance like dis een ah hurry again, Pooja pleaded. *We eh ready toh goh back hwome yet.*

Yeah please, Arya gyul, Chandini chimed in, *come nah, gyul.*

Meh eh wahn Pappy toh wake up and see we eh dey, Arya said, the weight of being the eldest there lying heavily on her. *Allyuh eh care wah goh happen to Mammy if dah appen? Is not only we behind we hah toh worry bout. Dharmendra, turn rung, take we hwome now.*

He pressed even harder on the gas pedal; the engine thundered below them. He clenched his jaw, ground his teeth; veins pulsated in his neck. The needle on the speedometer climbed to 70, 80, 90 . . . She pressed herself into the seat and held on with both hands.

Wheyyyy, Pooja whistled, *Dharmendra, boi yuh could rheal drive!* She slapped the back of his headrest as though spurring on a galloping horse,—*Yeah mahn, geh we dey fastah*—then threw her head back and hooted.

No, Dharmendra, yuh goin too fass, Arya said, *slow dung. Slow dung, Dharmendra.* But that just seemed to urge him on faster.

Yuh always sneakin whey foh ah lil bit, Dharmendra said. *Yuh eh hear dem awah? Dey eh ready toh goh hwome yet. Lemmeh enjoy meh damn self before ah shuttle allyuh ass back nah mahn.*

Arya, Chandini said, *we eh geh nuff baccanal, nuff excitement gyul. Arima hah de music and de big crowd. We goh hah fun gyul wid de float and dem.*

Arya again checked the hands of her watch and the road ahead. They approached the bend on Wallerfield Highway, a well-known corner that had overturned many an experienced driver.

Dharmendra, yuh eh goh make de cornah, Arya warned. *Slow dung.*

Mahn, wah de ass wrong wid yuh? he asked. *Yuh tellin meh how to drive? Ahgo make it no mattah how fass ah go. Ah is ah experience drivah.* He thumped his chest as he said this.

Right before the turn he sped up. Arya flung her arms out and clutched anything that she could hold on to. Looking back at her sisters, she yelled at them to do the same. Pooja and Chandini screamed with glee. Bouncing around in the backseat, they ignored their sister.

The corner came too fast. He took it too straight. Jerked the wheel. This way. That. Too late. Moments suspended, bodies straining, hair floating, arms adrift. They flipped once. Roof. Twice. Wheels. Thrice. Roof.

Arya was the only one conscious through it all—the grainy black asphalt pelting at her through the open window, the thunderous crumpling of the car's top each time it landed on the roof, the screams of her sisters followed by their silence. Her head was pressed against the hood, her neck twisted almost grotesquely. Shards of glass shimmered on her skin. Arya looked to Dharmendra. He hung by his seat belt, his eyes closed, blood flowing from his head. Chandini was on top of Pooja. They groaned, eyes still closed. But no sound came from Dharmendra. Though she feared he was dead, anger as thin as thread knotted itself in her mind. They were there, after all, because of him. Blood pooling around his head struck fear in her again, and she scrambled to break free of the car. Arya fell onto more shattered glass. She crawled through the open window. Looked back. Dharmendra was still motionless. Death entered her mind, an unwanted guest. She decided not to move him, convincing herself if she didn't, there was still a chance he was alive.

Crawling on bloody hands, she heaved one of her sisters out of the back window. Never before had she felt the dead weight of a person. Her sister didn't budge. They stopped moaning, and it was the silence that scared Arya the most. The car creaked as the hood crumpled more.

—*Krys*, my mother tells me, *ah was the eldess. It was meh responsibility toh bring dem hwome safe.*

Without knowing which sister she was holding on to, she hooked her arms around any body part that wouldn't resist and pulled, and yanked, but nothing gave. Arya screamed and pulled, shattered glass driving into her knees.

A man touched her head. Another crouched at her side. Yet another tenderly took her arms from around her sister. More and more men swarmed her. These men came with women, and their women uttered words to her that did not register. The crash was in her head, drowning out everything else. These women helped her to a patch of grass, pressed handkerchiefs into her crimson palms, dusted her clothes, patted her head, hugged her. This dreamlike state melted away. Their chatter penetrated the roaring in her head. It pierced straight through and was clear, almost painfully so.

Arya pulled away from them and sprinted to the overturned car. *Dharmendra! Pooja! Chandini! E dead! All ah dem dead.* One of the men pulled her into his chest, and something of his warmth, his touch, his affection, subdued her. His voice was like the low rumble of thunder after a storm has passed. *Deh eh dead. We gettin dem out now, all ah dem. Stay close but doh worry, we goh geh dem out.* She nodded into his chest.

Numerous cars had pulled over. People continued to spill out of them. They helped in whatever way they could, some tackling the overturned vehicle, others holding people back.

～

BACK AT THE FARM, Rebecca wrung her hands in despair. She tiptoed from one end of the kitchen to another.

—*Krys chile,* my grandmother says, telling me her version of this, *meh was hopin de mahn stay sleepin foh much longah dan usual. Boh when ah kyant wait no moh meh hah to go an see if ah could find out someting bout dem.*

After an hour and a half passed, she walked around the back and followed the gravel path to the main road. At the meeting of gravel and pitch, she shaded her eyes from the sun and swept her gaze in both directions. The road was deserted. Each time she detected the rumble of an engine she started toward it, hoping it was Dharmendra with her daughters. The afternoon sun blazed down on her, and soon the thin material of her dress was soaked in sweat.

Another vehicle approached. She jumped to her feet from where she sat, afraid to go back to the house. The front of a small car peeked over the hill—it wasn't them. Rebecca slumped against the wooden post of the shed.

Misrez Singh, the driver hailed her from his open window. Rebecca recognized him from her market trips. *Dem gyul and dem geh een ah accident wid de policeman. Meh juss pass dem on Wallerfield.* Rebecca froze under the sun.

SOMEONE GOT TO A PHONE FOR THEM. An ambulance arrived. Pooja and Chandini flanked Arya behind someone's car. They watched as the medics efficiently handled Dharmendra's limp body. A collective tremble passed through the trio as he was strapped to the stretcher. Before Arya could shrug off the towel someone had tucked around her shoulders and run to him, the medics had already shut him behind the doors of the ambulance. They sped off.

The girls were checked, then double-checked. Luckily, they were told, other than cuts and scrapes, they were fine. Arya heard a creak, a whine, then a crash. Several men took it upon themselves to flip Dharmendra's jeep right side up. The top and sides were caved in, the wheels askew. The men grunted and sweated as they pushed the broken vehicle onto the grass.

—*When meh see it like dat, Krys,* my mother says to me, *ah couldn't believe we was een dere atall. Let alone we make it out wid barely anyting.*

Eventually the clusters began to disperse after ensuring the girls were all right. Cars pulled back onto the road more conscientiously than they would have done prior to witnessing the accident. They took the turn with caution until the accident faded from their minds.

～

Misrez Becca, the man said in a gentler voice, *yuh gyuls an dem ahright. Meh see dem befoh ah leave. Boh me eh know bout de pohlice fella. E wasn't lookin so good nah.*

Rebecca nodded again, hoarsely said her thanks, and started wandering up the road to the house, wringing her dress in her hands. It had been two hours since they'd been gone. Shiva must be up and waiting for her in the kitchen. How was she to tell her husband that their daughters snuck away while he slept? Snuck away while they were supposed to be working. Snuck away *with* her permission. Without the last piece of information, he might beat them to death. Rebecca was resigned to sacrificing herself for her children once again. If she couldn't entirely protect them, at least she could take the first of his wrath, tire him out before he dealt them their blows. For surely this would be the day he started beating her again.

The house was in view. She saw a shadow pass on the verandah. Squinting against the brightness of the sun, she recognized the familiar smudge of her husband leaning against the parapet in the gallery. The low wall pressed into his thighs.

Ruuuuuubbbbby.

～

IN A TIDE OF DUST, Shiva skidded to a stop. Bystanders were still scattered along the median. Arya, Pooja, and Chandini stood in the basin of a semicircle. They were being doted on before return-ing home to face the inevitable.

—*We was dey ahready,* my mother tells me, *an dey givin we food and drink. Ah was hopin toh fin out wah appen toh yuh faddah, maybe geh ah ride to de hospital, yuh know, Krys, boh Mistah Shiva pull up papayo!*

They saw their father's contorted face as he slammed the jeep's door shut behind him. All three of them dropped their soda bottles and fried chicken wrapped in paper towels and foil, food intended for someone's beach picnic. His black skin gleamed under a film of sweat; his strides were long and purposeful; he snarled their names one by one starting with Chandini, the blackest of them and his least favorite, and ending with Pooja, his favorite because she was the fairest, leaving Arya in the middle, as ever.

The three girls turned and ran to the only sanctuary they saw—Dharmendra's smashed jeep. They scrabbled through the driver- and passenger-side windows, pulling and pushing one another up. They jumped into the backseat. Once again Arya was in the middle flanked by her two younger sisters. They didn't hear what their father hissed to everyone, but the group of help-ers dispersed, disdain showing on the faces of some, while others glanced sympathetically at the girls.

—*Everybody hah to mine dey own business,* my mother says, *nutten foh dem toh do now. Ah mahn come toh deal wid e dawtahs and howevah e wantah do dat is e right. Dah is how dey hah toh see it, no mattah how dey feel.*

He turned to them and strode to the jeep. Pooja clapped her hand down on the knob; Chandini did the same. Shiva yanked at Pooja's side first. *Pappy, it eh wokin,* Pooja said, *it geh mash up een de accident.* Though scared out of their minds, their attempt to

avoid the situation seemed too horrific, so much so it was comi-
cal, and Pooja let slip a giggle. She started a chain reaction—Arya
giggled too, and so did Chandini. They stifled the laughs beneath
their palms. Shiva snaked his arm through the shattered front
window and to the back where he grabbed Chandini by the head
and slammed her face into the headrest.

Geh outtah de cah now.

Chandini, hand to bloody face, tumbled out of the car first,
followed by Arya, then Pooja. Arya tried to shield Chandini by
stepping in front of her, but their father cuffed her around the
ears a few more times. Chandini screamed; he slapped her.

Geh een de jeep now.

They sat in the back of their father's vehicle with the buckets
and pails, sheets of metal and nails, axes and knives. By the time
they reached home the rooster was crowing to signal six p.m.
They leapt out of the jeep and cowered. Shiva looked at Pooja,
and she started crying.

—Pooja always like dat eh, my mother says. *All de mahn hah
toh do is watch she and she done staht toh cry. And not juss cry,
nah, is big big bawl like e done tryin toh keel she oh someting. And
so e use toh leave she and move on toh we. Plus she was the fairest
one ah we and Chandini was de blackess, so dat had someting toh
do wid it too.*

Pooja's yowls ricocheted off the walls and echoed on the
ground floor. She dropped down, covered her head, and started
rolling back and forth as though he'd already whipped her. Standing right by Pooja, Chandini knew she was next.

—Dat day Chandini geh de woss lickin meh see in a long time,
my mother says, *e eh stop nah. E beat she til e tyad. Gyul was on de
grung, done stop movin, and e din stop. Sometimes, back een dem
days we din hah pad and ting, we hah we period and blood soak troo*

*de rag, rollin down we leg, stain up we clothes, and dat mahn din stop,
e juss keep goin.*

Before Shiva had a chance to shift his gaze to Arya, she took
off running. Without looking back, she ran as fast as she could,
past the pomegranate tree, past the cocoa house, down the hill,
past the chicken pens, and plunged into the thick bushes. She
only stopped when the trees above were dense enough to block
the sunlight. The greenery surrounding her glistened. She leaned
against the trunk of a tree and held her chest. In the shade, a cool
breeze dried her sweat. While running, she'd kicked off her heels;
now the coldness of the earth where sunlight hardly reached
felt rich beneath her bare feet. Arya sat and leaned against the
rough trunk. It prickled her skin through the thin material of her
clothes. She listened. Birds whistled and chirped, the leaves mur-
mured, but nothing else.

The path that meandered around the property and back to
the house wasn't far off. For over an hour Arya sat with muscles
pulled taut, ready to jump and sprint at any sign of her father.
When she finally relaxed, her body ached; she slumped against
the dark bark. For a moment she considered scaling the tree
and lounging in its branches but banished that thought when
she looked up. The leaves overhead spun an intricate pattern
with the leaves of other trees, the branches spiraling big and
strong. Snakes, she knew, were most definitely camouflaged in
the web above.

Once when she was a little girl, Arya was stung by a scorpion. The longer she remained curled in the same spot, the more
thoughts of venomous creatures seized her mind. She rubbed her
skin where the scorpion once stung her and shuddered, thinking again of death and the many brushes she'd had with it in her
short life.

Arya looked down at her short, beaded skirt and wispy blouse. Both were torn. Beads, like breadcrumbs, led straight to her. Fabric from her clothes was undoubtedly stuck in the bushes, her blood on the branches, her shoes left somewhere in the dirt. Her father was a hunter. If she stayed where she was, he would find her. If he let loose his hunting dogs, they would shred her.

—*Now meh run away meh kyant evan tink bout goin back nah, Krys,* my mother tells me. *How? If ah gone back dis time ah know e goh keel meh.*

The only person who brought her solace, the one man who would do anything for her in that moment, was Dharmendra. She wondered if he was okay, if he was at home or at the Sangre Grande hospital, which was, coincidentally, right across the street from where he lived with his parents and siblings.

She walked with trepidation to the path. Even in the gathering darkness she could find her way through with touch and sometimes smell. With nothing to protect her feet, she stared at the ground praying she wouldn't step on anything that would bite or sting.

Blackness came swiftly. She picked her way through the trees to the path, which was lit by a silvery beam of moonlight. She scampered to the house. Frogs croaked and crickets chirped. She crouched by the cocoa house; the tall grass trembled. This was the last sanctuary off the track. Arya planned just how to jump from the bushes and dart to the main road. Just as she was about to move, a yellow light slid through the blades of grass. She flattened herself on the ground and rolled slowly back until she was touching the wooden beams of the cocoa house.

Gravel crunched beneath heavy footsteps. *Arya. Arya. Whey yuh dey Arya?* her father coaxed her in the same saccharine voice he saved for her mother. She cringed, pressed a hand to her mouth, and held her breath. He stepped off the gravel path and into the grass. *Ah see someting move hyah. Meh know is you, Arya. Come out.* Shiva swept the flashlight to and fro, passing over her with both beam and eyes. Eventually gravel crunched beneath his boots again and his voice faded.

She didn't know how long she lay there trembling, but it was long enough to see her father retreat to the house and extinguish the lights. Even then she didn't move. Only after the house itself seemed to take a breath for the night did Arya make a dash to the main road.

DHARMENDRA'S HOUSE was miles away in the bustling city. The light of the moon paved the way in blue and silver streams. It was approaching full moon, she noted, not yet bloated and yellow, but sharp and thin like a spinning blade. After she'd traipsed a couple of miles, a van's headlights flooded the lonely road, and Arya flagged the vehicle down.

—*Een doze days it eh hah nutten like rape and murdah goin on een de country,* my mother informs me, *nutten we know bout anyways. Yuh need ah ride, yuh flag ah mahn dung. People moh dan happy toh take yuh whey yuh wantah goh an it eh hah nutten like offerin money an offendin dem nah. Is tank yuh and yuh gone yuh whey. De island done so small yuh goh probably bonx im up een de mahkit oh someting nex time yuh goh.*

The man stopped in the middle of the road and beckoned her to get in the front seat; she did. *Good night, suh. If yuh doh mind droppin meh off by de hospital on Ojoe Road ahgo greatly appreciate it.*

They made small talk in the car, and she learned of his wife and kids and what he did for a living. Arya's bare feet, ruffled hair with twigs and grass sticking out, and dirtied clothes didn't go by unnoticed. He learned her story and said, *Doh mind yuh faddah sound like ah high class madmahn—and ah doh usually puh meh mout een people business boh yuh young enough toh be meh dawtah—ah tink yuh should goh hwome when yuh done. Is de right ting toh do. Wah yuh goh do runnin away like dis? Wah kind ah life yuh goh end up wit?*

At the entrance to the hospital, he tipped his hat, smiled, and continued on his way.

Arya stood across the street from the Sital residence. The familiar concrete wall of alternating green and white cement blocks bordered their shop and bar on the ground floor. A metal railing circled the gallery on the second. It was so different from the Singh home, half wood and half concrete, flimsy wire fencing haphazardly tacked into place.

She'd only met Dharmendra's parents—Harry and Jaya— a handful of times. Showing up on their doorstep like this, as embarrassing as it was, still felt more comfortable than returning home. The wooden doors to the Sitals' shop were bolted shut. Arya conjured images of brightly wrapped preserves and chocolates organized in their glass cases.

Tonight, noises belched from the rum shop next door. They'd continue until daybreak when patrons stumbled home to their enraged wives who sucked their teeth and screamed, *Who de ass care bout Carnival Tuesday when yuh hah chilren toh feed and chicken toh mind.*

Arya skulked to the side of the house, where she ran into Dharmendra's younger brother Som.

Aye boi, Arya said.

Arya? Wah yuh doin hyah, gyul? he asked, rubbing his eyes.

Ah-ah-ah come toh check an see if Dharmendra ahright, she stammered.

Oh Gawd gyul, dat couldah wait till mawnin. Come come come.
He led her upstairs. They tiptoed through the living room first,
past his father's room, and then past his mother's. A clock chimed
once. It was one a.m.

Dharmendra's head was wrapped in white bandages
stained brown with dried blood. Cuts and scratches marked
his cheeks and arms, but he grinned when he saw her. He
engulfed her in a warm embrace, and she wanted to break
down and cry. Instead she scolded him, told him to keep it
down before they woke his parents.

—*Is ah shameful ting foh me toh be dey so wid a boi een de
middle ah de night, yuh know, Krys,* my mother confides. *A gyul
chile always hah toh tink bout she reputation no mattah wah she
doin. Mahn an dem could do wah dey wahn, geh on bhad, geh lock
up and all kinda ting boh ah hah toh watch mehself an ah wasn't
doin dat enough dat night.*

But Arya had no one else to turn to, and she told Dharmendra
everything.

*Boh ah rheally wanted toh make sure yuh ahright, and it ease
meh heart toh see yuh happy and good,* Arya said, rubbing his
shaven cheeks with her thumbs.

Arya. Dharmendra's voice was calm and serious. He really
looked at her, a gaze so deep she wanted to turn away but couldn't.
*Lewwe geh mar-red. Come gyul, we eh goh trouble nohbuddy,
nohbuddy eh hah toh know nutten, nohbuddy eh goh giwwe no prob-
lem. Lewwe goh an geh mar-red.* He gathered her trembling hands
in his and kissed the tips of her rough fingers. *Come nah doo doo
dahlin, sugah plum. We goh goh een de warden office een de mawnin.*

They jumped apart when they heard the shuffle of footsteps and the sweep of a dressing gown flapping down the corridor. Dharmendra's parents filled the doorway. It was past two

a.m. Arya stared down at her hands. She hoped his parents had not heard the words he muttered to her only moments before. They were kind but curious as to why she was there so late. They assured her Dharmendra was well taken care of, asked her if she would be okay, and offered her a ride home.

The man who'd given her a ride to Dharmendra's house, though a stranger, seemed to know her better than she knew herself. Arya could get married to Dharmendra tomorrow without telling anyone but, as the man said—*Wah kind ah life yuh goh end up wit?* As much as they might not think her a good fit for their son, if she married him the right way they could show no hostility toward her without losing him.

It took all of her, but Arya held back her tears and shook her head. Arya knew their offer was polite and obligatory; she also did not want them to see just how deep in the bushes she lived. They gave their son a pointed stare before leaving them alone again.

Dharmendra, ah hah toh goh hwome. We eh doin dis ting behind yuh parents' back, Arya said.

He stared at her, this time with one question pulled taut between them. She shook her head. Without their parents' blessings their marriage would be cursed. This Arya believed more than anything.

—*Meh couldn't do it like dat nah, Krys chile,* my mother tells me. *Is important toh do dese things de right way, de propah way, uddahwise it follow yuh and yuh chilren and yuh chilren chilren foh de ress ah yuh life. So dat night meh leff and meh gone back hwome. Pappy eh hit meh nah. Foh de fuss time e leff meh so, e eh lay one lash on meh. Ah eh know why boh ah was happy. Oh Gawd, foh once meh geh ahwhey scotch free. Yuh doh question dat nah. Yuh count yuh blessin and goh yuh way.*

INTERIM

—*Well, yuh know how Trinis does say—yuh faddah and me, continue we goin arung,* my mother tells me as she stirs a pot of curried goat, then grinds split peas for the roti next. She smiles when she isn't cooking a meal for my grandfather, who usually takes up most of her thoughts; the act of cooking provides temporary respite. *Nobody was suppose to know anyting, boh is blind dey playin dey blind, because ah don't tink yuh faddah and me was de bess at hidin it nah.*

In the months after the accident, Arya and Dharmendra fell into a rhythm of dodge and embrace. There were certain places where Arya leaned against Dharmendra and he slipped both arms around her. Sometimes they swayed to the provocative beat of reggae at a bar, their lips brushing, every part of their bodies in tantalizing motion in this dance of seduction. Then there were open places where their fingers strayed to meet but they walked one step away from one another, places where it wasn't appropriate to be side by side, eyes trained to their every movement, vicious tongues lying in wait to destroy them.

Despite these complexities, Arya and Dharmendra fell into their own patterns, as precarious as some of them were. Even after the accident, Dharmendra maintained he was Amrit's friend and frequented the Singh house, not just as much as before, but now much more. Though her father hadn't seen Dharmendra on the day of the accident, he knew it was his vehicle. The local gossips were powerful, and Shiva had heard many versions of the story.

But it was as if parts of that day—her runaway disappearance from home, her late-night reentry—were sucked into a black hole, and her father continued to make no comments. She just prayed he wouldn't snap when she least expected it.

—*De only ting I could tink of, Krys,* my mother tells me, *is dat e di know. Mistah Shiva di somehow know bout yuh faddah de whole time, and de only reason e din say anyting chile is because e di approve.*

One day not too long after the accident, Pooja steered Nollie to the sink to wash dishes unattended. Cruel enough as it was to assign her such a chore, for the sake of efficiency they needed her out of the way, and they all knew she'd stand there until one of them stopped her, even if it took hours.

—*If yuh poh she to wash ah cup oh pot,* my mother tells me, *Nollie go stand dey foh twenty or tirty minutes just sayin undah she breath dat she hah to wash dis, she hah to wash dis, and she goh juss keep washin and scrubbin ovah and ovah again.*

Nollie continued to repeat the instructions to herself and scrubbed and rinsed while everyone milled around her, free to tend to their duties for the day. But within minutes loud voices rose from the front. Amrit, grown into a tall man, was now the same height as his father. Muscles from farm work rippled along the tops of his shoulders, down his chest, and across his abdomen. His voice became thunderous, and just beneath that they heard the rumble of their father's. Then the quiet.

How dare Amrit speak back to him?

Rebecca's first instinct was to guide Nollie away from the dishes and nudge her toward the stairs, where at least she could safely hide. But Nollie zeroed in on the silence, asking why her brother was shouting. Her words were filled with such sweetness no one would believe the brutality of the beatings he inflicted on her.

Ah juss hear bhaiya, Nollie told Rebecca, *lemmeh goan see wah appen.*

Nollie, frail looking and with the innocent mind of a child, always tried to stop her brother when he beat his children. Rebecca wanted to get her out of the way before she interfered yet again. Whenever Nollie tried to stop him, his anger intensified, resulting in even more lashes for the children. When the Singh clan once tried to stop their father from beating Nollie, he threatened to pull out his gun and shoot them all. They knew they had no choice but to allow his anger to run its course.

Even though she appeared fragile, Nollie was strong and sprang from Rebecca's grip with surprising spryness. They followed her just in time to see Shiva clout Amrit about the head. Nollie slid between them, willowy in her housedress. She pushed her brother with enough force to make him step back. Amrit gathered Nollie in his arms and tried to hand her to Arya to get her out of the way, but Shiva, in his twisted mind, saw himself challenged, and turned his rage upon Nollie.

Bhaiya. Nollie called him brother affectionately in Hindi. *Why yuh do dis? Is yuh chilren.*

More tender words dripped from her lips, but no one heard them, they never heard them, no matter how Nollie tried to reach out and, as senseless as she appeared to be, talk sense into Shiva. The screams of childlike Nollie haunted them all long after she'd passed away. She bawled like a baby, never understanding why she was being beaten, never understanding why her brother beat his children or his wife, always pleading with him to stop.

—*Is de kinda bawl dat make yuh belly tun,* my mother says, *de kind dat echo een yuh head till de day yuh dead.*

After he was done thrashing Nollie, then Amrit, the siblings, who had stuffed themselves into every corner, swooped in and cleansed Nollie's wounds, held her as she had held them many times before, hummed lullabies into her ear. It was the least they could do for this woman who had shielded them so many times before.

—*Believe meh, Krys,* says my mother, *if we couldah stop im we wuddah do it ah long time ago. Dat oman din deserve nutten like dat een life, she was so sweet. But if we try an stop im e show we e goh beat she moh befoh movin on toh we.*

The sound of his car starting and pulling away flooded them with relief. It was a comfort to know he was gone, and even more so to hear him return after his long drive, gather a few necessities, and retire to the cocoa house. As was often the case after one of his violent episodes, Shiva fell into a deep silence. He closed in on himself, packed up some clothes, clanged some pots and pans together, and moved into the cocoa house across the path.

Underneath the pyramidal structure was bare dirt and a low wooden wall, an unwelcoming place, even for stray animals. Galvanized metal sheets were pressed together to form the angles for the roof. Brown patches of rust glittered in the sun while the heat exacerbated the bitter scent of cocoa permeating the air. Round tree trunks formed the foundation of the structure. Even though it took a violent outburst to bring the calm, everyone looked forward to the quiet for as long as it lasted.

—*Meh eh know why nah, Krys,* my mother says, *e juss di go een this silence an move outtah de house, cook e own meals and wash e own clothes. And is always always aftah ah big blowout oh two. When e beat Mammy or Nollie or one ah we till we bloody and lifeless den e gone een dis calm like e vex or satisfy. We eh know which one it was, we juss happy e eh een de house. Sometimes it lass foh weeks.*

The house itself seemed to breathe easier. Brothers and sisters joked and laughed. They stayed up late at night and told stories of Papa Bois, father of the forest, who had horns and donkey's hair and could turn into a deer, or shared gripping tales of witnessing a douen beckoning a child that was never to be seen by its parents again, its soul claimed by the monster. With the absence of their father's looming shadow, they were free to be children, siblings to one another. They laughed with their heads thrown back, not having to check over their shoulder; they were affectionate, slinging an arm around a neck. For them, this was the height of their togetherness.

Their nightly talks took a somber tone one night when Amrit made fun of one of their cousins who lived right up the road from them.

Ah see Sachin walkin like dis, said Amrit, and mimicked Sachin's wide gait, made so from a greater girth and from squatting and carrying lumber.

Doh make fun ah im like dat, Amrit, Arya chided.

Arya came to realize much earlier than her siblings that her father had taken more than the lion's share of land his mother had left behind, had claimed more than was rightfully his.

Shiva was one of eleven children—seven girls and four boys. Because their father, under the pretense of caring for Nollie, snagged the most envied piece of property, the house they lived in along with the lands connected to it, animosity ballooned among the Singh children and their cousins.

—*Dere was juss so much dispute, Krys,* my mother tells me, *we juss keep ahwey from we cousins and dem. Even if we went toh visit one ah e sistahs who livin dung de road juss ah half ah mile ahwey she run we like dawgs.*

The history of the brothers was muddled. One disappeared, stories of him lost to time as well. Another was murdered, but no one knew how or for what reason, the stories changing with the sands of the shores. There was no interest in avenging his death, and so no arrest was made; the police were as uninterested in the case as the family was. And to no surprise, for disappearances in Trinidad were not unheard of; your connections were what mattered. That left Mitra and Shiva among the sisters.

In a house as small as a matchbox and as flimsy as chicken wire, Shiva's last brother, Mitra, lived with his wife and children. Because of the friction caused by the unequal distribution of land, to say the cousins didn't get along would be an understatement; this kind of strife is passed down through generations.

Mitra's house stood along the gravel path that led to the main road. To get to and from the house each day, the Singh clan passed by them without uttering a word, while Mitra's girls hissed and spat at them, their mother clipping clothes to a line, her lips pressed together. Once in a while a scuffle would break out among the girls from the two households while the adults weren't looking, causing a ripple of retaliative acts and more hurt and pain than could ever be repaired.

—*Ah use to feel sorry foh dem, Krys,* my mother says, *livin een dat small small house wid dey muddah and faddah. Right een front ah we. All dey hah toh do is look back and see we een we big house and land, so when Amrit makin fun ah im ah nevah like dat.*

Sachin, the boy Amrit mercilessly made fun of, was Mitra's eldest son and bore witness to his father's decline into the bottle, where his fears became his reality, consuming him until he started consuming his family. When there was no money to bring in, Mitra sold a piece of his land twice, collecting money but never delivering the deed to either party. This became one of his many failures. He blamed Shiva for his misfortunes, accusing him of having stolen their mother's land, leaving him destitute.

Alcoholism and depression were not terms yet widely known in the early 1980s, not in Trinidad, not on a Caribbean island where boys were bred to grow into men who drank rum the minute the sun sank below the horizon, to mark the end of a workday. This was a place where rum shops stayed open all night, where a teething child's gums were rubbed with brandy. Women grew up knowing that, one day, they would be debating whether or not to show up at the bar to beg their husbands for money for food.

Mitra had been an alcoholic who was also severely depressed, but no one connected those dots, not until it was too late.

—*Everyting di juss appen right on top ah one anuddah*, my mother tells me, *fuss de accident wid me, den Amrit beatin, and now dis*.

Sachin was the one who delivered the news to the house. He approached with trepidation, uncertain now of where they were in this family war, and asked for their father. There was something in the way he asked that made Arya point him to the cocoa house, no questions asked.

Mitra had pulled up a chair in his house, slid the barrel of a gun into his mouth, and pulled the trigger, leaving his eldest son to find him.

—*Ah remembah goin toh de viewin to see wah e di look like*, my mother says, *and I juss kyant bring meh mind toh go back dey right now*.

In the wake of such violent loss, their entire house trembled under him. They rode the wave of the aftermath of his wrath for close to a month, holding, holding, holding while he almost destroyed them all. At last, he again moved to the cocoa house, and while they didn't know how long he'd stay, they needed the relief now more than ever before.

In this interim, Arya and Dharmendra seemed to glide together, smiling and laughing. Their romance was finally everything she wanted it to be. With her father out of the house, Dharmendra could sneak in and lounge in the living room with her siblings. Sometimes they were even bold enough to drink liquor while Arya's father was off tending to his other properties during the day. Staticky music filtered through the speakers of a busted-up old radio while the boys smoked. Laughter touched them again, and on a farm atop a picturesque hilltop, they swayed their hips to the beat of the islands.

TRADITION

~~~~~~

DHARMENDRA PULLED OFF the main road and onto the familiar gravel pathway that led up to the house. He waved to Shiva, who'd just arrived at the shed after a day's work, and Shiva tipped his head in acknowledgment. Rebecca was up at the house alone.

Ma, Dharmendra called her for the first time, and Rebecca knew what was coming next. She tenderly caressed his chin and smiled.

Yuh hah to tawk to Mistah Shiva, Dharmendra boi, not me, she said to him. *E muss be dung by de shed by now. Yuh wahn someting toh eat son?*

Ah wantah ax yuh permission fuss.

Rebecca nodded her head. *Now goh,* she said, flapping behind him with a towel, *befoh yuh make meh drop some tears een dis soup.*

Dharmendra went back down to the shed and asked Shiva for Arya's hand in marriage. He was the only suitor of any of Shiva's daughters to do so.

Arya knew the proposal was coming after the night of their car accident, but she waited for it to come the right way—Dharmendra came to the house when she wasn't there, chatted with her father, charmed him the way he charmed everyone else. He explained how he was from a good family, had a stable and respectable job, was madly in love with Arya, and assured Shiva that not only would he treat his daughter the way she should be treated, but by marrying him, her social and economic status would rise. Shiva agreed, and with her father's endorsement, Arya couldn't risk saying no. She'd already tried everything, down to applying for her visa to leave the country, before even meeting Dharmendra and had been denied over and over again. Dharmendra was her chance of escape, and so he and the blinking lights of the city were the only thoughts in her head.

—*Oh Gawd Krys,* my mother says, *dem Indian weddin an dem eh play long no ass nah. All ah know is dat it was too long.*

As tradition would dictate, the wedding was to be held at the bride's home. Of the seven Singh children, Arya's was the only wedding in that house, an important distinction for both Shiva and Rebecca. Rahul, Reeya, and Gita had already emigrated to America, leaving Amrit, Pooja, and Chandini still at home. Gita, only a handful of years older than Arya, had followed in their mother's footsteps; in her early twenties, she was already pregnant with her fourth child. Rahul, now living in rural Pennsylvania, already had two children with two different women.

Avinash arrived early with all his records in tow. He embraced Arya in a hug warmer than all her siblings combined, eager to be the DJ for the wedding. To no surprise, he told her their father had instructed him to play only classical Indian music.

—*Rheal ole time ting, eh Krys,* my mother tells me, laughing. *Only Hare Rama Hare Krishna, Krishna Krishna Hare Hare,* she says collapsing into laughter, making fun of a quintessential Hindi song that has now become synonymous with American cults, *when all we rheally wahn to hear is some nice hot chutney and soca music to dance up toh.*

But Shiva wanted no dancing and frivolity under his roof today, just the strict ceremonial giving away of his daughter to a man he thought would make a fine husband for the integrity of his family. Arya joked with Avinash, telling him, *Oh Gawd boi, slip een ah lil chutney nah mahn,* but even though it was a joke, Avinash, as always, was very serious about following Shiva's orders. She studied him closely, noticing for the first time how much Avinash resembled their father, more so than any of her other siblings.

Arya retreated upstairs, which was empty save for a stray family member running up to grab something. She wanted the comfort of her mother in these moments, but Rebecca was banished to the kitchen, or anywhere else her husband told her to be.

—*She kyant be wid meh,* my mother tells me sadly. *De mahn wahn de oman een de kitchen and dah is whey she hah toh be. Dere was not one minute ah closeness wid me and she dat day. Ah wanted it but nevah geh it.*

Rebecca rinsed and cracked the spines of hundreds of fig leaves for people to ladle channa and aloo, globs of mango takarie, curry pumpkin, deep-fried dhal balls soaked in curhee, string beans dotted with masala, paratha roti followed by the sweets to placate the spices—sweet rice with cinnamon and raisins, vermicelli steeped in nutmeg, parsad, ladoo, burfi, and gulab jamon bobbing in honey sauce. All of this and more Rebecca had a hand in preparing for her daughter's wedding, with guests bringing more dishes to add to the tables that were constructed for the occasion, both outside and in.

The morning of the ceremony passed by in a blur of saris, bells, and people. Arya rented her sari and all the jewelry that twinkled on her ears, nose, wrists, and ankles. Her father offered to hire a make-up artist and hairdresser, but she insisted upon doing this herself. Even then, Shiva sent a family friend up to her room to help tie her sari and apply her make-up.

—Yuh know how dem ole head and dem is, my mother tells me, *when dey oldah and come up toh do up yuh face and ting she only wantah do it she whey, what **she** tink goh look good on **me**. Ah juss hah to send she awhey aftah ahwhile.*

With henna-painted hands, Arya curled her hair and pinned the veil, vermillion stitched with gold thread, to the crown of her head.

Arya was twenty-two and Dharmendra was thirty. It'd been three years since they first met, and though this outcome was inevitable—and one she yearned for—sadness seeped in. Arya started to cry before the ceremony even began. She tried to wipe away her tears, but upset her jewelry and smeared her make-up. *Wah de ass yuh doin?* someone chided. *Look at yuh messin up yuh whole damn face.*

—Meh was cryin, Krys, my mother says, *not because ah wasn't happy, ah was happy, boh it was ah sad day too. Meh was leavin meh parents' house. Ah was toh be ah oman now.*

Arya looked at the three siblings she was leaving behind, and thought of the laughter and conversations only brothers and sisters could have in the happiest and also the most terrifying of times. Memories as sweet as the smell of freshly halved coconuts drifted to the forefront of her mind—going to the market and sharing sweets together, reclining in the arms of mango trees, stealing away to watch a movie while their father slept. When she looked forward to her future with Dharmendra, she feared the loneliness she would find far away from what she'd always known. Once she left, she would never be able to return. Yet she knew Dharmendra loved her, and Arya had to be pragmatic.

—Only yuh faddah di know what e wahn, my mother tells me. *E was tirty—ah grown mahn—and ah was only twenty-two. Ah was ah lil gyul still. Dat wasn't no kinda courtin me and e do*

nah. We nevah went toh de movies, barely togeddah by weself, always arung uddah people, a lil bit a time hyah, a lil bit ah time dey, teefin time like criminals. Meh still feel like ah din know dis mahn ah was marryin, and ah know foh sure dis wasn't de kinda ting ah wanted foh meh chilren.

In the home where Dharmendra pretended to be Amrit's friend, and earned Shiva's respect, he led his bride around the sacred fire seven times; then they placed garlands of flowers around each other's necks—Arya's was white to match his kurta, and his was red to match her sari. They sat cross-legged on a pink blanket with a pattern of red hibiscus and yellow hummingbirds while listening to the pundit chant in Sanskrit. He flicked water on them, chanted some more, and then beckoned their parents. Both sets of parents gave their children to one another. Arya wept.

—*Krystal,* my mother tells me, *is ah blessin toh hah boat yuh parents gih yuh away. Goin forward wid yuh parents' blessin is de right ting toh do an yuh goh hah ah blessed life. Widout yuh parents' blessin yuh goh only see trouble.*

UPSTAIRS, AWAY FROM THE CROWD, the chattering, and the cheering, Arya took off her jewelry, unwound her sari, and unhooked her bells. On the bed was a gossamer white gown overlaid with lace that she had paid a seamstress to create for her. From magazines she had seen in the dressmaker's shop, Arya told the woman how the shoulders should be puffed and shiny, the sleeves long and lacy—not appropriate for tropical weather, but it captured the delicate beauty she wanted for her wedding day.

Dharmendra's meddlesome sisters said she shouldn't wear any dress at all, because it went against tradition. Dharmendra, high off the celebrations, paid them no attention, even when they threatened to leave if Arya put it on.

—*When dey leff nohbody miss dem,* my mother says. *Who rheally miss dem? It was meh weddin day an I eh miss dem one ass.*

Her mother did not come to the room. In fact, she stayed away most of the day, present only when she had to be. Rebecca had given Arya her blessing, had nudged her in Dharmendra's direction, had lied for them, was beaten for them. She wanted her daughter to escape this life as much as Arya did, but once the hour of their parting dawned, the pain that came with it was swift. They both felt it.

Alone in the room, Arya slipped the dress over her head. A murmuring drum mixed with the plucking of a sitar filtered through the open window. The satin was cool and smooth against her skin. She fluffed the dress around her shoulders and then tucked a beaded clip of pearls into her curls. She glanced in the mirror. It was time to make her entrance.

Downstairs, friends and family congregated around wooden picnic tables and ate mounds of food with their fingertips. They cracked the spines of fig leaves and used them as plates. When they caught a glimpse of the bride at the top of the red staircase, they stopped and gazed. It was unheard of for an Indian woman at the end of an Indian wedding to don a white dress, the color traditionally worn at Indian funerals, the color of widowhood. Through doing this, Arya threw superstitions to the winds that whipped the sands on their islands, and declared herself free from their rules.

Arya held the railing as she walked halfway down the stairs in her white satin shoes. The chattering stopped when she was in full view of everyone. She turned around on the narrow ledge. Her sisters and their friends, married or not, gathered at the bottom of the staircase. Clasped in her hands was a bouquet of red and white carnations. She tossed it into the air behind her. It arced, the ribbons unlacing themselves and floating before landing into the hands of one of her sisters.

It was time to say goodbye. Faces bled into one another as tears swelled to the surface. Rebecca's tears mixed with her daughter's as they held on to one another, cheeks together. Her mother's chest heaved against her own, and Arya opened her mouth to release a howl that perfectly matched the pitch of Rebecca's. They would never again be a cushion for one another against her father. Once she left, everything would change. People pulled them apart until their fingertips gave way reluctantly.

—*No werds di pass between we dis day,* my mother says to me. *Dat was it foh me and she.*

Shiva too was sad as he gave away his daughter. Food, invitations, tents, fires, music, festivities. The family had indulged, and these memories would buoy them.

All the guests gathered on both sides of the staircase with rice in hand. They made a narrow path to the car for bride and groom. Dharmendra, waiting at the bottom of the stairs, eyed the grains in their hands and dashed to the car without waiting for his wife. Arya's footsteps to the car were heavy. She looked back. Rice rained down on her. Tears sprang again. When she reached the car, the door was shut, and she opened it for herself. Dharmendra was grinning inside as she slipped in and arranged her gown.

—*Krys . . .* my mother's words change over the years after my grandfather's surgeries from *is leff e leff meh to haul ass so e eh goh geh no rice on im* to *ah shoulda know den wah kinda husband e wuddah tun out toh be. Ah shouldah nevah marry no mahn dah goh run awhey an leff meh so.*

Dharmendra's grin faltered, but he picked it up again. One too excited, the other too nervous, they both ate nothing after the ceremony. They headed straight to the airport for their twelve-minute plane ride to Trinidad's twin isle, Tobago.

DESPITE ARYA'S WHITE DRESS, the couple followed many wedding and early marital traditions. As was customary, they were wed on a Sunday and endured the smoky ceremony that dragged on for hours, the intense scent of incense seeping into their skin. Arya permitted all the little things to happen— Dharmendra not seeing her, the draping of her jewelry, orchestration of food.

The white dress was followed by the premeditated decision to leave for their honeymoon right after the wedding. They were newlyweds locked in one another's gaze, and Arya was aware of each decision she made, never having had this much freedom in her life.

They both thought they would skip right over one of the most absurd practices they were expected to follow. Directly after the ceremony, the bride is taken home with the husband. A female elder, called a lookanny, is stationed in between the couple that night and every night until the Wednesday after the wedding, when the father then comes to collect his daughter and take her home. On the following Sunday, the husband can come back and get her. Most traditional Indian Trinidadians followed these rules punctiliously, never questioning why or how they came to be. It was simply the way it was done. By escaping to their honeymoon, Arya and Dharmendra thought they could skip the lookanny too.

—*Not wit meh honeymoon waitin foh meh, chile*, says my

mother. *Dese traditions and customs dat eh make ah lick ah sense. Yuh tink I wahn some strangah sleepin between me and meh husband?*

They stayed in a hotel on the beach in Tobago, and in two decades of marriage to come, it would be their only vacation. Arya unwrapped a bathing suit from tissue paper. She had saved up to buy it from a local shop. A lascivious breeze swept through the open French doors of their hotel room and lifted her dress up around her. Dharmendra grabbed her around the midsection, threw her up in the air, and started kissing her everywhere. At first she giggled, but when his hands started reaching body parts previously untouched, she stiffened.

—*Krys,* my mother says, *me eh know nutten bout sex. Nohbuddy tawk bout dem ting back een de day nah chile. Meh gone intoh marriage blind like ah bat. It hut. It hut so rheal bhad. Ah scream like someboddy was killin meh.*

Arya's screams were so intense, they drove a maid to unlock the door with her employee key only to discover a young couple tangled in bedsheets, hair disheveled and faces flushed.

—*Dat was it,* my mother tells me, *one time and yuh conceive. Yuh faddah family din believe ah was a virgin when dey here ah pregnant so fass, buh if dey do de matts den dey goh see yuh come exactly nine monts latah from July toh April. Besides dat, who een dey right mine goh wahn geh pregnant so fass? Lun from meh mistakes, eh chile.*

Dharmendra and Arya luxuriated in Tobago's silky waters for an entire week. As a young girl from the bush who had barely set foot outside a twenty-minute radius of her farm, Arya was euphoric. They took a boat out to the Nylon Pool—a shallow area in the middle of the ocean and one of the main attractions in Tobago. They walked on white sand with goggles on, careful not to step off the sandbar, as neither of them could swim. Arya squealed when she looked into the water and found fish swimming all around them. Bits of coral and starfish littered the sand, and Dharmendra, the braver of the two, snatched them out of the water for a closer look.

They sailed on a glass-bottomed boat above the glittering Buccoo Reef. Arya pressed her face against the glass as fish darted just inches away from her. Schools of fish paraded past, and she, like a tourist, pointed in awe. Dharmendra had been here many times before and was content to lean back, crossing an ankle over a knee, his body lounging, while Arya babbled and squealed beside him. The pool at the hotel, the trek through the rainforest, their visit to Little Tobago—Arya absorbed it all.

Tobago, which is mostly rainforest, is home to some of the world's most beautiful birds. As Dharmendra and Arya sipped rum and twisted pieces of roti into curry shrimp, hummingbirds flittered all around them. The gentle whizz of the birds' wings as they hovered and dipped their long beaks into a flower's nectar was music to Arya's ears. On the last day there, Dharmendra took her to Bird Island, where one lone scarlet ibis caught her eye. There was an elegant curve to its beak that was both seductive and dangerous. Its legs seemed to be stuck in a pool of mud, and Arya, entranced, couldn't take her eyes off it. The scarlet ibis spread its majestic wings, tipped with feathers of the deepest black Arya had ever seen. With great flapping, the bird soared into the air, high and far above them.

On the day of their return, their families tried to salvage whatever they could of their traditions. Despite Arya's reluctance, a lookanny was installed in their bed. On Wednesday her father came to collect her, and on Sunday Dharmendra brought her home.

—*Meh eh know why we do all dat nah Krys,* my mother says. *Ah din even believe een any ah dat nonsense.*

FOUNDATION

~~~~~

—*AH DIN WANTAH END UP like Gramma,* my mother says to me as she tucks the sheet around my grandfather, who is still in the hospital, his condition after the failed brain surgeries leaving us all in a state of uncertainty. *Yuh know how she move een by Grampa muddah and all de tings she hah to put up with. Ah juss wanted to start diffrant.*

Arya quit her job before her wedding and, as was the norm, returned with Dharmendra to live in his parents' house, even though Arya had explicitly said she didn't want to. They began their life together in a small bedroom at the back of the house. Arya fumed, and Dharmendra attempted to pacify her. *Ah juss need ah lil moh time dahlin. We eh goh be hyah long Arya, not long atall. Lemme juss make it moh comfortable for we.*

—*Ah di feel like ah outsidah livin dey,* my mother tells me, *and ah din know what toh do wid mehself. E promise de house wuddah be done by de time we geh married boh meh feel as though e di plan dis all along. Geh meh een e muddah house and hope ah wuddah stay dey. Nah mahn!*

There was one other daughter-in-law residing in the Sital residence, Dharmendra's younger brother Vipin's wife. Her name was Ivy, but she told everyone to call her Sugar.

—*Sugah, yuh could believe dat?* my mother says. *Sugah. She di wahn everybody toh call ah grown oman Sugah. Huh!*

Ivy had married Vipin one year earlier and had been living with the Sitals ever since. On moving into the house, Arya had hoped to forge some kind of connection with her, but those hopes were dashed when she walked into the living room one day to discover Ivy whispering with Dharmendra's three sisters. They hushed one another upon her arrival, grinning and offering her a seat next to them.

Arya was reminded of why she shouldn't have even tried. Months back, right after Dharmendra had proposed to her, his sisters invited her to a barbecue at their house. Arya had dolled herself up as usual with heels, tights, teased hair, and make-up. Glancing at herself in the mirror, she rubbed off some of the make-up and muted the lipstick, assuming his parents would be there as well. At the door, the youngest sister took her upstairs and into a room.

Ah tinkin it was ah bah-b-que, Arya started.

Doh worry yuhself wid dat. Tak ah seat, one of them said to her. The three sisters sat in a circle in front of her. Confused, Arya dropped into the chair.

We bring yuh here today, the youngest started, before the eldest one interrupted, *We wantah know yuh intentions wid we bruddah. Allyuh been going ahrung a while now an ah tink is time toh hah dis conversation.*

Arya flew out of the chair, sending her heavy pocketbook crashing to the floor. *Excuse meh,* she said, *dat is de pretense allyuh bring meh undah hyah for? Meh intentions wid Dharmendra is mine and mine alone and frankly is none ah allyuh damn business.* Arya *steupsed* at them, and they gasped. She grabbed her purse before exiting, her posture ramrod straight.

—*Krys gyul,* my mother tells me, *ah was so furious boh wid mehself too tinkin dey was goin be nice toh meh. And den ah move een*

dere and ah tinkin Ivy and me goan get along but it moh uncomfort-
able dan anyting de way she stick up een dey behind so, grateful she eh
de new one een de house anymoh.

So instead of taking the seat they offered her now that she
lived there, Arya declined as gracefully as she could manage
and said she'd rather take a walk. They scoffed at the thought of
a walk, exclaiming the midafternoon heat was too much, and
exchanged looks as Arya walked past them. But Arya eyed their
flabby arms and fleshy hips and resolved to walk every day.

DHARMENDRA RETURNED HOME past midnight every day,
only to wake up at five in the morning to start all over again—
police work, the house, his parents' rum shop, then home. He
snuggled into bed next to Arya, the damp fragrance of Irish
Spring soap and Brut clinging to him.

How de house goin? Arya asked him, unable to contain her
excitement at the thought of moving into a large house in the
city. Dharmendra was ecstatic too. Though tired, he told her
of each day's accomplishments, detailing for her the work he'd
done on the land his father had blessed them with to start their
life together.

But with no one to talk to and nothing to do, Arya wandered
around Sangre Grande, hearing the sirens and cries at the hospital across the street, the roar of inebriated men in the rum shop,
and smelling the stench of the open drains. The blaring sirens
gave her such piercing headaches, she had to lie in bed all day. The
smell of the drains, and of everything else, made her vomit. Arya
knew she was pregnant.

The silence and loneliness were dizzying; the walls of their
cramped room spun. Arya begged Dharmendra for them to

move into their unfinished house in Chaguanas, about a forty-five-minute drive from his parents. He was reluctant, but Arya needled him day after day until he relented.

It eh ready, Arya, he warned her. But she didn't care.

—*E din wantah go nowhey gyul,* my mother tells me, *happy hwome dey wid everyting, comfortable no ass while I done give up everyting.*

When they announced to his family they'd be packing everything up and moving in the next few days, everyone was surprised. A string of cautionary words followed them, *No plumbin... No electricity... No furniture... No nutten... Allyuh crazy... Bettah off stayin right hyah.*

Despite the dismal picture everyone had painted, despite her new home sounding very much like her old home, Arya wanted to go, wanted to get away from Sangre Grande, where there was nothing for her but loneliness and utter sadness. She wanted to get away and move into something she could help create each passing day, and at the end wipe her brow and say, *Dis is mine.*

It goh take a while toh move yuh know, Arya, Dharmendra said to her. He told her it would probably take a week or two, not the few days they had told everyone it would. His parents assured them they could stay as long as they wanted. But while Dharmendra was at work, Arya locked the bedroom door behind her and packed. When his mother called her for breakfast, for lunch, for dinner, Arya said she'd eaten and that she was okay. Their things fit into fewer boxes and bags than they both expected.

Dharmendra returned that night to find no clothes for him to change into and their entire room stripped from the bedsheets to the curtains.

Lewwe goh now, Arya pleaded. She picked up a box to take downstairs to his jeep, but he removed it from her hand, warn-

ing her to be careful. They had yet to tell his parents about their
new grandchild.

Dharmendra's mother was still awake in the living room,
waiting for her husband to get home from work. She begged them
not to go, told them it was the middle of the night, they could
wait till the morning. Arya knew the morning would bring with
it more and better excuses for them not to go; they had to leave
now. Convinced his mother was right, but also because he was a
bona fide mama's boy, Dharmendra cocked his head to the side
and lifted his shoulder, the universal language of *let's give in*. Arya
put her arms around her mother-in-law's shoulders and promised
they'd visit often. She hugged her and planted a kiss on the top of
her graying head.

They made the drive to Chaguanas in just under half an hour.
It was one of the busiest cities in Trinidad, and Dharmendra
weaved in and out of back roads to get them there faster. They
pulled into the driveway of Lot No. 22 Pepper Place in Montrose,
Chaguanas. Arya clapped her hands and squealed.

She set her eyes on what was merely a skeleton of a house.
There were no windows, no locks, no doors, no water, no electricity, yet Arya beamed as she strolled through the house with an
oil lamp in hand. This place, crusted with mortar that had dried
unevenly, Arya called *hwome*, the happiness in her voice foreign
to her own ears.

Dharmendra lugged their meager belongings from the car
to the second floor of the house. *Dis*, he said throwing his arms
out, *is de mastah bedroom*. It was an enormous space at the
front of the second floor with a smaller room connected to it.
Dah is de batroom. He caressed her belly and led her down the
corridor where their child would have her own bedroom and
bathroom too.

For now, they slept on a piece of tarpaulin, the cold of the concrete invading their bodies and making them sore by morning. But Arya dreamed just as her mother did—there was paint on the walls, furniture in the rooms, cabinets in the kitchen, dishes in the cabinets, and every single thing was chosen by her hand. She would make this house what she wanted it to be.

Dharmendra woke earlier than usual, for now his commute was longer. He cursed the stiffness of his bones but didn't disturb Arya as he gathered himself together in the darkness and left. Arya didn't stir until much later. When she awoke, she knew exactly where she was and smiled at the sun pouring through the window openings. Birds were calling and chattering outside, and people were doing the same.

Brushing her teeth proved to be a bit of a challenge with no water in the house, but in the backyard was a water tank. She filled a bucket and lugged it to the house, where she brushed her teeth and cleaned herself. Upstairs, she searched through boxes for clothes she could easily move around in. A foul smell assaulted her while digging through the box closest to the bathroom. Flies buzzed around an uncovered bucket of excrement and urine. Arya threw a ratty towel over the bucket and heaved it down the back steps, through the yard, and to the lip of the river. The contents sloshed over the sides, but Arya turned her mind to pleasant thoughts of the house and its big kitchen while she dumped the contents of the bucket into the river. The brackish water briefly turned a darker shade of brown.

There was much for her to do throughout the day—sweeping and dusting, scrubbing and mopping the walls and floors. It would only become layered with dust and muck again when her husband and his friends returned to work in the evening, but better to clean every day than to let it build up, she thought.

———

DHARMENDRA RETURNED HOME with his friends at five to a sleeping wife. He woke her, his mood changing from tired to sour to grouchy. Arya was still in a haze from dreaming of her home and of their tranquil honeymoon with its glorious sunsets, of Dharmendra slipping into bed next to her and nuzzling his stubble into the back of her neck. His hunger made her defensive. How was she to cook? There was no money, no refrigerator, no goods, no utensils. Dharmendra's friends stood outside smoking cigarettes.

Allyuh goh ahead and staht, he told them. *We goh be right back.*

They set out in the jeep to buy the cheapest items. Though everything they purchased was plastic, Arya held their bags tightly because these were the first things they would buy and own together. They chose a large iron pot for her to cook in over the open fire downstairs, plastic utensils, plates, and bowls that could withstand rough handling for a while. For tonight they bought Chinese food—fried shrimp wontons, vegetable fried rice with half a chicken doused in pepper sauce, and whatever else the guys wanted to eat.

Dem doh wahn payment oh anyting, Dharmendra said. *Dem fellahs and dem juss helpin meh out. Boh we hah toh feed dem. Mammy used to send food and ting foh dem boh now yuh hah toh cook. How it lookin ah hah wife hwome boh no food when me and dese fellahs reach hyah?* The plastic bags whipped between them in the breeze. Arya said nothing.

Before they curled up on the ground that night, Dharmendra handed Arya his wallet; it was filled with money he had withdrawn from the bank earlier that day. *Take wah yuh need toh buy grocery and ting tomorrow. It hah ah grocery store right out de road.*

It eh fah atall. Geh some tings so yuh could hah someting ready foh me and dem bois when we reach back tomorrow.

Arya took the worn leather wallet he slipped into her hands. He turned the oil lamp up for her, the yellow flame licking high and gleeful. Dharmendra lit a candle to take with him to the bathroom. Massaging the leather between her hands, she felt the warmth from his pocket. When she opened it, she did so slowly, pushing up his laminated policeman's ID with her thumb and then sliding it down. She went through all of his cards this way, most of them serving only the purpose of identification, and then his sole bankcard. The money was pressed into a slit at the back. There were seven electric-blue hundred-dollar bills. She counted the amount several times. This was enough to hold them over for months.

Take wah yuh need, was what he said. She extracted a single hundred-dollar bill, folded it in half, and placed it beneath what served as their mattress. Lying back with her hands tucked beneath her head, she followed the flickering shadows the flame cast on the unpainted walls. The belch and cough from her husband's rectum in the next room, accompanied by its smell, didn't faze her; her mind was on the glossy fruits she would choose from vendors at the market tomorrow, haggling over a better price, the brightly packaged goods she'd purchase from the grocery store, a snow cone or two doused in condensed milk to devour on her way back from food shopping.

How much yuh take? he asked her, slipping his wallet into the pocket of the uniform he'd be wearing tomorrow. *Oh Gawd gyul, ah so tired,* he said without waiting for an answer. He knelt on the floor next to her.

Ah hundred, she whispered.

He sat up and grabbed his wallet.

*Ah take out all foh yuh rheally boh ahgo keep ah hundred foh me.
Tak de ress. Yuh goh need it.*

He handed her the remainder of the money, and the crackling bills remained askew in her palms. Dharmendra extinguished the flame and lay back.

Poh it away, lewwe sleep.

She folded them in her hands and tried to fall asleep but couldn't for a long time. When she did, the money was within her grasp beneath her pillow.

THE NEXT DAY Arya went through what would become her morning routine before her husband installed plumbing and electricity. She dragged the bucket down to the river, tossed its contents in, rinsed it with water from the well, filled another to clean herself and brush her teeth, scrubbed away the mess they'd made the day before, stuffed herself with fruit from their back-yard, and went to the market and store with bills tucked under her armpit where no one could snatch them from her.

For her trip to the market downtown in the morning, Arya wore flats and tights that accentuated her body in all the right places. Only two months pregnant and with no baby weight yet, she could still wear the stylish clothes she'd always worn. As she walked, she sashayed her hips from side to side in a fluid motion, capturing even the eyes of the women who passed by. Men hooted and whistled; Arya smiled. They didn't yet know who she was, but soon enough she'd be *de policemahn wife,* and respect, not whistles, would follow her, though the lascivious thoughts that undoubtedly entered their minds wouldn't end.

Arya took a ten-minute bus ride to the market in Chaguanas where vendors sat wilting, along with their produce, in the sun.

She gazed at heaps of mangoes of all different varieties—julie, donkeystone, doo-doose, starch, long—alongside bundles of bandanya, bags of rice, sacks of flour, ground peas. Though there was no need, she haggled with the vendors anyway, getting a great price for their stash. Her eye for fruits and vegetables was keen. From the shake of an avocado she could tell if it was ripe or if it would ripen nicely, if it was plucked too young, or if the inside was rotten. She rapped her knuckles on a watermelon, ran her hands along its skin, and shook it before deciding it was good enough to consume later that night. Without a fridge or icebox there was nowhere to store anything extra or left over.

At the butcher's she ordered salted beef—Dharmendra's favorite in rice dishes, though his Hindu parents couldn't ever know—and eyed the man's hands as he placed the meat on the scale. She was unknown in the Chaguanas market, her style too new, her face too fresh, so he tipped the balance in his favor.

A A wah yuh tink yuh doin? Yuh feel ah dotish awah? Me eh blind. Gih meh ah bettah price now oh else ah leave yuh blasted meat juss so.

The man put his hands up defensively. Arya *steups*ed, getting used to this small defiant act toward people who pissed her off. The butcher wouldn't make that mistake with her again. And to hook her into coming back to him now that they'd done this dance and knew where they stood, he lowered his price and threw in a little extra for good faith.

A bit high off of being able to get anything she wanted for the first time in her life, she wandered to the section of sweets and indulged in a milky piece of burfi, the sprinkles crumbling and melting in her mouth. She sampled blocks of peera, the rice and sugar grainy and pleasant on her tongue. The taste of sticky honey from the rasgulla remained long after she was on a maxi taxi.

At home, she prepared her meal on the back steps. She ground seasoning with two stones, chopped meat on a tree stump, and seared everything over the open fire on the ground floor. When Dharmendra and his boys came home that evening, they gathered around the pot, spooning this meat dish—something Dharmendra's mother would never have sent—onto their plates. They cracked the watermelon and devoured the whole thing in minutes before returning to their work with vigor.

BLOWS

~~~~

ONLY TWO MONTHS HAD PASSED, but Arya and Dharmendra had transformed the place. There were now some doors and windows, lights, a toilet, fridge, sink. No more lugging bodily discharge out of the house in that godforsaken bucket. Once the grass started towering in the backyard and Arya could no longer see, she started to fling the contents of their bucket over the grass and somewhere beyond.

—*It eh hah nobuddy toh check up on meh oh anyting,* my mother says, laughing, *an if dey gone lookin and geh stick up een shit den dey was lookin foh it. Is my house now, ah di hah propahty gyul.*

Their home was becoming comfortable. Arya was comfortable. Enough that she took pity on her younger brother Amrit and his sixteen-year-old girlfriend, and offered them a place to stay for a while. A while turned into a week, then two, three, four.

Arya was downstairs at the stone sink scrubbing clothes against the washboard with her knuckles. The suds built around her arms, soaking her dress as well. She strung pants and shirts, nightgowns and sheets on the lines, clipping them with wooden clothespins to dry. On such a hot day, she knew everything would dry quickly.

Her belly had begun to show, her gait had changed, and she could no longer hug the basket in front of her as she liked but instead fastened it to her hip. As she was walking upstairs to change into dry clothing, her brother and his girlfriend skipped down the stairs giggling. They were going to a bazaar they'd heard about through the grapevine.

Dharmendra doh need no help on de house Amrit? Arya asked.

Karen pouted, and Amrit shook his head. They were off.

Upstairs she passed by the room that was to be for her child. Arya jiggled the doorknob and tried to get in. Amrit and Karen had installed a lock. In *their* house. *Dammit Amrit!* she said. Footsteps sounded on the back staircase. Thinking it was Amrit returning for something he forgot, she said, *Amrit, why yuh put uh lock on dis door? Yuh hah no right.* When Dharmendra's voice was the one to reach her ears, Arya knew he'd seen them leave. She walked away, not wanting to deal with her husband's anger, despite how right he might be.

They stood in the middle of the narrow corridor that cleaved the entire second floor in two. She saw how Amrit's reluctance to help with something as easy as setting cinderblocks had rankled Dharmendra. He threatened to kick them out. Arya leaned against the wall and placed her hands on her belly. At four months pregnant, her belly protruded round on her slim body.

Dis muddah ass, ow long e goh eat off meh? Eh Arya?

Dharmendra, watch yuh mout bout meh bruddah.

E is ah nasty, ungrateful son-of-ah-bitch. E eh eatin and drinkin off meh no moh.

Dharmendra, ever irrational when enraged, wouldn't calm down now. Arya suspected he'd even had a few drinks in him already, as he was wont to do when working on the house all day on the weekends. She *steupsed* as she walked past him, long and loud. Irked by his wife's blatant disrespect, he grabbed her and shoved her back into place.

Wah de ass wrong wid yuh? Yuh mad awah? she flared up at him, ready with a torrent of vituperations. He cracked a blow to her jaw. Her head ricocheted off the concrete wall. Black splotches stained her vision. Her sight blurred; her knees buckled. Instinctively she cradled her belly. Arya fell on her side. Dharmendra turned and left.

She lay on the cold, dusty floor and heard the slap of his leather slippers hitting his heels as he walked away. Here in this place she had fallen in love with, Arya now knew intimately every creak and rumble on 22 Pepper Place. She heard the laundry billow, then stop as he broke through the wet sheets hanging on the clothesline. He sauntered over a carpet of lush grass at the back of their house, and she heard nothing for a minute. Separating their house from his brother's was a tongue of gravel, the same path she often crossed to gossip with her sister-in-law next door. Through the gaping holes in their walls where windows had yet to be installed, the gravel crunching beneath his slippers reached her on the second floor. It was so quiet where they lived, where the humming of a bird's wings could easily be heard through an opened window. But today she found no comfort in the quiet of nature's melody. Arya wondered if he was going to his brother's or the rum shop down the street. Would he return? Would he gather her in his arms? Kiss away her tears? Promise to never do it again? She'd never told him about her father beating her mother, and he'd never been violent before, why now?

—*Meh nevah tell im nutten bout Rebecca gettin lix so,* my mother tells me. *Din wantah plant no seed een e head toh beat me too plus yuh nevah suppose toh talk bout dem tings back een de day. Ah tell mehself, eh Krys, no mahn goh evah put deh hand on meh as long as ah life een meh body.*

The rumble and thump of the loose cesspit cover ground

below his weight as he crossed their yard into his brother's. Prana, the eldest Sital sibling, said, *Aye boi, come come come ahgo meet yuh een di front. Wah yuh wantah drink today?* Already six in the evening, it was time for their routine fraternal drink.

Arya slapped the floor with her palms and blinked the tears from her eyes. She rolled onto her back and lay supine. The grooved plywood ceiling Dharmendra had recently installed swam before her eyes. Getting up, a pain pulled on her right side; she kicked the front door, but it didn't budge. She leaned against the walls, the coolness quenching the heat in her body. Looking down at her belly, she cradled it in her hands.

—*We di juss find out yuh was a gyul chile, Krys,* my mother tells me. *Ah wasn't bringin yuh intah ah wherl whey yuh goh watch yuh muddah geh beat up like me.*

Arya slid back down to the floor. The impact of her butt hitting the ground jolted her. She clapped a hand to the back of her head, the other palm never leaving her belly. His hand cutting through the air replayed over and over again in her mind. No remorse. No reaction.

His laughter traveled up to her ears. He laughed louder. It became deafening. Arya tore at her hair, scratching her ears in the process, drawing blood. No more waiting. He was never coming back. Not to do what she needed him to do.

She pulled herself up. Perspiration beaded along her upper lip and between her swollen breasts. From the verandah she watched him. Shirtless, he sat on the low wall in his brother's front yard. They exchanged something. Dharmendra flung his head back and laughed. Both his hands were on the wall with him, supporting him from tipping over. A bottle of beer sat sweating beside him.

To get to the back of the house took less than thirty seconds. At the back door, she looked through a pile of wood but did not find

what she was looking for. Downstairs she spotted a piece of two-
by-four in a corner. The one she selected had been varnished carefully by her husband's hands, no doubt for the bed he was making
them. She tested it by slapping it into her palm. It was solid.

Arya walked through the clean laundry, over the cesspit, and
around to the front of the house. Nissi, her sister-in-law, was in
the kitchen adding the finishing touches to dinner, something
Arya would've been doing herself on any given day. Giving them
a wide berth, she approached her husband and his brother from
behind. Prana stood up, hooked the necks of the empty bottles
between his fingers, and disappeared into the house for more.
Arya tightened her grip around the wood. Behind Dharmendra
now, she raised it high over her head and in one sweep of strength
clapped it on his back. He grabbed the sides of the wall tighter,
trying not to topple over. He knew it was his wife. Over and over
she arced her weapon, bringing it down on his back. Hit after hit,
he sat there, his clenched fists supporting him on the stone wall.

Prana emerged from the house with beers in hand. *Aye aye aye
gyul, wah yuh doin?* He got closer. Without stopping she warned
through ragged breath, *Prana, if yuh come closah ahgo beat yuh too.*
Prana didn't move.

Nevah, Arya spat at her husband, *in yuh life,* she hit him, *hit meh
again.* Spent, she allowed the two-by-four to clatter to the ground.
She turned and walked away, the image of her husband hunched
forward, red welts forming on his back, burned into her memory.

—*Krys chile, e nevah lay so much as ah fingah on meh again.*

MY
GRANDFATHER

2006–2008

LEGACY

〰〰

—Ah couldah see de greed een all ah dem eye, my mother says to me, *dey eh care one ass bout Pappy.*

My mother is right: after three brain surgeries in November of 2006, no one cares for Shiva's life. They just need him to stay alive long enough to figure out who has his last will and testament. With no concern for his condition, my mother sees how her siblings count his money, inventory his land holdings, and tally their possible values. Who will benefit most from Shiva's death? Who will inherit hundreds of thousands of dollars in verdant land stretching across Trinidad? Who will Shiva bequeath everything to? If my grandfather chooses to follow tradition, then only one person, his eldest son, will inherit everything. But no one has proof, and so they all ask underhanded questions of one another, sometimes directly accusing: *So **you** hah e lass will. Dat is why yuh could go bout yuh business so.*

Several of Shiva's children have a will in their possession, but no one is forthcoming, each hoping theirs is the most recent. Shiva was fond of visiting his lawyer and drawing up wills based on who had won his favor for the time being. My mother has a will of her own that names her the executor and gives my grandmother power of attorney. With him incapacitated, my grandmother is able to make all decisions on his behalf, and my mother bears the burden of carrying out the legal provisions of his will. But that will is ten years old, and if Rebecca and Arya plan to wield it, they have to do so swiftly.

In our apartment, my mother unfolds papers from our fireproof safe. They resemble ancient parchment, yellowed and creased. She's protected the will for ten years, from Trinidad to America, a piece of paper that unevenly divides Shiva's legacy among my mother and only two of her sisters.

—*E di always makin will,* my mother tells me. *Wah frame ah min e was een when e mak dis one meh doh evan remembah, boh is mad e mad wid Amrit and Rahul and dah is why e leave dem out. Boh de uddah gyuls and dem is wutless dey wutless refusin toh help im when time foh im to move up hyah een America, so e cut dem out too.*

The family set the current in motion, and it pulls them along, Rebecca signing every document that comes her way to keep her husband alive.

—*We di need im toh stay alive,* my mother confides to me. *Toh fix it, e hah toh stay alive.*

Three sisters meet with my grandmother at her apartment.

My mother reveals to them the will in her possession. One of them pulls Arya aside.

Arya, we hah toh make ah will ah we own, she says.

We kyant, my mother responds, *it eh right.*

Ah know somebuddy back hwome in Trinidad, she continues, ignoring my mother. *Ahgo call im. Me and you goh geh everyting.*

No, meh eh doin nutten widout Mammy.

Ahright, come back tomorrow, Pooja says before she leaves.

My mother does not return the next day. The idea of fabricating a will gnaws at her conscience, and so does her eldest brother's lack of interest in trying to keep their father alive.

—E was so cold, Krys, she says to me, *so cold. Meh doh undahstahnd how e could be money hungry so, e eh care if e own faddah dead oh* **how** *e goh dead if e goh suffah oh anyting. All meh see is de greed een everyting e doin.*

They all agree that their eldest brother must have the last will and testament, but he never produces it. Since my mother's is the only one that surfaces, Rebecca has more power than anyone.

My grandmother calls my mother. *Arya, meh geh ah lawyer willin toh make ah will foh meh on Pappy behalf. All e need is e tumb-print. We hah toh geh im out ah dat ospital.*

Wah lawyah yuh geh, Ma? Arya asks her mother.

Meh geh one eh. E not so good boh e good enough foh wah ah need.

Rebecca tells my mother she has divided everything Shiva owns between their two sons, she too thinking only of the crippling tradition that pretends women do not exist.

Ma, how **could** *you?* Arya says. *Rahul* **nevah evah** *come toh see im, treat im like ah dawg. E nevah even come toh see* **you!**

Arya, Rebecca interrupts, *if de bois and dem evah sell de estate ah puh someting een de will dat say dey hah toh gih each ah de gyuls an dem $10,000 TT.*

Some of my grandfather's properties can sell for close to a million Trinidadian dollars, approximately $170,000 each. The stipulation my grandmother includes in the will for the girls will give them around $1600 each.

My mother insists on seeing this will, goes to my grandmother's house straight away and holds that paper in her hands. After reading it, she brandishes the stapled papers in front of my grandmother's face and says, *Dis is enough foh all yuh gyul chilren toh nevah tawk toh yuh oh see yuh evah again.*

As the bickering swirls around me, my grandfather now a mist vaporizing in the background, I wander back in my mind to lazy Trinidadian days, where the heat lingered at the backs of our knees and around our necks.

In our open living room in Trinidad, we sat on the couch as we often did when he visited. I learned to spell his name, finishing the round letters and curves with a flourish. He enunciated each letter with a calm in his voice that was reserved only for me, something I understood even at this tender age. *S-H-I-V-A S-I-N-G-H*, he spelled. I didn't know then, as I practiced my writing on our floor, that my grandfather was illiterate.

Lun meh dis and lun meh dat, was what he said to me with each visit. *Is **teach** meh, Grampa, **teach**, not lun.* He grabbed a pencil and wrapped his fingers awkwardly around it, unsure of what to do next. He stared at the crooked letters that I'd pressed into the page, my handwriting that of a little girl still learning the alphabet. With a shaky hand, he copied what I'd written, but his fingers trembled from fatigue by the time he wrote the last letter. This man, who had labored with his hands well into his later years, collapsed from trying to write the letters of the alphabet.

When my mother walked into the room to scoop me up for a bath, he shuffled the papers together and cleared his throat. Ever gruff, he said, *Pass meh de remote dey,* and she did as she was told, obsequious in her compliance.

Wah allyuh was doin? she asked as she spun me from one end of the towel to the next. I told her, *Nutten, juss writin. Meh show Grampa how to sign e name.* I laughed as she flipped me upside down then right side up again. *Yuh know why e doin dat, chile? E practisin foh when e write e will. Yuh goh geh someting. Truss meh, e leavin yuh someting.*

In a place like the islands, where land begets identity, power, and wealth, children pick up on these subtleties, and I knew what this meant.

Boh you is e dawtah, Ma, I said. To which she replied, *Boh Krys gyul, e hah a special love foh yuh and everybody know it, chile. Everybody.*

I grinned and grew up assuming I'd be included in his legacy, but Shiva deceived us all.

BOND

GROWING UP, we regularly visited my mother's parents on the farm, leaving the city behind, following roads as thin as veins into the mountains, until we got to a narrow gravel path that our car hissed and spat over.

On one of these visits, my mother's older sister was at the house with all six of her children. As we were all close in age, we often spent time together. Yet my grandfather took me alone with him around the farm in the mornings, and I ambled behind him, tired but happy. After food and a nap—sometimes while he was still asleep—I would jump on top of him reminding him that I wanted ice cream. *Grampa, Grampa, Grampa. Wake up! Doh play yuh fohget yuh know, cause meh wahn meh ice cream and meh wahn it now!* In one sweeping motion, he pulled me into his arms and leapt off the couch, laughing. Going for ice cream was a ritual of my visits. I didn't choose the most convenient location, but he took me anyway because I wanted peanut ice cream and there were only a few places that sold it.

He grabbed his keys, holding me on his hip. We passed my parents, my grandmother, my aunt, and my cousins. They knew where we were going, and while my cousins were too young to hide their yearning, their bodies leaning toward us, their fear kept them in place. I wrapped my arms around his neck, pulled myself up higher on his hip, and turned to them. *We gone toh geh we ice cream. Ahgo be back in ah bit. Doh miss we nah.*

We traveled in his sleek new car: a Blue Bird the color of liquid gold that shimmered in the sunlight, a car that was envied for miles around. He buckled me into the front seat, a place where only adults had sat before. I knew my cousins' eyes were on me, but never did I turn to look at them. We peeled off. My grandfather allowed me to eat ice cream in his car, though he never permitted anyone else to bring in food or drink, far less to eat or drink. I knew what a special privilege this was and was always careful to let the ice cream drip onto my skirt, shorts, or top instead of on his seat. By the time we returned, I was almost finished or already done, jumping around everyone with a smeared face and sticky clothes. My mother made a halfhearted attempt to stop my gloating, but she herself was pleased that my grandfather favored me, and so after a while her chiding faded to laughter at my naughtiness.

We returned to the city in the early evening, before the sun touched the horizon. My aunt and cousins lived close, but we had at least an hour's drive. *Okay gih Gramma and Grampa ah hug, lewwe goh now. Make sure yuh tell everbuddy bye, yuh hear?* my mother said.

I bounced around kissing and hugging everyone, leaving my grandfather for last. When I broke away from him, he leaned against the wall with a smile on his face. *Okay, lewwe goh,* my mother called to me. *A A Grampa,* I piped up, *boh whey meh money? Yuh does always gimmeh money. Whey meh money?* Everyone turned to look at us. My mother marched toward me and grabbed me by my arm. *Krystal! Apologize now.* My grandfather's face betrayed no rage, not even a hint of displeasure. He winked at me. I wrenched my arm free from my mother's grasp and put one hand on my hip and one palm out. With his soft *heh heh heh heh heh*, a laugh only discernible in the silence, he plunged his hand into his pocket, extracted his wallet, and gave me a red dollar bill. Already saucy, I waved it around and said, *Wah is dis? Dah is all? Meh wahn twenty.* He pulled out a green five, and I shook my head. He gave me the purple twenty-dollar bill; it was crispy new, straight from the bank. *Okay gimmeh back de dollah since yuh geh yuh twenty.* I flounced away saying over my shoulder, *A A dah is wah yuh geh foh foolin meh. Ah takin de extra dollar.* My mother stepped in again. *Krystal give it back now before ah give yuh ah good cutass in yuh skin.* I stopped and turned to my grandfather. He said to my mother, *Leave she nah, is ahright. Allyuh reach hwome safe.* With that he turned and left, only reappearing when he wanted his dinner. My cousins, I knew, never got anything from him.

ANXIOUS, I ASK MYSELF why there is a special bond between my grandfather and me. What does that say about me? Did he see something of himself in me?

—*Is because we do everyting right, Krys—me and yuh faddah.* My mother tries to explain it away. *E get toh gih meh ahwey de way e was supposed to and everyting between me and yuh faddah was done de right way. Parents on both sides give we ahwey to each uddah. It was a blessed marriage. Dat love and blessin di juss pass on toh you.*

But not my sister. Throughout our entire lives, she was invisible to him. She never kissed him on the cheek, got money from him, or settled in the crevice of the couch next to him. They just never connected, his indifference to her matched by hers to him. I never point out to my mother that this love she attributed to her traditional marriage didn't pass through to my sister. She either didn't want to acknowledge this or couldn't see it.

I think of how I'd speed through the chicken pens with him from the time I could walk, plucking one yellow puff of feathers after another off the ground, feeling their bellies squirm against my palms. I think of how much I wanted to squeeze them, to squish the fluffiness and stop their squirming. Did he recognize something in me at those moments, and did it please him? Was he grooming me? Did I make it easy?

A memory, wave-like, washes over me: back up at the house in the living room, while my grandfather took a nap, I waggled my index fingers at my captured birds, ones he'd allowed me to herd into a tall cardboard box and bring along.

My mother appeared and whispered, *Yuh hah toh feed dem and gih dem watah, Krys, oh dey go dead.* She went downstairs and tiptoed around the room, trying desperately not to wake and anger my grandfather. I was oblivious, falling into the safety of his love for me. The gray pellets she carried reeked, and I retched when she handed them to me.

My grandfather grumbled from the couch, and my mother stood pin straight, glanced in his direction, and patted my head. *Ah gone downstairs, come nah.* I refused, knowing I could stay up here and do what I pleased.

The chicks scrambled for food, climbing over one another. I tripped them as they skipped from one end of the box to another, I petted their heads while they pecked my hands, I picked them up and squeezed them, I played and played until they shit everywhere, and then I left them alone.

I went to my grandfather lying on the couch. *Grampa, Grampa, Grampa, ah bored, rheal bored.* He unhinged his arm from over his eyes and glared at me. *Stan up dey by meh foot and kill any mosquito yuh see. When ah wake up ah wahn see plenty dead body.*

—E use toh do dat to meh, Krys, my mother tells me, *make meh watch and make sure no mosquito bitin him while e sleepin. If meh hit im too hahd is lix, if de mosquito bite im is lix, if e wake up and it eh hah no dead mosquito is lix, everyting is lix, lix, lix. Beatin was e ansah toh every question. So I use toh find dead mosquito all een de cornah and just put it juss so on e leg so when e wake up e see dem dey.*

I situated myself at the end of the couch and watched. Mosquitoes flittered around, but they were too small and too fast for me to catch. I started slapping his legs with my palms. *Ah geh one two tree! Foh fih six, meh geh plenty plenty plenty.* He sat up and laughed. He reserved this part of himself for me. My mother had never seen it.

The midafternoon heat mingled with the fullness from lunch settled over me. *Come hyah,* he said, patting the cranny next to him on the couch. I clambered over his legs and nestled comfortably between him and the cool sheets over the sofa. He sang his special song for me, *Dodo popo dooodoooo, yuh Mammmy gone toh Toco toh buy ah bunch ah moco so dodo popo dooodooo.* My mother never went to Toco without us, and I undoubtedly wanted to sleep but still managed to mumble, *Grampa, wah is moco?* I dozed off before I could hear him tell me it was a bundle of cooking figs.

Sometimes he dozed off again, and unable to sleep, I left via the balcony steps, the same stairs my mother and her sisters checked before going to Carnival. I skipped quietly down and slunk off the gravel pathway so no one downstairs could see I was leaving the property. I jumped over the yard chickens and crawled through the bushes, following that meandering road until I got to Radica's house. She, her brother, and I were almost the same age, and though we sensed we were not supposed to play together, we did it anyway.

They lived in a tiny, one-bedroom hut at the entrance to my grandparents' property. Radica was sweeping the ground with a coconut broom, and her brother was feeding the chickens. They told me they still had to milk the cows and gather the goats. Their arms and legs, though thin, were muscular from farm labor. Their skin was caked with dust and grime from working all day long.

Boh come, Krystal gyul, she says, *Mummy and Daddy gone dung de hill foh ah lil bit, lewwe goan inside before dey come back and see we togeddah.*

Radica and Raj's father is Sachin, my grandfather's nephew. There was a feud between the brothers, and though Sachin wasn't a part of it, the animosity traveled down through the generations, touching but not infecting us. We knew enough to understand we shouldn't play together.

I knew they couldn't come up to my grandparents' house, or *de big house* as they called it, to visit me, so I always snuck away to play with them. They tried once and got a beating from Sachin, so I now steered clear of him completely.

There were two beds in the corner of the room with only a narrow gap between them. We jumped up and down, touching the ceiling and then cannonballing from one bed to the other. At first I didn't notice how we dirtied their sheets, and even once I did I didn't think about the trouble they would get into, or wonder if they had money to afford soap to clean them.

—*Dem eh bet see trouble,* my mother later tells me. *Dey was rheal poor and ah know yuh juss wantah toh play dahlin, boh yuh grandfaddah din wahn it so nobody couldah hah it.*

Over our squealing, Radica heard something and shushed us. She rushed to the window and saw her father and mother clanking up the hill with pails.

Krystal, she said, *jump troo de window, walk to dat bush right dey, yuh go see ah tall tall tree, just walk straight and it goh lead yuh back to de gravel road. Yuh hah to goh now.*

I didn't have time to hug or say goodbye; I just did as she said, and sure enough I was back on the gravel path in no time, weaving my way through the grass back up to the house.

We were caught a handful of times, and it was always worse for them than me, as though Sachin punishing them before my grandfather's eyes was what they deserved, what pleased him.

UNSETTLING

～

AT THE HOSPITAL ONE DAY, in response to the words *Lewwe juss leh him go, doh hol on toh nutten,* one brother lunges at the other.

—*E suy dat because ah de will, Krys,* says my mother, *so Pappy could dead now.*

The sisters attempt to claw them apart. Their fight, my mother told me later, was a buildup from years of animosity stemming from Rahul treating his younger brother like his servant and taking advantage of him once they were in America.

My mother screams for security. They show up with their batons, pulling Rahul one way and Amrit the other. *Ahgo keel yuh,* they holler to one another as they're dragged down the corridor. *Ahgo keel yuh, ahgo keel yuh dead!* Though Amrit is now a cook and Rahul a postman, neither has lost the muscles and build they earned in Trinidad.

Two strong men wasting their energy like that, and sadder yet, brothers.

—*Rahul use toh treat Amrit rheal bhad,* my mother tells me, *use toh hah im like ah caddy when e fuss move hyah een America, always hah toh hol im dung, tellin im take meh hyah take meh dey, goh do dis, goh do dat. When Amrit hah toh go off by eself—and foh e own good too—Rahul din help im one ass. Rheal rheal treat im bhad.*

Amrit cools down and is allowed back into the hospital,

where he drags a chair closer to my grandfather's bedside and wrings his hands as though they are soaked sheets.

I pity my Uncle Amrit as I watch him, for he has the most complicated relationship with my grandfather: the son who has been shot at and beaten worst is the one now struck with a sense of obligation.

—*Krys,* my mother says, *e beat some ah we woss dan uddahs and Amrit geh it de woss. When e staht on Amrit ah do everyting toh juss protek im. Someting een Amrit make im not wantah stop.*

They were younger than sixteen when my mother heard my grandfather yelling at Amrit one day. She ran outside, and that's when her father said, *Arya, goh an geh de gun foh meh now.* But my mother couldn't do it. As dangerous as her father was, he hadn't yet crossed that line of life and murder. But the hatred he had for Amrit made her think he could do it one day. She wouldn't be the one to place the gun in his hands if today were that day.

Amrit looked at his sister, and Arya mouthed the word *run,* and he did. Amrit turned and ran with everything he had, weaving his way in and around a stray chicken, a startled cow, a tire-filled garden. Shiva leapt after him.

Dozens of young coconut trees anchored down by their heavy base hadn't been planted yet. They littered the escape route Amrit chose. Shiva seized one of the delicate stalks and lassoed a coconut palm above his head before aiming and flinging the coconut at his son.

—*E look like ah real madman dat day,* my mother says to me.

The solid shell landed on Amrit's ankle, crippling him, and sent him rolling over and over, writhing with pain. While his son was incapacitated, Shiva darted into the house and returned, gun aimed and ready to shoot.

Amrit, run nah boi, git up and run, oh Gawd run! Arya screamed.

Her father clipped her with the gun round her head for trying to protect her brother, and in response Arya pushed the barrel to the side, buying Amrit as much time as she could. Shiva positioned himself and leveled the shotgun on his shoulder. He aimed. Shot. Gravel and dust pitched up. Missed. Amrit was still running.

—*Oh Gawd Krys,* my mother exclaims holding her head in her hands, *ah know een meh haht if e ketch im e wuddah shoot im dat day. No doubt about dat.*

Amrit kept running, weaving like a drunkard until he was out of sight. Shiva kept shooting long after Amrit disappeared, but Arya didn't wait around for him to beat up on her. She slipped away to finish her work along with her brother's.

A mind that would think to shoot at its own child is certainly lost. Shiva shot with every intention of killing. In my grandfather's world, where he held his family against their will, was nothing sacred? Was human life, the lives of his wife, children, siblings, really so expendable? What happened to this man as a young boy, as a baby? *Did* something happen, or did he enter the world this way? The unsettling feeling of never being able to know burned in us all.

GLINT

UNABLE TO TAKE ANY MORE TIME away from work and school, I fall away from the hospital visits after the third surgery and leave my mother to go by herself each day, even on the weekends. There is freedom, a lightness, in returning to a semblance of routine. I go back to my waitressing job, where no one really knows or cares about what's going on.

Hey Krystal, someone says, *you okay? I heard someone might've died in your family?*

And after a little explanation and an awkward silence, the moment is gone, sucked into the vortex of the past. We are free to lounge and laugh around the soda machine in our downtime. Here, I am able to breathe.

At home, my mother continues to empty herself into me, a nightly cleansing ritual. Away from my grandfather's bedside, my mind is less cluttered. As I learn about the men in my life—my father, my grandfather—men I've been enamored with and admired, they take on dimensions I've never imagined. I can no longer see them as just my father and grandfather; they are Dharmendra and Shiva. Fathers, yes. But also husbands. Perpetrators.

Yuh know wah appen wit dis lass surgery, Krys? she asks me.

The doctors had removed the cranial bone on the left side of my grandfather's head. She'd told me this countless times already.

I look at my mother's gaunt face, her eyes sunken above black crescents, her hair unkempt and clothes disheveled. I search for a trace of her effervescence and am frightened to think it hasn't just diminished but has evaporated altogether. I also realize I've been staying away from the hospital because I am afraid to find my grandfather broken, the conqueror of snakes already gone.

I know I have to return, so we start going to the hospital together again. My mother warns me he no longer has a private room, and griefs clash in the limited space.

From outside the room, I notice the shades are drawn, though I can't see in with my mother in front of me. We have to walk past the other occupant, a woman lying unconscious on a bed, with a man weeping over her chest. My strong, sturdy mother deflates before me; I see the strength drain from her neck and down through her arms. Her broad shoulders tremble and curve inward. She hugs herself before she walks into the room. It is always awkward, tiptoeing past someone else's pain, ignoring theirs to tend to our own.

In the weeks my mother and I spend in that room, we draw back the flimsy curtain that separates us from my grandfather's roommate, Valentina. They're a Spanish couple in their forties with no children and no family, only each other. She was his life. *Mi vida,* he screams. This man pours his heart out to us, complete strangers, because he has no one else.

Valentina, he tells us, was fond of slipping her dainty feet into the slippers he calls *chancletas.* They were the only shoes she ever wore. These netted slippers, in 2006, were the most popular footwear for little girls, teenagers, and adult women in New Jersey and New York. Made of fine mesh decorated with sequins and beads, they were backless and had smooth rubber soles. They were being sold everywhere, from street corners to department stores, and could be found everywhere I frequently shopped. Because they were stylish, but more because they were cheap, I owned a pair in every color and stored them in a large container underneath the bed I shared with my sister. One day, as Valentina hurried across the street, her fingers loosely intertwined with her husband's, the smooth bottoms of the slippers slid on the concrete and she fell, hitting her head on the sidewalk. It had been months since she'd last awoken.

The sight of that man wailing over his wife makes me hesitate before I sidle over the threshold, clinging to the walls to get past them. His anguish spills into the hallways. That feeling of pain sticks to me as my eyes land on my grandfather.

A feeding tube vanishes into one of his nostrils; his breathing is raspy through the transparent oxygen mask over his mouth, which clouds as he breathes out and clears when he breathes in. His cheeks and lips quiver. The stench of his breath is thick and heavy, musty from abandoned teeth and foamy saliva buildup. Thin lips hang loosely around his toothless gums. They are cracked and dried with spit. His body, like death, is ominous and still beneath the austere whiteness of the crisp bedsheets.

I stumble backward but keep my reaction in check when I see my mother's eyes on me; I step forward again. I need a breath, some air, my freedom from this image of him, but I feel imprisoned in that room. From deep within his throat, his breathing continues to rake the silence. It is intense but hollow, summoning death. Wisps of breath escape his oxygen mask and wilt my nose hairs; I can help it no longer and turn away.

My mother nudges a copy of the Upasana into my hands. I thumb to the most popular bhajan, and when I start singing, my voice is slow, unsteady, like wings flitting, attempting to stay airborne. *Om Jaya jagdeesh hare, svaamee jaya jagdeesh hare / Bhakta*

janan ke sankat / Kshan me door kare / Om, Jaya jagdeesh hare /
Maat-pitaatummere, sharan gahoo kiskee, svaame sharan . . .

I follow the transliteration of the Sanskrit; the language itself, though beautiful to behold, is foreign to me. I sing these words to my grandfather without knowing their meaning. I cantillate a rhythm instilled in me from when I was young, the melody of a sacred song, one—I was told—that was supposed to remedy, revive, sustain.

I had only used and seen this bhajan performed at the ends of events. When prayers were done, to signal we were finished, we fed the fire with everything leftover from the ceremony— ghee, samagree, parsad—while intoning the Aarti bhajan. This chant was indicative of the end. My mother felt in her heart that my grandfather should go peacefully now. She regretted having forced my grandmother to let the doctors perform brain surgery. It had only tortured him.

A doctor enters and scrapes the bottom of my grandfather's feet with a pen, saying out loud, *Mr. Singh? Mr. Singh? Mr. Singh,* but the only response is the haunt of his hollow breathing echo-ing in the narrow room. When the doctor unveils his feet, their suppressed stink rises into the air. His yellowed toenails are long and curled, and fungus cobwebs his heels and toes.

—Meh kyant believe e own chilren leh im get like dis, my mother tells me. *We was suppose to take turns takin care ah im boh not one ah dem do dey share aftah me.*

Garish staples hold the collapsed side of his head together; hacked hair grows unevenly along the incision's edge. The cranial bone removal had left behind too much skin; it sagged and set-tled, a pocket in his skull.

Instead of my grandfather's rehabilitation bringing him back to his former self, his progress is now marked by his screaming the

199

word *no.* If my grandmother enters his hospital room, his glassy eyes slide over her and he howls *NO! NO-NO-NO-NO-NO-NO-NO* until, unable to take it anymore, she leaves and sits in the waiting area. I refrain from asking him any questions, especially everyone's favorite: *Yuh recognize meh?* He shrieks *no* at everyone, and *no* is his answer to every question. But he is awake now and will continue to heal, so the hospital begins the paperwork to get rid of him.

There are two options now—home with my grandmother or a nursing home.

E hah toh stay wid Mammy is the consensus their children reach without consulting Rebecca. Not one of his children offers to take him home. Though it is culturally expected of them to take care of their parents when they're ill, this isn't even an option; he is my grandmother's responsibility. After hearing horror stories about nursing homes from friends and family, they can't bear to put their father in one. But that isn't the truth. Thinking of nursing homes make them uneasy, forces them to consider their own uncertain futures.

He needs round-the-clock help, a nurse informs them, but they don't think about what this will do to their mother; they make the choice that allows their consciences to rest the easiest. My grandmother sits outside the circle of her children. I know she doesn't want to take on yet another burden from this man, but no one else cares. They don't ask her what she wants, what she's thinking, how she feels. Her husband will be thrust upon her once again, stealing whatever life she has left.

Rebecca sits by for weeks while the doctors monitor her husband and her children fill out paperwork for her, acknowledging her presence only when they need a signature. All talk of the nursing home has long since been laid to rest.

The day of Shiva's release, Rebecca tells no one. She travels to the hospital because, without her signature, they can't do anything.

I'm changing my mind, Rebecca explains to a nurse while looking around her, checking for her children. *I would like my husband to be taken to a nursing home instead,* she says in a flawless American accent, so there is no mistaking the words coming out of her mouth. *I've already taken care of everything. Here is the paperwork from the nursing home right by my apartment. They're expecting him today. Just give me what I need to fill out from the hospital. I would like to get this over with as quickly as possible.*

The familiar nurse is taken aback. This is the first time she's seeing my grandmother assertive. With everything already arranged, she says, *He'll be well taken care of there, Mrs. Singh. It is very difficult to take care of someone in his condition.*

My grandmother nods. This stranger understands, and wants this freedom for her too.

What my grandmother doesn't know is that Pooja decided to take some time off from her job of cleaning houses and is on her way to the hospital with her three young girls in tow. It was time for them to visit Grandpa now that the worst was over. When they arrive, Shiva is already on his way down to the ambulance that will transport him to the nursing home.

We din know it was today, Mammy, she says. *Yuh ready foh im hwome? Yuh need we help?* My grandmother says no, the whole time praying nothing will slip about where she is taking her husband.

They wheel his bed over to the back of the van.

Come Katie, Meghan, and Ellie, gih yuh grampa kiss, says Pooja to her girls. *Tell im yuh goh see im soon. E goin hwome now.*

Shiva is loaded into the van. The driver comes around the

back of the truck with his clipboard. He speaks with two medics who will travel with Shiva, then shuts the doors and clamps a lock into place. The driver checks some things off on his paperwork and says, *Okay, we're all set, Mrs. Singh.* Pooja and her daughters start to go.

Just one more thing, the man says.

Pooja stops to listen.

Goan, Pooja, Rebecca said, *ahgo see yuh latah.*

The driver flips through a few pages. *I just need one more signature here, please. This just says you know he is being transported to the nursing home instead of—*

Pooja shrieks.

After that, Rebecca is attacked by one unified force. All of her children band against her, brutal and unrelenting. Rebecca's children bring her to tears for wanting her freedom from a man she hoped to escape her entire life. With no strength left to fight, Rebecca gives in.

Oh Gawd Krys, my mother says later that day, *wah she do today is what yuh call unbelievable.*

I listen to her without comment, and when she is done I say, *None ah allyuh eh tinkin bout Gramma. Ma, allyuh eh gih Gramma ah chance, ah choice. Not one. E beat she, yuh fohget dat? E beat she till e tawt she was dead. And not once oh twice, countless times. She sacrifice everyting.*

Krystal, my mother says, *e is meh faddah.*

Ma, Rebecca is e wife. Puh yuhself een she position foh once. Yuh goh take care ah mahn who beat yuh yuh whole life?

I want to kill Shiva myself when I think of how he'd beaten everyone. But his image flickers before me again, and I try to reconcile the two images I have of him: Shiva my grandfather, and Shiva the man.

*E is meh faddah. E was good toh we no mattah wah he do. E put
clodes on we back and food een we mout,* is all my mother can say.
Dere was people woss off dan we. E was meh faddah no mattah what.

We leave the table, neither one of us willing to capitulate
to the other's perspective. With his children entangled in their
history, my need to defend my grandmother is strong.

Because in the end, the only person who can be forced to have
him is his wife.

I MEDITATE ON MY GRANDFATHER'S LIFE and the question of
how he came to be this way. My mother and I drive to my grandparents' apartment in Jersey City. I am reluctant and anxious to
step inside once we get to their door. It is 2008, two years since
my grandfather was well enough to welcome me himself, two
years since his procedures. After the last surgery, we'd all given
up hope of him ever truly coming back to himself. I'd never again
make him laugh at the memories of me playing with the baby
chickens. We'd never again share a hearty Sunday lunch of rice,
dhal, and stewed fish with boiled figs and plantains, spoonfuls
of watercress salad bordering the rings of our plates. I can't even
remember our last games of checkers. In all the years I played
him, he never let me win. And now my chance is gone.

When I arrive that day, my grandmother bustles over from
the couch to welcome my mother and me with a hug. She is warm
and soft. Looking around her neck, I glimpse my grandfather
sitting in his hospital chair in front of the television.

The last time I visited, what I saw struck me all at once: my
grandfather in a gated bed, the left side of his head caved in, white
sheets slipped off his black body. He was naked, and his hands
clawed his crotch; his face was sunken, eyes wild and crazed,

black birthmark on his left cheek, his eyes vacant and rolling in all directions; his mouth had no dentures and it hung open, a dark hole.

That birthmark on his left cheekbone beamed behind my eyelids. I thought of how I used to point at it as a little girl and laugh, *Grampa, it look like shit. Ewww.* No one else seemed to zero in on it except me, but to me it marked him as different, distinctive. He would join in my laughter and move my hand from in front of his face. Now his eyes are subdued and glazed. I can't bear to stay in the room with him.

In the bathroom, various contraptions line the sink, the toilet, and the inside of the bathtub, things to help my grandmother with the tedious processes of caring for my grandfather: helping him to use the toilet, to wash his hands, and to give him a shower. I lean against the door, incapable of holding myself up, and close my eyes. I press my cold fingers to my eyes and slide to the floor.

It takes me some time to collect myself, but when I emerge from the bathroom, the apartment seems even more cluttered with apparatus to help my grandmother help my grandfather. With all of her added responsibilities, there is no decadent Sunday spread of curried peas and oxtail poured over rice, mountains of dasheen chunks sautéed with smoked herring and onions on the side. I rummage around the fridge, surfacing with a sandwich and some forgotten strawberry ice cream. I eat while watching my grandfather.

His body is buckled to the chair. My mother sits on the arm of the couch next to him. On his child's tray she places a sippy cup and two bowls of food, both mashed into mush. I try to convince myself he looks better than the last time I visited, but other than his incision healing and hair growing back, he remains the same: reduced to a child in an elder man's body. His hands are of no use to him, and his legs can't hold him up. He is gaunt. A shade of the person he once was.

Every time my mother tries to spoon food into his mouth, he writhes and twists away from her.

E too damn stubborn, my grandmother says, *even when e like dis. E eh eatin nutten lately.*

Rebecca takes the spoon from my mother. With her left palm, she pushes his chin down, and with her right hand, she pries his gums apart. My grandmother shovels food into his mouth with the mechanical emphasis of a person who hates that she has to do this for so long. She then holds him by the jaws and forces him to chew. Satisfied, she barks, *Swallow. Swallow now.* And he swallows.

My grandmother glances at his side of the living room, where she's jammed as many of his things as can fit, and joins me back in the kitchen. My mother, much gentler, resumes feeding him, coaxing, *Pappy, come nah. Yuh hah toh eat. Open yuh mout nah Pappy.*

I came with questions about my grandparents, and my grandmother is the missing piece. I see how tired she is of taking care of her husband. I want to know stories my mother can't tell me: How did my grandparents meet? Were they ever in love? Why did my grandmother stay with him? How could she stand to take care of him?

Gramma, I ask, *how yuh takin care ah dis mahn aftah all e do toh yuh?*

My grandmother clasps her hands and looks down before she answers.

Krys, de mahn ah always beat meh, you know. Some days was foh e spray kyan. Uddah times it was foh ah hose, ah pump, ah rope. E hunt meh like ah animal foh it. Din matter wah, e di always fine someting toh beat meh foh.

My grandmother's story begins with the same beating my mother had described, from when she was eight years old.

Gramma, how you di meet Grampa?

Her hands fly through the air as the words gush from her mouth. She grabs my face with both hands. Her eyes glint alongside the golden edges of her glasses. No one has ever asked her before. This is the release she's been yearning for.

Mistah Shiva was a tall mahn. Ah rheal tall mahn. De day ah meet im e was someting toh watch. If yuh di evah see im den, Krys, Mistah Shiva was someting toh watch.

In the narrow space between us, she conjures her life for me, repeating a single haunting phrase she's held fast to for decades. *E hah house, lan, and motocah and foh ah young gyul like me een dem days ah couldn'tah dream ah nutten bettah dan house, lan, and motohcah, chile.*

REBECCA

1954–1980

COFFEE

~~~~~

THEY'D GOTTEN THE NEWS about Rebecca's uncle, her mother's brother, from a messenger who arrived in the middle of the night, and her mother had wailed until she'd awoken their entire small village, Coal Mine, deep in the hills of Trinidad. The funeral would be later that same day. But grief had no place in the homes of the poor, and they would have to venture to work as normal. At eight in the morning, they were late to leave.

—*Een dem days, Krys, de year was 1954,* my grandmother tells me, *messengahs an dem was anybody yuh know. Ah poor boi een yuh village. Vagrant, bruddah.*

George Ali, Rebecca's father, roused himself from a drunken stupor. He babbled incoherently, spittle catching in his beard. Within a few seconds, he lost consciousness; his chin met his collarbones, and his thin frame slouched back onto the couch. Jacinta and Rebecca slipped quietly around him, afraid he'd wake up and start thrashing them both for their late start.

Rebecca and her mother gathered necessary things for their day of work—two baskets and bottles of water refilled from the nearby well. Her mother pulled a battered towel around her head and rubbed her eyes with the knotted end. Rebecca only observed as her mother choked down her anguish.

They exited the wooden house, which was stacked on bricks.

Rebecca glanced back at the table and chairs cramped together before shutting their front door, which had no lock. Her mother stumbled across the gravel, spraying dust into the air and into their eyes. Rebecca kneaded away the particles from her eyes and bent forward in frustration.

She knew nothing of this uncle, had only distant memories of visiting her grandparents when she was a child. This man her mother cried for was dear only because he was blood, a brother. They had been estranged for many years.

Jacinta and Rebecca, mother and daughter, trod alongside the main road, which curved around plantations of coffee, cocoa, bananas, and oranges. Rebecca led while her mother stifled sniffles along the way. Rebecca thought of the flower-arranging class she had to attend later that day and of the man her friend Lacey promised to introduce her to. The class was the only thing her father allowed her to do other than the plantation work she must do with her mother.

Rebecca had failed the Common Entrance exam when she was thirteen, then fourteen, fifteen, and finally sixteen. The exam tested one's capabilities in math, English, and science. Without passing, one couldn't move from standard five in elementary school to form one in secondary school. After she had failed the final time, there was nothing left for her to do but work.

In the government school she attended, the principal felt sorry for Rebecca and allowed her to repeat standard five three times, but at sixteen Rebecca was too old to continue her education with ten-year-olds. Unlike the principal, who viewed Rebecca's return year after year as a way for her to redeem herself, to forge a path ahead through education, the teachers scorned and ridiculed her. They used her as a cautionary example for the other children. Every year, they singled her out, commanded her to stand up and walk to the front of the class, where she was forced to recite how often she'd been left back and how many times she'd repeated standard five. But her parents sent her back every time the principal offered, until all her opportunities had been used up.

The principal was a man with a bald head and severe eyes, but beneath these features Rebecca discovered compassion. The results of the students' exams came in envelopes, with each name scrawled across the front. The last time Rebecca took the exam, instead of letting her teacher humiliate her in front of the class again, he called her to his office to give her the final results himself. It was toward the end of the school year then, months after she'd already sat for the test with the pencil her mother had whittled to a crude point with a dull knife. He explained that she was much too old to repeat standard five again. This, he said, was the end of her educational route, but there were others she could take, and he offered her a handshake and a smile along with her opened envelope.

Again she had failed. It didn't sink in until after she left the principal's office. Only after she passed her teachers, triumph and contempt stamped on their faces, did Rebecca truly realize she was leaving school for good.

Girls hugged one another and cried because they'd been accepted to schools at opposite ends of the country. Their long hair hung down the backs of their uniforms in tightly braided plaits, blue satin ribbons looped lovingly into tidy bows against their dark hair. They clutched their exam results to their hearts, some wailing, others smiling. The wailing ones were the daughters who would inform their fathers they would be attending junior secondary schools; the beaming daughters would be celebrated because they were accepted to the number one all-girls school in the country—St. Augustine Girls. If you passed through there, you were expected to become a doctor or a lawyer, the only two professions of substance and respect in Trinidad.

She walked through the open courtyard, not bothering to finish the term—what was the point? There were no friends to hug her as she left, no one to miss her. The image of the girls in their crisp blue-and-white uniforms holding on to one another stayed with her.

She told her parents that evening. Her mother hung her head in shame. Her father beat her and, as he did, told her it was what he'd expected from her anyway. Their neighbors in the little village of Coal Mine peered through their windows to watch her humiliation.

Soon after the school term ended, Rebecca's father ordered her to work the plantations with Jacinta. He told them they needed all the money they could get and that sending Rebecca back to school all those years had been a waste, when she could've been working like all his other children. Rebecca didn't point out that, of his ten children, only three were left at home.

—*Krys,* my grandmother says to me, *Mama was always tryin to help meh, all ah we. She din wahn none ah she chilren toh stick up dey een de bush like she, she din wah we toh wok de fiels like she atall. She put it in meh head toh get out, toh goh.*

After six months of working the plantations Monday through Friday, and cooking and cleaning on Saturday and Sunday, Jacinta told Rebecca about the flower-arranging class she had secretly found for her daughter to take. The class convened three times a week, and Rebecca could attend after their daily work on the plantations. Jacinta assured her daughter it wasn't expensive and showed her the money she'd been keeping back little by little from her husband so Rebecca could take the class. Jacinta lined coins at the bottom of the basket she used for collecting coffee pods in fields and taped them down so they wouldn't jingle and betray her. On top of them she taped a flattened paper bag and then layered a towel.

This was how Rebecca came to appreciate the basket rocking back and forth on her mother's arm as they trudged to work that day. The woven wicker caught on the cotton threads of her mother's dress, and the anger Rebecca felt toward Jacinta—for crying over a dead brother who never cared to visit them—subsided.

The details of the union between Rebecca's parents, Jacinta Garcia and George Ali, were lost memories. No one remembered and no one recorded. The details she knew were: Jacinta had an elder sister and George an elder brother. Their brother and sister were in love and planned their wedding at the Ali residence.

—*Yuh know it was customary back den toh hah ting like dis,* my grandmother tells me. *De priess use toh come toh de house an perform de ceremony nah. It was durin dat Mama and Pa di staht cryin toh geh mar-red too. Oh so ah remembah when Mama di tell meh di story. Dah is juss how it appen.*

Rebecca did not know how her parents met. She did know they'd been seeing each other for a long time, and when they begged to get married on the day of their elder siblings' marriage, the celebration turned into a double union before the priest under the Ali roof. Protestants were one of the largest religious groups in Trinidad. Theirs was a Presbyterian wedding, one that embraced the Christian religious beliefs of the Venezuelan sisters and dismissed those of the Muslim Indian brothers, something that turned George Ali sour till the day he died.

In a land where cultures and religions remained as neatly cleaved as the dry season from the rainy, George and Jacinta's union was an unusual one. Though there were different nationalities on the island, they were expected not to mix. And though the nuptials were sanctioned and both sides were present, George's family did not approve. They thought Venezuelans, from the neighboring country they could see off the coast of Trinidad, were below them. Their skin was too dark, not like their olive undertones, which they tried to protect from the sun; and their hair too coarse, cropped close to their heads, not like theirs that spilled past their shoulders.

For two first-generation Indian-Muslim men to wed two first-generation Venezuelan women in Trinidad was to invite severe social disapproval that would traumatize their families for generations to come. Snubbed, whispered about, and ignored by family, friends, and strangers, Jacinta and George were pushed out of civilization, well up into the mountains where others like them—poor, mismatched, disabled—had cobbled together the nine houses they called their village.

EXPOSED TO GLASS SHARDS, bottle caps, nails, and other dangers, Jacinta and Rebecca—and later, Arya—traveled many of the same roads in Trinidad. When the rare car passed Jacinta and Rebecca as they walked along the side of the road, they hid behind bushes or trees. If she was too tired to drop and roll down the embankment, Rebecca looked for a leafy banana tree, pulled down the leaves, and encased her body in a wall of green.

—*We eh wan people toh see we nah*, says my grandmother. *We eh wahn dem toh know we was rheal laborers. Yuh di hah toh hide dem ting back in de day.*

But that never stopped Rebecca from staring at the car as it chugged away. She yearned to be in a car, to be driven somewhere instead of having to walk everywhere barefoot. These cars that puttered past must have belonged to majestic households, she thought, houses with their own wells and private latrines, unlike the community ones they all shared. People who had houses with doors and locks, furniture and rooms. Houses deliberately planted on their own land, not a haphazard village set up in the middle of the forest. There would be land aplenty with farm animals to care for and reap from.

—*House, lan, and motohcah,* my grandmother says, *dah is all meh evah wanted.*

THEY WALKED TO THE CHECK-IN and check-out shacks located at either end of the fence. Her mother took both their baskets and marched to the check-in shack. An attendant pulled out a piece of twine with increments blackened along its length. He measured the width and depth of their baskets, then issued paper passes with numbers for the day. Rebecca remained behind, dawdling until the measuring was finished. Almost everyone else had arrived hours ago.

Jacinta handed Rebecca back her basket. Within a week of Rebecca leaving school, her mother had scrounged together enough money to buy her one of her own. It wasn't new, but the glaze over the woven wood was intact. To preserve it from sun, rain, and coffee stains, her mother told her to wrap a plastic bag around the thick handle and layer the base of it with a towel. After Rebecca's failed attempts to cover the handle, her mother showed her the basket she'd been using for over five years. She pointed out where she wrapped the plastic around the midway point and held it at two-inch increments with fraying twine. Rebecca knew they couldn't afford another one, but she didn't want to follow her mother down the same path either; to treat this basket the way her mother had treated her own would trap her in Coal Mine forever. But at her mother's insistence, the plaited handles of her basket had been wrapped and stripped of plastic bags several times over the past year. Only the twine remained, yellowed and unraveling. The towel, folded and patted on the bottom, was streaked with reds and browns. No matter how many times Rebecca scrubbed the towel against the stone grate in the washbasin, the pungent smell of damp earth mingling with sweet leaves and coffee never deserted it.

Today, Rebecca looped the handle on the inside of her elbow. They entered.

Because this field had been open to harvesters for two weeks, the trees had already been stripped of coffee bunches for miles. Nevertheless, they searched outstretched vines for blushing cherries, but all they found were green pellets budding along the leaves. A full basket fetched only a dollar, and they had to fill both.

Their work was split into two categories—day's work and task work. Day's work was picking from eight a.m. to three p.m., and it was during these days that they each had to fill their basket to earn a dollar. For task work, Jacinta and Rebecca hoed, clumped, and cutlassed branches around the bases of eighteen trees in one section of the plantation until they were clear.

—*It eh play di hah plenty snake dat ah hide up een dem bush nah,* my grandmother tells me. *Big-big fat-fat snake. Yuh fine one so yuh bettah cut off e head quick and doh play nah. Mama was ah strong oman, she use toh mash up e head.*

Because her mother was older than other laborers and seemed to droop with each passing day under the sun, Rebecca tried to shoulder most of the labor. She worked fast, trying to finish early so she wouldn't be late for class. The man her friend Lacey had promised to introduce her to was rich. *Rheal rich Becca, doh worry ahgo take care ah yuh,* Lacey said to her.

Of the coffee, cocoa, banana, and citrus trees they combed, the coffee was by far the most difficult to obtain. Coffee trees were spaced ten feet apart. Running all around them, resembling little squares on graph paper, were deep drains in place for irrigation.

Rebecca, along with her mother and other workers, toiled on the prosperous land owned by the wealthy of Trinidad.

Today they started at the beginning of the plantation at one coffee field, searching between branches for bunches that might have been left behind. Rebecca and Jacinta methodically searched clusters, turning the green stems over carefully, hoping some would be red. After an hour of burrowing into trees and twisting stems where the sun had no chance to touch and ripen, their pace quickened from a stride to a trot. They scrambled up and down still-moist ditches. Worms wriggled before they were severed between their toes. Black earth built under their nails and around their cuticles.

The walls of some drains were too steep for Jacinta to climb without help. Rebecca took their baskets, ran up the side, dropped them at the top, and skidded back down to help her mother. With each pull up, Rebecca kicked and patted dirt to form footholds for her mother to grasp or step on. At the top, they collapsed at the base of a sparse tree. Sunlight filtered between skeletal limbs and threw the burden of heat onto their depleted backs.

—*We was tryin toh geh toh de uddah side ah dis cauffee fiel,* explains my grandmother. *We nevah rheally do it een conditions like dis befoh because it was so dangerous boh sometime we hah to cross one oh two rivah to reach ah nex place whey we goh geh some stock.*

Some time later, they stood beside the river where a tree had fallen across as a bridge between two plantations. Neither Rebecca nor Jacinta knew how to swim, and today the river was full. The large tree trunk rose and fell with the current. In November—the rainy season in Trinidad—the river overflowed often. More than a few times, Jacinta had told Rebecca, the river swallowed an overturned tree, making quick passage from one field to another impossible. The trunk could be glimpsed rolling backward and forward in the swirling water. Some men (family men, hard workers) who couldn't afford to let go of a single day's work would wade into the muddy water, home to snakes and alligators. Cheered on by others who stood back from the dangerous water, these men felt their way to the base of the fallen tree with their bare feet. When the water reached their ankles, they rolled their pant legs up to the knees. When the water reached their knees, they tightened their belts. When the water reached their waists, they crouched into a fighting stance, their opponent the river whirling all around them.

Jacinta witnessed men fight their way into the water up to forty feet only to stumble right before touching the trunk and be whisked away by the sandy-colored water. Some were able to grip the ridges of the bark, where they held on for dear life, only to be knocked unconscious by a log and stolen by the river's depths. Others reached the opposite bank, but were bitten by a startled snake before they could wade out of the water and suck the poison out. Families and friends of these men searched the calmer outlets of the river's path only to find bloated bodies or none at all. Of course there were men who battled the river and triumphed, but Jacinta said they were few. Still, it was because of these few that there were always willing challengers.

—Toh goh in da watah, yuh signin yuh own deat cetificate, my grandmother says.

Today Rebecca was skeptical about crossing. Her mother didn't ponder or converse with Rebecca about this decision, as she was accustomed to doing. Instead she secured her basket on her shoulder once again, hoisted herself onto the trunk, and lay across it. Rebecca couldn't bring herself to object. Images of her mother flailing as the river took her while Rebecca stood helpless on the bank flashed through her mind. Convinced there was nothing she could do or say that would dissuade her mother in her grief-stricken state, Rebecca followed. In the same pattern, Rebecca secured her basket and climbed onto the trunk. They knew intimately the deceptive quality of this island's water, and today the turbulence was harsher than it looked. The bark was slippery with wet moss. Living things teeming in the wetness squished beneath her grasp, but she ignored them.

—Krys dahlin, my grandmother says, *we din hah to goh dah way. Dey was ah bridge toh cross ovah boh it was miles ahwey and we know when we reach dey all dem tree done pick. Is ah rheal chance she was takin dey.*

Halfway across, her mother stopped. Above the rushing of the river, Rebecca could hear her mother's heavy breathing. Jacinta tilted a little to the left as the water attacked on their right. Rebecca screamed, *MAMA!* Jacinta continued across with her arms and legs wrapped around the trunk.

When they reached the other side, Rebecca collapsed. Jacinta wrung water from her dress and emptied her basket. *Chile, git up,* Jacinta said, *we hah wok toh do.* But Rebecca didn't yet trust herself to stand and examined the cuts and scratches on her arms and legs. This was the first time they'd crossed the river while the water flowed around them. In the past, her mother only ever led her over the tree when it was dry.

Jacinta trekked ahead knowing her daughter would follow. Rebecca pushed herself off the ground when she saw her mother wasn't looking back. The light fabric of her dress was made heavy by the water. She tried to wring it dry as best she could, but it stuck to her skin. She shook her basket and wobbled toward her mother. The scare from the river wouldn't leave her as fast as she wanted it to.

Jacinta frantically beckoned her daughter. Rebecca jogged over to discover her mother pointing at a branch above their heads, laden with bunches of blushing coffee cherries. But she couldn't reach it no matter how high she jumped. Rebecca, taller than her mother by three or four inches, crossed a longer, drooping branch over the one they wanted to reach, and pulled until the fruit hung right above Rebecca's head. Jacinta yelled for Rebecca not to let go until she'd plucked every pellet. After, they scoured the ground, prying apart thick blades of grass until Jacinta was satisfied they had collected every last one. Even then, their harvest filled only half of one basket.

The sun rose higher and crept across the sky. Sweat mixed with the dirt on their skin. Everything became sticky and hot. For relief, Jacinta and Rebecca intermittently sought the cool shelter of a tree. But Rebecca was scared to linger in its shade. When her mother asked her why, Rebecca recounted all the stories Jacinta had told her over the years about snakes biting the unsuspecting as they sprawled beneath a tree for a quick break.

Oh Gawd Becca, Jacinta said, *nah worry bout dat nah. Meh take kyare ah meh pickney. Meh keel de snake good an dead. E nevah see wah come. Watch nah, like dis,* and Jacinta picked up a rock, *yuh hah ketch e head.* She ground the rock into the earth with such force it spun a hole. *If yah nah grung e head like dat den de ting eh dead. E jus like mahn. E come back toh keel yuh. Make sure when yuh keel ah snake yuh take ahwey de ead an do wah say.*

—*Meh muddah was a sweet sweet oman, eh Krys chile,* my grandmother says, *ah sweet sweet oman. She only wanted to look out foh she chilren.*

Their work was laborious, especially without food all day. Many times they drained their water supply and had to work without. Sometimes friends among them shared, but with a disapproving *steups* and the cock of a hand on a hip. Today there was no help; workers had scoured these grounds hours ago, leaving nothing behind but trampled grass. Leaves flapping low in the trees slapped their skin. It was a sickening sound, one that lingered in their ears. By the time both baskets were filled, the sun had crossed the sky and was beginning its descent.

DOUGLA

⟿

—KRYS CHILE, my grandmother says, *meh muddah was consume wid she grief. Poor oman, all-doh meh din see it den. Ah was inna diffrant worl. Meh was tinkin bout class latah dat night. Yuh see ah di hah one friend rheally and truly and she name was Lacey. And Lacey di hah ah surprise foh meh latah dat day. Meh only friend, Lacey.*

Rebecca had met Lacey a few months before in the flower-arranging class Jacinta had found for her. The class met three times a week in the evenings, and three times a week Rebecca found herself looking forward to seeing Lacey, especially that night, since the two of them had hatched a plan to leave class early so they could go to an Indian celebration.

Too shy and self-conscious to talk to anyone, Rebecca welcomed Lacey's stream of chatter as their fingers fumbled with silk roses and baby's breath on their first day. No one in class spoke to Lacey. The other students blamed Lacey's obnoxiousness, but they didn't talk to Rebecca either, and she was quiet. Both knew it was because of their racial backgrounds (for Rebecca it was her racial mix, and for Lacey it was her Spanish roots), but neither girl ever mentioned it to the other. For them, their exile was also their acceptance of each other. All the Indian girls in the class thought they were too good for Rebecca and

Lacey, shunning them to the back of the room—all the seats up front taken, bags and sewing cases flung onto any empty space left over. But neither girl cared.

Rebecca, usually uncomfortable with her own round appearance, relaxed in the company of Lacey's vastness. Where Rebecca had thick thighs and creases down her side, Lacey's legs were flabby, she had rolls beneath her armpits and back, and her breasts drooped in ovals over her swollen belly. At twenty she already had four children. There was always a chance she could be pregnant with her fifth child, but Rebecca never asked. When Lacey sat on the sturdy chairs in class, she seemed to plop her weight down onto four flimsy legs, and Rebecca always checked the slightly splayed posts to see if they would splinter under the pressure. They hadn't yet.

Lacey had black hair cascading in ripples over her shoulders, delicate features, and brown skin like everyone else on the island, but hers was infused with a light that made her caramel skin look sheer. Rebecca felt a particular magnetic pull to Lacey's hair. Unlike her own, which became a knotted mess when allowed to grow free, Lacey's looked soft, as though her fingers could easily slip their way to her white scalp. Rebecca's own hair was coarse and cropped close to her head.

—*Krys chile,* my grandmother says, *Lacey surprise foh meh today hah meh excited. Rheal excited.*

Rebecca burst into class, and though she was only a couple of minutes late, some girls had already started on their floral displays. Lacey sat at the back of the class commenting on and laughing at other's festoons, oblivious to everyone's disdain. They shot her dirty looks every time she opened her mouth.

Their instructor was a bony, brown Indian woman. She strolled up and down the aisles of the classroom with her glasses perched atop her nose. When her eyes landed on Rebecca, a sneer wrinkled her onion-thin skin. Lacey liked to whisper things about their instructor when Rebecca obsessed over the woman's dislike for them. *Doh min she, Becca. She eh hah ah mahn oh no chilren. She goh dead by sheself. Meh eh know why she eh try toh put on some weight and find ah mah toh bull nah.* While Rebecca loved to listen to Lacey, she never added anything to her stories.

A A Becca gyul, Lacey bellowed from across the room, *meh tawt yuh wasn't comin today. Yuh eh wantah meet de mahn awah?* At the mention of Rebecca's mystery man, her heart fluttered. She smiled. Someone was interested in meeting her, excited even, according to Lacey.

E hah cah, Lacey had told her. *Me, Jamal, and di chilren went somewhey and ah hear Jamal say someting bout ah fahm.*

—*Krys chile, ah see it,* my grandmother says in what will amount to an incantation, *house, lan, and motohcah.*

As Rebecca weaved her way around the termite-riddled desks, everyone turned to stare. She hoped Lacey would say no more. An Indian girl who had never spoken to either of them before piped up, *Wah mahn go wahn you? E muss be rheal blind. Tell im come and see me, ah nice and pure, meh eh no dut poor dougla.* She flipped her ponytail over her shoulder and ran her hands down the front of her body. Her friends snickered. Their instructor suppressed a smile. Rebecca stopped. The sound of silk being folded and twisted ceased; there was the thump of scissors on the desks, the popping of pins in cushions. Their teacher said nothing.

Dougla—half African, half East Indian—was a mix Rebecca was not, but she did not yet have the strength to stand up for herself. Her short, coarse hair revealed her as someone of mixed racial descent, but the only word hissed at her back then was *dougla*. Trinidadians eventually created more names as races intermingled, but *cocopanyol*—half East Indian and half Venezuelan—had not yet been invented.

—*Mama di come from Venezuela,* my grandmother tells me. *She di tawk Spanish rheal good and she is one ah de few people ah know who could tawk de true patwah. Boh wah me goh say toh dese people, Krys? Dey eh care. Is mix ah mix up an dat is all dey need toh know toh shun meh.*

The derogatory word, *dougla,* was given more heft the longer the silence lived.

Lacey was flushed for Rebecca and started getting to her feet to defend her, but the same girl said, *Wah appen, Rebecca?* and she dragged Rebecca's name out in the crudest way possible. *Yuh kyant say nutten cause de Africans eh goh claim yuh and de Indians eh go touch yuh.* Lacey erupted, but now the instructor intervened. *Dat's enough, let's get back to our projects.*

It took Rebecca a few minutes before she sat. She swiped at tears both angry and hurt. The image of her blubbering mother trailing behind her earlier flashed before her eyes. She thought of the shack they lived in and how much of nothing they had. That made her stop crying. She refused to indulge in pitying herself.

Lacey's eyes lit upon her again and again during class, but Rebecca's eyes stayed down. All the questions she'd been on fire to ask Lacey had been extinguished. She was fixated on getting away and leaving everything and everyone behind.

—*Meh was tinkin,* says my grandmother, *meh kyant stay hwome, meh kyant stay whey ah is, so meh hah toh run. Ah di tinkin too maybe dis mahn goh help.*

Rebecca was prepared to leave before she even met him.

———

IN NOVEMBER, the month of Kartik, Hindus across Trinidad and Tobago gathered on the banks of rivers and the shorelines of beaches to join in the festivities celebrating the passage to the New Year. Women donned saris in varying shades of reds, yellows, oranges, and whites. The older women were wrapped in demure folds of blues and greens with hints of gold or silver. Music jingled from the thick bands of bangles lining arms and the delicate bells tied around ankles. The young women tossed their veils to the wind, untying coils and braids, gold and silver sequins glittering in the waning sun. Older women fastened their veils to dignified buns set low at the backs of their heads; the intricate designs of dark brown henna stained the bumps of purple veins. Some watched their granddaughters, daughters, and nieces wave fingers and toes trellised with crimson patterns of flowers and leaves, a tug of the past pulling them toward memories of when they danced by the water's edge, drawing the eyes of men.

Rebecca wore a flower-printed dress with a scrunched waist-line. The tenuous fabric barely concealed her large cotton under-garments. Though her father was raised by Hindus and Muslims, he never took her or her siblings to a temple, a mosque, or any of the ceremonies scattered throughout the year. She eyed the saris draped on the young and the old, deftly folded and neatly tied by the expert fingers of older women. Slender midsections exposed beneath sari blouses swayed to sultry rhythms of classical music emanating from radios set along the banks.

Once when she was a little girl and her father had walked with her and her mother to the market, she pointed to a lady wearing a hoop through her nose that was connected by a string of gold to her ear, then her hair. *Pappy, why she wearin earring in she nose?* She

had turned her neck to follow the woman as she passed by with
a parcel of Indian sweets dusted with sprinkles. The lady turned
and smiled. Her father roared with laughter and explained it was
a *nathani*, worn by married women in his culture. He cupped her
head in one of his palms and told her she would wear a *nath* when
she was a little older. The *nath*, he said, was a glass bead through
the nose for girls, and as she got older he would replace the bead
with 22-karat gold studs and then hoops. When she reached the
realm of adulthood, he promised, he would buy her a *nathani*. She
jumped up and down begging him to buy her one now. When her
mother emerged from the throng of people haggling under the
canopy of vegetables, Rebecca searched her mother for a *nathani*.

Pappy? He looked down at her, the rare smile lighting his face.
Whey Mammy nathani? His face dissolved. He said, *Yuh muddah
kyant weah dat. She eh ah true Indian wife. She Creole. My muddah
is ah true Indian an she does weah de traditions ah she culture. She
does weah de mangalsutra, sindur, an ah nathani!* Her mother had
veered off to another vendor for supplies to make green seasoning for meat. When he said *my muddah* he emphasized the *my* and
slapped his shirtless chest with the palm of his hand.

—*Meh grandmuddah din wahn nutten toh do wid we,* my
grandmother says. *We juss mix up so she disown we.*

Pappy, wah is ah magali and sinda? This time he didn't laugh.
He didn't place his hand on her head. Nor did he glance down at
her. Strolling along the outskirts of the marketplace waiting for
her mother, he scanned the antsy crowd of women till he found
one woman carrying a basket.

*Watch she dey. Yuh see dah oman? Yuh see wah she hah tie
rung she neck?* Rebecca strained to see who he was pointing to.
De oman widdee red sari. The woman he was pointing to wore a
necklace spun of yellow thread, gold pendants, and beads. She

nodded. *Well meh chile, dah is wah a mar-red oman does weah. She does hah toh weah dah all de days ah she life till she husband dead. Dah is ah mangalsutra. An yuh see how she paht she hair een de middle so? Dah red duss she put on she skull is sindur. Every mawnin meh muddah use toh getup and paht she head wid coconut oil an puh sindur on she head like dat.*

When her father spoke of his mother, a sourness lurked in his eyes as bitter as raw cocoa, yet a slow smile softened his features. Her mother returned to them soon, and he became his gruff self again, silent as they walked home.

He never did buy her a *nath,* and by the time she was old enough for a *nathani* she had given up all hope of ever getting one. Now, standing right off the road with Lacey scanning the crowd for Jamal, Rebecca hungrily stared at all the young girls' jewelry she had once been promised, and all the older women's adornments of marriage that she still hoped to receive.

Rebecca didn't know why Lacey chose for their first meeting to be on Kartik. The extravagant atmosphere made her feel distraught. She felt out of place and looked around for Lacey until she spotted her by her hair, quite unlike all the straight hair dancing in the breeze around them. If someone saw the way Rebecca eyed Lacey's hair, they would accuse her of casting *najar* or *maljo*—the evil eye. Whenever Lacey turned, her hair swayed with her, the tips of it clinging to her right or left hip. It was a different color than the hair of any of the Trinidadians she knew. While all Indians had hair as black as the fathoms of the night sky and all African coils were even darker, Lacey's hair was the color of coffee beans, reddened by sunlight. And the longer Lacey stayed in the sun, the lighter her hair became. But Lacey would never stay in the sun. *Meh hah toh protek meh color, Becca.* And Lacey had nice skin. It always looked like darkened honey trickling from the bark of a tree, as though if Rebecca licked her, she would be sweet and sticky. It was true that Lacey would always be classified as a bona fide *boboloops*—an obese woman—but nonetheless she had characteristics coveted by females on the island.

Lacey's eyes moved from side to side, up and down, searching for her husband. Exasperated, she ran her hands through her hair, sweat glistening on her fingertips. She never soaked her hair in coconut oil as all the Indians on the island did. When Rebecca asked her why she said, *Wah? An spoil meh head? Meh eh wahn it toh look greasy greasy so nah gyul. Foh dem Indian an dem igo be broughtupsy buh mine good juss so.*

Rebecca's mother never tried to flatten her children's coarse hair. Her mother's hair grew in tight corkscrews, while her siblings' varied in texture. Only her younger brother Kamal had inherited her father's hair, and he wore it long. He was proud to have the hair of an Indian man, because with that he could slip among them, unchallenged. Rebecca's hair fell right in the middle of her father's and mother's, caught between silky and knotted. It never grew more than six or seven inches, and though it was considerably softer than her mother's, it only spiraled upward. Every day she vigorously brushed away the offending curls, abrading her scalp in the process. Sometimes her mother would help her brush and other times just yell, *Wah nonsense yuh doin? Stop wastin time and goh do someting.*

Her father talked at great length about his mother's hair, how long and luxurious it was, how it matched the color of her eyes, and the way it shone in the moonlight. He would always say that's why his father had fallen in love with his mother. Rebecca wanted to meet this woman, whom she gathered bits and pieces about, but her father's bitterness when he spoke of her kept Rebecca from ever asking to meet her.

When Lacey finally spotted Jamal, she waved both arms about her head, her sleeveless top unable to hide the fat rippling along her upper arms. She jumped up and down, her breasts, belly, and buttocks jiggling. Jamal was among a group of girls now entering their teens. They wore vibrant colors that shone against their brown skin. Some wore their black hair in buns encircled with garlands of white flowers, while others wore theirs loose with no adornment but the setting sun. Jamal's eyes were trained on them, a smile depressing his nose and lifting the corners of his mouth. He didn't see Lacey for a few seconds.

At thirty-five, Jamal had a thick beard. Fifteen years Lacey's senior, he seemed to ravage her youth, impressing age and hard work upon her with each child. Jamal raised his hand to signal he saw her. Lacey waddled to him. On the few occasions Lacey had mentioned being Jamal's wife, Rebecca gleaned she was proud of herself for having the ability to steal a man like Jamal. Rebecca couldn't see why. He was a tall man whose bones were visible even through his floor-length khobe. His eyes and skin were just as light and radiant as Lacey's, but that was as far as the comparison went. Beneath a brush of brows were eyes deep set and moody. He always seemed to sift through women, discarding the ones he deemed physically undesirable, and Rebecca knew she was discounted the moment they met.

The first time Rebecca met Jamal, she and Lacey had taken their time gathering their things together before leaving the cramped classroom. By then everyone else had left for the evening. Jamal was outside leaning against wooden crossbeams, a box of du Maurier cigarettes unopened in his hands. Their giggling interrupted him, and he looked up as they strolled through the darkening corridor. He approached them and yanked Lacey by her arm, her bag slipping off her shoulder and onto the floor.

Pins, needles, and acrylic cases clattered on the concrete, rolling in various directions.

Wah takin yuh so long?

Lacey cowered against Rebecca, covering her head, her stance no mystery to any woman: she feared his fists. When Jamal registered that someone else was there, he stepped back and cleared his throat, pocketing the red box with his other hand.

Lacey recovered and introduced Rebecca as though their violent exchange had never happened. *Doh be shy Becca. Deez Jamal, de one ah does tell you bout all de time, gyul.* But Rebecca heard the forced lightness in her voice. They still stood among the debris of her purse. His smile made her insides stiffen. In the shadows of the hallway, they couldn't read each other's faces. Lacey dropped to the floor to pick up her things. Jamal loomed above her. When Rebecca tried to help her, Jamal said, *Lacey ah remembah yuh tellin meh bout she. Come nah gyul, lemme see yuh in de light.* Lacey urged them outside, assuring them she would be right behind.

He walked slowly at her back, creating distance between them. *How yuh hair so shaht?* She didn't respond. *Wah happen toh yuh? Yuh kyant tawk?* She felt his eyes roving her body. By the time they exited the corridor, she could hear Lacey panting along behind them. He sneered, then smiled. Lacey appeared next to him, and he slung his arm across her shoulders. *Lewwe goh home, gyul. Sombody hah toh watch dem pickney.* Something he saw made her no longer visible. What made him think of her when it came to Shiva, she'd never know.

For the occasion of Kartik (though Jamal was Muslim and didn't celebrate Hindu customs), he had donned a red sash tied into a knot around his head, the two ends drifting to his waist. Upon closer inspection, Rebecca recognized the sash as an orni veil taken from a shalwaar kameez outfit, but didn't say anything to Lacey. She looked to the cluster of girls kicking their feet into the air, spraying dust everywhere, the same group Jamal had just been standing with. A young girl of fourteen or fifteen stood still staring at Jamal and Lacey. Rebecca couldn't help but notice that while all this girl's friends and family had ornis tied diagonally across their bodies, she now had none. What could Jamal have possibly said to this girl to have her pining after him with her teenage eyes opened wide? How long had Jamal even been with them? How could Lacey ignore the young girl's veil now around Jamal's head? Or did she know it and couldn't say anything about it? The actions of these men and the blind acceptance of women tormented her. Was this what would be expected of her?

Aye Becca gyul, wah appenin? Long time no see. Yuh like de Indian festivities? She nodded. Lacey shook her hips to the elaborate music. Rebecca was dying to ask about Shiva but waited for Jamal or Lacey to bring him up.

Lewwe goh an dance nah, Becca? Lacey was in a party mood. *Lewwe goh and rub dem up, kick we bamsee in de air.* From the little of Hinduism that Rebecca knew, Kartik was a holy month for these people. Her dress was out of place. She was out of place.

Neither Lacey nor Jamal cared that they were intruding upon a time of renewal. Though their eyes constantly scanned the crowd, they didn't see the unwelcomed stares that lingered on them from passersby. It was clear people knew they were outsiders. Jamal held Lacey by her neck, the hilt of his hand resting at its base. Every way he turned, she looked as well. People milled around them, carrying wicker baskets piled with freshly picked hibiscus, lotus, marigold, jasmine, and chameli flowers. Their glass bangles clinked with the swaying movement of their arms. The women who carried the flowers were matrons of their households, and they held their chins high.

There was a flutter of motion around Rebecca. Jamal moved away from them to embrace someone. Lacey grabbed Rebecca around the waist and hissed, *He hyah, Becca, look he hyah.* Her breathing quickened as she waited for Jamal to step aside. The arms encircling Jamal were covered in white sleeves; the fingers were smooth and dark, the nails well groomed. They let go and Jamal revealed Shiva. He introduced Lacey and Rebecca in one breath.

Shiva was statuesque, broad shoulders draped with an intricate sherwani, the proper formal wear for a man. The long coat over the kurta fell just below his knees, the edges of it embroidered with fine gold thread and its matching gold buttons fastened all the way up to its Nehru collar. Beneath was a pair of white churidar, tight-fitting trousers, the edges also stitched. Patterns of waves lifted and curled in crests diagonally across his chest. A thick sash, matching the sherwani in texture and detail, was hung around his neck and folded flat along his front. His hair was thick and black, each strand straight and oiled back. His skin was the same color as his hair and just as shiny. His face was long and drawn downward, the creases around his mouth prominent. When he looked at Lacey and Rebecca, he didn't smile but nodded his head curtly in their direction, his angular jaw stiff.

Rebecca stood frozen, unsure of whether to smile or step forward and extend her hand. In the end, she did neither. Shiva and Jamal started wending their way down to the water's edge. When Lacey followed behind them, Rebecca figured there was nothing else to do but follow as well. A hibiscus flower fell from a woman's basket as they were walking. Jamal bent to retrieve it. Its petals were ivory with a purple-stained center. Sand stuck to the pollen even though Jamal tried to shake it off. With an exaggerated flourish, he planted the blossom behind Lacey's right ear. She giggled. Rebecca looked to Shiva, hoping he would smile or do something of the same for her. In the time she stopped to watch them, Shiva never glanced back. He was already about thirty feet ahead of them, becoming one with the crowd.

Rebecca rushed past them. The next time she glimpsed him, water was already lapping his dark feet. She wanted to call out his name but refused to draw attention to herself. She hurried forward, hoping she reached him before he started his descent into the water's depths. By the time the sand swept the bottoms of her feet, a pundit was praying over his head and he was already waist deep in the sea.

The waves were small on this side of the island, which made entering and exiting the ocean easy. Women emerged with a smile and men with a look of determination. Their clothing was soaked, the flowers in their hair damp and drawn, but their belief in the power of the cleansing water superseded all. Fathers and mothers showed signs of reverence with their palms pressed together, their lips forming the word *Namaste,* their bodies bowed at the waist. They rose from the waters seamlessly, swells of waves lifting them as they glided from the sea. Girls and boys fought the surge, delving into the waters and surfacing with as much vigor. They kicked and slapped their way out, laughter erupting from their throats, laughter that blanched when they were in view of a pundit again.

Shiva walked past the pundit, his arms spread, fingers trailing the surface of the sea. Neck-high in water, he raised both arms to the sky, pressed his palms together, and brought them down to his chest. After a few minutes with his head bowed in prayer, he sank below the water. When he resurfaced, he searched the water with his hands to retrieve the shawl that floated away from around his shoulders. Walking back to shore, he held his head high. The pundit blessed him again as he walked by, and he nodded his head in acknowledgment. His heavily embroidered clothing clung to his body, his movements dragging and deliberate.

When he reached the shoreline, he approached a group of women gathered around the silver and gold thaali platters. Each served a different purpose: some for burning incense, some for flowers, several for food offerings, and one for prayers. Shiva directed himself to the eldest woman, possibly the grandmother or great-grandmother of the family gathered around her. Curious eyes did not slant and follow his actions, for he was welcomed here. He was one of them. He knelt before an elder—the woman wrapped in white—touched her exposed feet with both hands, then pressed his hands to his head and heart. He kept his head inclined until she leaned forward and cupped his cheeks in her gnarled hands. Her orni slipped from her hair, unveiling white and wispy strands. They exchanged *Namaste* before they began to talk animatedly.

Over the various strains of music and the gentle rolls of waves, Rebecca heard only fragments of a conversation she couldn't understand. She buried her feet in the smooth sand, feeling a layer of coolness beneath the heat. Sounds from his mouth intrigued her, and she listened in surreptitiously. He was speaking Hindi.

—*All ah tinkin een dat time,* my grandmother tells me, *is oh Gawd meh faddah hah toh be happy bout dis. Meh muddah too. See, foh we, it wuddah be like ah was movin up. Improvin de bloodline. Meh chilren and dem wouldn' tah problems like me.*

She continued to watch as he turned to other members of the woman's family, introduced himself, and conversed so easily with them all. He gestured toward the thaalis, a question stitched across his calm face. Two young girls raised the platters, obscuring her line of view with little mounds of food. He kissed the tops of their heads and scooped food into his left palm. With his right, he breached their circle and chose three flowers. One of the flowers he tucked into the old woman's hair. She smiled, spaces where teeth were once rooted, now a black gap.

Shiva turned back to the water. He walked in ankle deep and knelt again. Rebecca hoped one of the flowers was for her. The food he littered in a line in front of him and waited for the water to claim it. When the currents receded, he placed both stemless flowers in a shallow pool of water at his feet. Something curled up within her, but she suppressed it. Within seconds, the sea claimed them too. He leaned back on his knees, his folded legs resting on the curve of his toes. The stark whiteness of the bottoms of his feet against the black of his skin disturbed the pastels of the sunset.

He stood. Water rushed off his clothes. He walked to her. His dark eyes stared at her. She looked down, fiddled with her fingers, clasped them behind her back, and wiggled her toes. She looked for Lacey and Jamal, but they were lost in the swell of people behind her.

Rebecca shifted her gaze from the wet sand clinging to the bottom half of his pants to the water droplets pearled along the oil on his hair that now hung in strings around his face. There was an amoeba-shaped birthmark along his right cheekbone. It was raised, and the cool wind on his wet skin pimpled it. He stood close to her, his breath cooling her scalp.

Not knowing what he was waiting for her to do, she felt pressured and bent to dust sand from his knees and shins. He waited for her to finish before saying, *Meh slippahs ovah dey.* His matching sherwani shoes were neatly paired together. She picked them up and shook sand from the sequins as she returned to him. But he didn't make a motion to take them, and she felt she was being tested, so Rebecca stooped to place the correct shoe in front of the correct foot. After he slipped both feet into them, he strode away, up the steady incline from the beach to the road. She scrambled after him, her insteps sliding sideways on the sand. Not once did he turn around to check and see if she was still following him.

Lacey and Jamal were leaning on the steel barriers at the road. Lacey was playing with Jamal's hair while Jamal buried his feet in the sand. When the men saw one another, Jamal shook Lacey off and called out to Shiva, *Aye bruddah, you gone een de watah den?* Shiva nodded at him and then signaled that he had to go. *So soon? Yeh eh evan goan enjoy de festivities, bruddah? Dance up and ting widdese young gyul?* Shiva shook his head. He told Jamal that he would drive Rebecca home.

Rebecca's heart fluttered. She looked to Lacey, who was oblivious to their conversation. She wanted to mouth to her, *Oh gaadoi, e rheally hah cah*, but Lacey never looked her way. Their goodbye was brief and ended with a hug and a slap on the back. The couple waved to Rebecca as they trotted along the highway. Again, Shiva turned and strode away, the heavy movement of his damp clothes murmuring as he led the way to his car.

Having never been in or near a vehicle before, Rebecca approached it curiously, awed by its beauty. Shiny. Black. Spotless. Her clothes were dirty; her hair was sandy. She felt filthy and in need of a shower. He caressed the door before unlocking it. A whiff of Pine-Sol and lemon wafted over her.

—*Mistah Shiva di assess meh from de moment e lay eyes on meh chile*, says my grandmother, *meh know dat now. A young gyul like me so? Only sixteen Krystal. Leg like tree stump, tough ahms, and broad back. No shoes, meh dress dutty dutty dutty from de fiels, meh*

*hair kinky. E know ah was somebody toh wok like ah horse. Boh meh
know from Lacey e hah house, lan, and motohcah. So e din know ah
was usin im too.*

He extracted two towels from the bowels of his trunk and
tucked them around the front seats. He settled himself in and
motioned for her to join him, but Rebecca stood there unsure of
what to do. He reached over and rolled down his window. *Opan
it widdee door handle. Push dung de button wid yuh tumb fingah.*
Circling her fingers around the door handle, she felt the warmth
of the silver from sitting in the evening sun. She yanked, but it
didn't open. *Press de damn button.* Using her thumb, she pushed
down on the button, and the mechanism released the door. It
swung toward her, and she had to jump out of the way.

Rebecca clambered into the car and pulled the door shut
with a touch too much vigor. The car shook, and silence followed.
Afraid to look at him, she stared straight ahead. He slid the key
into the starter and peeled onto the highway, spraying gravel and
sand in their wake.

THEY ENTERED THE VILLAGE of Coal Mine after the sun had
set and darkness had settled in an amorphous mass around them.
She directed him where to go. There was no path in her tiny village where a car could pass, so he dropped her off as close to home
as possible. The whites of his eyes floated in the night. They said
goodbye to one another. She fumbled with the handle before tripping out of the car. Without a backward glance, he drove away.

Rebecca was late. She was usually home before the sun set.
With the excitement of the day simmering down, fear seeped in
once again. Her father would beat her for this. He would rouse
the whole village from their homes for a show. As frightened as

she was, her mind strayed to Shiva's clothes, how beautiful they were, and the sophisticated way he carried himself.

There was a flicker of light through the window. Only now Rebecca wondered what time it was, recalling she was supposed to have accompanied her mother to her uncle's wake. Inside, her brothers and sisters were seated around the only table they owned. Her father was standing by the door, his eyes ablaze. *Where de ass yuh find yuhself? Yuh class done finish hours ahgo. Yuh fohget yuh was suppose toh be hwome toh take yuh muddah toh de wake?* From years of confrontation with her drunken father, Rebecca knew silence was the best option. *Yuh eh goh say nutten? Yuh goh geh lix een yuh muddahass till yuh loosen dat tongue.* Rebecca edged back to the door. Her brother wouldn't look at her, and her sisters gulped in her embarrassment with delight. *Who was dat mahn who drop yuh hwome?* Silence. He unbuckled his belt. *Yuh bettah say fass.* In one smooth motion, he whipped the belt from his waist and folded it in half. He cracked it, and the sound was so sharp they jumped collectively. *Dis eh de only ting ah goh cut yuh ass wid, yuh know. Kamal goan bring meh ah guava whip from oudside.*

Kamal stood to go and get the whip, and Rebecca shrieked, *Pappy, it was ah taxi, ah taxi.* He glowered at her and signaled for Sonia, her younger sister, to come to him. In Sonia's hand was a piece of paper. *Yuh sistah was smaht enough toh take dung de license plate. Dat wasn't no taxi, yuh nasty, stinkin, dutty liah! Who cah yuh come hwome een? Wah mahn yuh gone bullin?*

For the first time, Rebecca did not cry, nor did she want to. She stood upright, her back to the hairy boards of their one-room house. She knew what was coming next. He'd accuse her of all the salaciousness his intoxicated mind could conjure and call her names no father should ever utter to a daughter—*jagabat* and *wahjang oman*. Eventually he'd fling the door open and tell her to get out of his sight, she was too shameful for his eyes. All eight other households in Coal Mine would come alive to see their drunken neighbor drag his daughter down the steps by her neck. Sometimes he thrashed her and left her on the barren dirt to crawl back inside, and other times he stood on the steps and addressed everyone in their village. *Allyuh see dis ungrateful bitch of ah dawtah?* He was mortified, he continued, that such a tragedy had sprung from his loins. Her mother never ran to help or protect her. Instead she chose to block the eyes and ears of her other children inside.

Rebecca's oasis was her drive home with Shiva today. She'd found the straying of his hand from the gearbox to her thighs exhilarating. Coolness cascaded over her. A pleasant sensation pooled below her hips. His hands moved from the stick to her leg, back and forth, tugging her dress up her thighs, never stopping.

Her father seized her by her neck and pulled her head close to his. The pungent scent of beer rolled in waves off his breath. The door was already open. Her siblings were sitting at the table with no mother to usher them to a corner tonight.

In the middle of his tirade, Rebecca wrenched her neck from his grasp. *Yuh wahn meh toh leave?* she asked. Shock stopped him for an instant. He slapped her. Her head reeled to one side, her cheek stinging. *Get out! Get out yuh bitch yuh!* Faces were already pressed to windows, and some people had their doors wide open. With her back straight and her head high, Rebecca walked down the steps. Her father stumbled behind her.

She'd go to Lacey's, she thought. And wait there until they could get in touch with Shiva for her. With a plan in place, maybe it was a good thing her father was kicking her out now. He hurled so many words at her, but nothing penetrated. The only person she thought of was Shiva. His name fluttered her breast.

She walked through the darkness until it swallowed her.

She walked until her father's voice was an echo of the past.

She never looked back.

DAYS

～

REBECCA TRUDGED ALONG the Eastern Main Road for miles. She passed fields, orchards, and groves, until she reached settlements and towns. Stones were embedded in her feet, wedged deep in her cuts. She was searching for Lacey and Jamal's house.

Her thighs began to tremble, and numbness spread to her knees, shins, and ankles. Her back ached. Doubt seeped in. How would Lacey and Jamal react to her showing up on their doorstep in the middle of the night? Did Shiva even want to see her again? Thoughts and pain mingled. She stopped for a breath, kneading a spasm in her side.

Up ahead raucous laughter spilled through the open doors of a rum shop. She passed it, and eyes slid over her. Their flat was right off the main road. There was no verandah, no backyard, no grass. She knocked on the door. Footsteps slapped concrete. She hoped Lacey was coming. Jamal answered the door with a baton within his grasp. He called for Lacey and disappeared into the shadows. When Lacey saw Rebecca, she squealed and hugged her as though she hadn't seen her in weeks.

They stood outside. Lacey shut the door behind her. Rebecca could hold her anguish inside no more. Years of tears flowed. They held on to one another until Rebecca's sobbing had subsided. Lacey waited until Rebecca had composed herself before ushering her inside.

The house was even smaller than it looked from the outside. The ceiling was low. There were only two rooms—a kitchen and a bedroom. From the flickering light of the oil lamp on a table, she saw a narrow bed shoved into a corner. Lacey seemed to have pressed everything into corners—stove, icebox, chairs, clothes. There were no windows.

Their children slept in the middle of the floor beneath a ratty cover. Jamal sat at the table smoking a cigarette. Lacey pressed a finger to her lips as they walked past the sleeping children.

Sorry Becca, meh eh hah blanket and pillow yet, juss ah ole ratty sheet. Rheal sorry, gyul. Yuh goh sleep right dey, is de only place we hah. She pointed to a spot just inside the door— other than under the table, the only available sleeping spot. Jamal flicked his cigarette outside and fell into the bed. Rebecca wrapped herself in the sheet and slid down to the floor. Lacey extinguished the flame. Rebecca was plunged into darkness once again.

~

REBECCA WOKE TO Jamal nudging her out of the way with his boot. He sneered at her before walking away. She pulled the sheet tightly around her shoulders. In the kitchen, three chipped enamel mugs were on the table. Settled at the bottom was Nescafé instant coffee mixed with sugar. Over the fire was a dented pan warming water. A cloud of heat rose.

Aye Becca, mawnin, gyul. Lacey's voice was thick and hoarse. *Whey Jamal gone, boi? E eh drink e coffee yet.* Jamal reappeared, then disappeared again, fingers crooked around the handle of the enamel cup.

Lacey stirred both their drinks. Rebecca fixated on the swirl of bubbles spinning in the middle of the cup. A shroud descended on Rebecca's thoughts. She wondered if Jamal could get in touch with Shiva today. Not wanting to ask him, she asked Lacey to do it for her.

Both women went outside and sat, Lacey smoking a cigarette, letting the end dangle from her mouth. They talked, whittling away their time. When the children woke, she ignored them. They ran around outside digging holes and flinging gravel at one another. They ate nothing because Lacey had nothing to cook. The only thing other than coffee Lacey could offer her was water.

They stuck together all day except when Rebecca used the latrine at the side of their house. As Rebecca walked down the steps onto their barren land, she knew that no matter how much it was tilled nothing would grow here, nothing could flourish.

Jamal didn't return until late in the evening. Hungry, and spent from the heat, they sipped water and moved to stay in the shade of the house with the waning sun. It was difficult for her to tell the time, but when Rebecca saw Shiva's car, time mattered no more. He was wearing a suit; she smiled. The children swarmed the car. One of them tried to touch it, and he barked, *Doh touch dat*. They jumped back, returning to Lacey and tugging the folds of her dress.

Jamal carried a couple of containers of food into the house. The children were scrawny. They batted at their father with their arms trying to get to the food. Though ravenous, Rebecca hung back from the meal as the whole family devoured what was in the boxes. Rebecca glanced away as they delved their dirty fingers into chicken, rice, and peas, tearing at whatever they could find until she was offered some food.

Shiva and Rebecca slept together that night. Wrapped

together in the sheet she slept under the night before, in the same clothes she met him in, on the same spot she curled herself on. He was on top of her, around her, inside her. She was his now. He had taken ownership, and now he couldn't leave.

THE MEN LEFT EARLY IN THE MORNING. No one mentioned anything of the night. Lacey persuaded Rebecca to try a cigarette. She told Rebecca to hold it in her lungs. She coughed and spluttered, but didn't hate it and asked for another. Rebecca wanted to ask how they could afford cigarettes and flower-arranging classes, but not food. Even asking in the blunt way Trinis asked everything, she knew it would come out the wrong way.

As the day grew hotter, they sought the shelter of the cool room. They lit the oil lamp if they needed to see, as the place was dark. Jamal, Lacey told Rebecca, stole the oil from his job. Rebecca never learned what Jamal's job was, and she wondered if Lacey even knew.

At midday, there was a knock on the door. Lacey hushed the children. A soft voice traveled past the crevices. *Becca? Becca, is Mama. Come meh chile, opan de door.* Rebecca made to go to the door, but Lacey grabbed her arm and whispered, *No, she goh take yuh hwome an yuh goh neva see im again. Yuh wahn dat?* Rebecca hesitated.

She shrugged off Lacey's hold and walked to the door. Her mother walked around the house. At the back door, she pounded louder, calling for her daughter, then pleading with her to let her in. Rebecca looked from Lacey to the door. Jacinta's voice pierced the shroud enveloping her, and for the second time she started to the door. Shiva's face swam past her eyes. She thought of his shiny car, his well-pressed clothing, the smell of farm around his fingernails. All these material things came first, followed by the warmth of his skin on hers and the heat being lifted from their bodies as they lay down to sleep. She shut her eyes against the path to the door. She clenched her fingers into fists until her mother left.

—*Krys chile,* my grandmother tells me, *it hut meh haht toh not ansah dat door dat day. Ah muddah searchin searchin foh she dawtah an me eh ansah. Meh haht still hutten.*

The night rolled in. They were starving but forced to wait until the men returned, *if dey come,* said Lacey. Sometimes days passed before Jamal showed up again, and without groceries, Lacey was forced to go and beg for food. Sometimes Shiva's mother sent food for them. *Rheal nice Indian food, gyul, dat oman could cook!* Jamal had another woman whose food they also ate. Lacey told her she loved to cook but only got a chance to when they had enough money to buy groceries. *Meh juss sorry yuh come durin one ah we dry up times. It does be good eh gyul, it does be good.*

They waited outside for the men to return. With a storm threatening the sky, the breezes were cool in the crooks and crevices of their arms and legs. The heat from the day left them parched for food and water. Rebecca could barely contain her hunger. When the men pulled up to the house, it took all of her self-control not to barrel toward them and grab their food.

Again Shiva stood in a corner while everyone dug in. Jamal didn't extend an offer to him; Rebecca didn't care why. Just as yesterday, Lacey gave her a plate. She was the only one to eat from a plate.

He stayed again. They slept together, but something felt different.

SHE CRIED. Lacey consoled her, but she continued crying, fat beads of tears squeezing between her fingers. They sat out front, and even after a cigarette, the tears kept coming. She was suffocating, and the only thing she could do was choke out tears. She wanted to go home. She didn't. What she really wanted was to leave their desolate place behind.

The men came earlier than usual. Rebecca went to Shiva and explained to him as best as she could. She asked him to accompany her home. She needed clothes. His silence spelled no, and she steeled herself for his answer. It didn't come. Instead, he nodded his head and gestured for her to get in the car.

In her father's home, Shiva stood just inside the door. The two men eyed one another but said nothing. Her mother was standing in a corner in front of her siblings, forever protecting them. She watched Shiva, not a word crossing her lips nor an expression passing her face.

So dis is de mahn we hear yuh goan shack up wid? her father started. *Is ah shameful ting wah allyuh doin. Is not right. Yuh muss mar-red meh dawtah. Do de right ting and mar-red she.*

Shiva stared at her father. *No,* he said. *Ah will do what ah wahn on meh own time.*

—*MEH STAY WID LACEY and dem seven days, chile,* my grandmother tells me, *and dem seven days di feel like ah lifetime. Aftah dat tird day everyting geh mix up.*

Everything started to blend together. Rebecca entered a

constant state of nausea. She couldn't live with them here, not like this, and though Shiva came to her every day, he spoke of no change.

—*Ah was rheal fraid, Krys,* says my grandmother, *now e might wantah keep meh like some concubine lock up dere een dey house.*

On the seventh day he told her he would take her to meet his mother. Rebecca looked down at her old clothes, broken nails, and uncovered feet. *Ah doh tink ah should meet yuh muddah like dis,* she said. He slapped her. In front of Lacey, Jamal, and the children. *Yuh go see meh muddah if ah say yuh go see meh muddah.* It stung—the strike, the embarrassment. She nodded her head; she would go. After all, she had no other choice now.

Shiva tried to say her name, but his tongue doubled up on itself. He rolled the *R* as though there was a succession of three *R*'s before he finally came to the *E* in Rebecca that he pronounced more as an *O*. It was funny but she dared not laugh. The sound of the *E* was like a retching in his throat, and though he only tried a handful of times to hack it out, none of them came close. *Rrrroooob,* he started.

Lacey interrupted him, *Nah mahn Shiva, wah appen wid yuh? Reeee, Reee-beck-kah. It easy nuff toh get it.*

Shiva shifted an imperious gaze from Lacey to Jamal, and Jamal chastised her, *Mind yuh business, oman. Yuh tink anybuddy wahn yuh in dey business? Why yuh eh geh yuh fat ass up and cook some food oh someting?*

Lacey *steupsed* and said, *If yuh could buy food foh dis place ahgo cook.* She waddled away, Jamal close behind.

Shiva turned his dark eyes upon Rebecca once more and said quietly, *Ruby.* Her gaze was inquisitive, but he didn't offer to repeat himself, and so she was forced to ask, *Wah yuh say dey?* He pulled away from her and smoothed his hands over his suit, this one a powder blue, white ruffled shirt inside, shiny gold buttons twinkling like stars. *Ruby. Meh kyant say yuh name so from now on meh cahl yuh Ruby.*

Ruby like de stone? Meh like it, meh li—

No, like blood.

～

HE STEERED THE CAR along the mountains. They followed the road that led to his estate, vegetation on both sides. *All dis yours?* she asked. *Yes.* The two-story house loomed into view, and she fell in love. Never mind who she had to meet inside or all the deficiencies one could immediately detect, she knew she wanted to live here. She wanted to call his place her own.

—*Is true, Krys,* my grandmother says, *de mahn hah house, lan, an motohcah. Wasn't juss talk nah. Foh somebody like me to meet im oh gaddoi ah was rheal lucky. Meh was gettin outtah dat bush.*

The land sprawled on for acres and acres—ten, twenty, thirty, forty, fifty acres around the house, away from the farm, in other parts of the island. Rebecca wanted to walk through the house slowly, absorb everything she saw, but he hustled her through to meet his mother. There was a garage for two cars, an open space downstairs, a kitchen, a bathtub out back, a drawing room, and at least three bedrooms.

His mother and one of the three sisters who lived with him were sitting on a couch upstairs. They were all dressed in traditional Indian garments woven from silk. Shiva exchanged some words with his mother in Hindi. *Meh muddah doh speak English,* he explained. *She say why yuh doh poh some oil een yuh hair and comb it dung flat?* Rebecca touched her hair. *It doh do dat,* she muttered. *Meh try it befoh.* While Shiva and his mother continued to talk, his sister wandered over to her and started playing with her face. She pinched her cheeks, rubbed her chin, and massaged her face.

—*Dat sistah e di hah, she name was Nollie,* my grandmother tells me, *she wasn't een she right frame ah min nah. She was nice, rheal nice, was evan alive when yuh was born, di hol yuh undah de pomegranate tree een de front boh someting di wrong wid she and nohboddy di know.*

As family stories were often passed along the female line, Rebecca shared a morsel of Nollie's history: Shiva's mother, while pregnant, stood beneath a tree and tugged at a branch for fruit. A much larger branch overhead cracked and crashed into her belly, knocking her over, pinning her down until someone could get her out. They attributed Nollie's mental state to that single accident. It meant taking care of Nollie for the rest of her life, and whoever did that once Shiva's mother was gone also inherited her share of the estate.

REBECCA LEARNED HER WAY around the house—the ground floor with its garage, the open sitting area with only a chain-link fence separating her from the outside, and the kitchen that stuck out like an appendage. On the second floor were rooms upon rooms, a maze of bedrooms all linked to one another by a doorway, a living room, a verandah. Shiva slept in the only room with glass doors that opened onto the verandah. Stone steps led from the gallery that opened into the bedroom to the side of the house where his car was parked.

She slept in his room; they shared a bed. Every night she succumbed to his calloused hands tearing at her clothing, his grunts and groans as he sank into her, then collapsed next to her, sweaty chest heaving until his breath evened out and he fell asleep. She lay naked next to him, staring at the wispy floor-length curtains swaying gently before the windows and doors. Curtains, a luxury her parents could never afford. Sometimes the moonlight shone like mercury through the translucent drapes, and the silhouette of the dresser in a corner of the room conjured thoughts of dresses and pantyhose, things she'd soon own. She lay there with her arm tucked under her head, drinking in the richness of her surroundings.

Sometimes she threw on the ratty dressing gown she'd brought from home with her and left the bedroom to explore. She unlatched the doors quietly and strolled into the gallery. Her breasts swayed to and fro underneath her gown; she allowed the cool night breeze to caress her ankles, play at her toes. On a farm tucked well into the hills and mountains, the Trinidadian sky was brilliant at night. Though it was the same where her parents lived, hidden behind thickets where roads didn't reach, never before had she just sat outside and reveled in the celestial beauty of a starry sky. She learned the moon in all its variance—bloated, crescent, purple, silver, clouded—until the month's cycle was as familiar to her as the lines on the palm of her hand.

While Shiva slept, she slipped into the living room and sat on the couch; it was fluffy and soft. Rebecca traced the cabinets, the tables and chairs, her fingers trailing each thing as a lover would. She returned to their room sometimes hours later. She slipped out of her dressing gown, slid into bed next to him, and put his hand over her bare stomach. There she finally succumbed to sleep.

HIS MOTHER AND THREE SISTERS all spoke Hindi to one another, his mother having migrated from India late in her life. There survived no stories of her husband or how she came to live in Trinidad as such a wealthy woman, owning much of the island. She left the handling of all the day-to-day affairs to Shiva alone.

The stream of Hindi his mother shrieked scared her at first. This gnarled old woman circled her, her knotted fingers poking and prodding Rebecca in places she didn't expect. Though she couldn't understand the language, Rebecca grasped everything when his mother reached up and tugged at her hair, only to wipe her hands distastefully on her white sari. In the end she spat on the ground and walked away. His sisters swung in the hammocks squealing when her mother would do this. None of them ever spoke to her, with the exception of Nollie, the one who looked as though she could be Shiva's twin.

—*She couldn't rheally tawk, Krys,* my grandmother says. *She use toh juss come up toh meh and play wid meh face. Once in a while she use toh pick flowahs and ting and wantah put it een meh hair. Boh when de muddah see dat is lix foh Nollie. And dat mahn too, e eh play de beat dah oman plenty nah. Poh Nollie, she eh do nutten wrong but e beatin she foh so when e geh vex.*

Rebecca tried to talk to Nollie but realized she couldn't respond; loneliness settled in deep once again. Shiva continued to talk to his mother in Hindi. He never offered to teach Rebecca, nor did he draw her close to his side when he and his mother conversed. His mother just glared at Rebecca from beneath the hood of her sari shawl.

Meh muddah go teach yuh how toh cook Indian food de whey ah like, Shiva told her. *Ah does reach hwome dis time every day foh dinnah. She does usually prepare everyting. From now on you goh do it.*

He waited for Rebecca to nod.

Hah everyting ready when meh walk troo de door. Bring it upstairs on ah tray. And meh doh like plenty salt on meh food.

And so Rebecca was taken under the wing of this indomitable woman who sneered and spat constantly. Rebecca realized quickly enough that this woman had every intention of showing her things only once. If she didn't commit it to memory, there would be no second chance.

One of the first meals she learned was tomato choka and roti, a staple meal of Indians on the island. His mother took her to a vegetable garden near the house laden with tomatoes and eggplants. Baigan and roti was another meal she'd have to learn to perfect soon. All the herbs she'd need to grind her own seasoning sprouted from narrow beds. Springing forth from the black earth were sprigs, knots, and wires of thyme, bandanya, celery, parsley, chives, and the tops of garlic. The fine array of greens against the rich earth pulled Rebecca like a magnet. Where she lived with her parents in Coal Mine, the surrounding land was barren, and to plant one had to venture far away from their village, deeper in the forest. Jacinta eventually did, but traipsing back and forth was no easy feat, and with no help, the garden struggled. If others found it, they trampled it spitefully or stole its bounty for their own.

Rebecca rubbed her coarse thumb over the thin skin of a ripened tomato, and her fingerprint left ridges on its surface. She turned it in her hand, and the red orb parted readily with its vine. The eggplants were so purple they shone black under the pulsing sun. When his mother turned her back to grab a basket, Rebecca, unable to help herself, gnashed her teeth into the tomato. Juice spurted, ran down her chin, hand, arm; seeds splattered her dress. It was warm and sweet, the fleshy insides bouncing from one side of her mouth to another. Rebecca tried to hide what she'd done, but the red mess wasn't easy to wipe away, and the slap across the back of her head startled her into dropping the rest of the tomato.

His mother shrieked Hindi at her; Rebecca cowered, though this frail woman was much smaller than she. His mother flung the basket at her and put up her ten fingers twice then, pointed at the tomatoes. Rebecca gathered twenty tomatoes while this woman tittered at her with arms folded over the pleats in her sari.

In the kitchen, they roasted these fat tomatoes over an open fire until the skin turned black and crackled. Seams broke; the hissing and spitting over the open flame revealed red insides. They pulled the charcoal skins off using two forks; the older woman demonstrated. Rebecca chopped onions, garlic, and scotch bonnet peppers; she tossed them together and chunkayed the mixture with hot oil. She squashed the tomatoes with vigor, sweat dripping from her face in the sweltering kitchen.

In the flurry of making the tomato choka—a meal she'd never before prepared—his mother scooped flour from a sack and into a basin, assuming Rebecca was paying attention. Next she added a pinch of baking soda and salt, sprinkling, considering, sprinkling again. She added water to a well in the middle and skillfully rolled the mixture together with her fingertips until it was a full mound in the center of the silver bowl. Draping a damp cloth over it, the old woman made the hand motions to signal it had to sit before further action was required.

Rebecca tried desperately to remember these things. She started lists in her head, but her attention was divided, and she lost track of necessary steps and ingredients. With a mortar and pestle, she ground seasoning to add to the food.

One of the workers on the farm rapped on the wooden kitchen door. He stepped inside and tipped his head to Shiva's mother; they smiled at one another, a familiar routine. He looked inquisitively at Rebecca but didn't ask questions. He hoisted a bag onto the table, and with a thump oranges spilled out. The man bowed before backing out through the door. Shiva's smiling mother turned upon Rebecca once again with a scowl that made her jowls quiver. She chopped an orange in half and squeezed the juice from it, preventing the seeds from entering the jug with a closed palm. Rebecca was to finish juicing the entire bag before Shiva got home.

After a couple of hours, Rebecca watched as his mother uncovered the loya for roti. It had swelled to more than twice its size, pushing at the edges of the basin. She was pleased to see it had done what she wanted it to do. The woman separated one after another, tucking the excess pieces into balls with her fingers. She made seven smaller mounds and sprinkled flour over them before covering them to sit for a while longer. When they were ready, she pressed them flat and rolled them out with a rolling pin, spinning them one at a time over the fire. They swelled and burst, emitting steam in a puff of white cloud and a shrill whistle. His mother, Rebecca had to admit, was a master at making Indian food.

They owned enamel plates and cups—dishes that did not break, and though this was something Rebecca didn't ponder right away, she would soon know why. Shiva had his favorites, and his mother showed her which ones to serve his meal in. The cups and plates were dented, flaked off in places to reveal a blackened skin beneath. Rebecca spooned tomato choka into one and heaped roti cut into triangles into another. She filled one cup with orange juice and another with water. His mother, done with her tutelage for the day, retired upstairs for some rest.

The eldest sister called to Rebecca from the front of the house. Rebecca covered the food to keep it hot and went to see what she wanted. But she pretended she hadn't summoned her. Frustrated, Rebecca took the food up on a tray to Shiva. The dishes rattled on the tray. He was sitting on the long couch in the living room waiting for her. She was so focused on memorizing what her mother-in-law was doing she hadn't realized how much time had passed and was surprised to find him bathed and dressed with his legs crossed on the sofa. She set the food on his lap and backed away.

He uncovered each plate and smiled at her. Not sure how to react or where to go, she stood off to the side, fidgeting with her clothes. He tore off a piece of roti and scooped up the tomato choka with it. After he plunged it into his mouth, the pleasure on his face faltered and his mouth puckered. He dipped his index finger into the red mush and sucked on it. His mouth puckered again. Without a word, he upended the tray from his lap, flinging everything in a fit of anger.

Wah de ass wrong wid yuh? Dis ting poison wid salt! Whey yuh lun toh cook?

Rebecca backed away from him, stammering, *Meh-meh-meh geh help from yuh muddah. Meh din evan puh de salt een in de food.*

He glowered at her with eyes as black as a pit of fathomless depths. *You goan blame meh muddah? My muddah yuh goan blame? Eh?*

The blows began. The women of the house congregated to watch. Nollie was the only one to try to stop him; she was beaten too.

—*Nollie was like dat, Krys,* my grandmother says. *She always tryin toh take lix foh uddah people. She use toh do it foh yuh muddah and all ah dem too boh e di juss beat she and den move on toh dem when e done.*

It took a few more beatings, careless mistakes, trust placed in the wrong hands, but Rebecca realized the sisters were the ones to salt his food on purpose before she took it up to him.

—*Dem was wicked and wutless,* my grandmother tells me,

lettin im beat meh foh nutten so. Dey use toh do it even aftah we hah chilren. Meh know is cause dey tawt ah was black eh, dey tink meh mix wid African. Boh it doh mattah wah, meh nevah do dat toh meh wuss enemy.

WITH EACH PASSING YEAR, Rebecca was pregnant again.

—*When ah give birt toh one,* says my grandmother, *meh pregnant again wid ah nex one. One on one bress and de nex one on de uddah. When me eh hah milk ah gih dem flour pap.*

Pregnant or not, she toiled on the farm with cutlass and sickle, bags draped over her back. His blows were no less brutal when she was with child, perhaps worse, as though rage could drive him to rip the baby bloody from her insides. He left her after he beat her. Blood spilled from every orifice, and as he walked to his car, she prayed he wouldn't turn back. She knew when he left it was to sink into the flesh of another woman.

Rebecca had long stopped wondering if his caresses could resume the tenderness they once had in the car that night. Or when he took her virginity on the floor of Lacey and Jamal's years ago. She often wondered about Lacey, but since saying goodbye to them, she almost never left the house and farm lands. Was her common-law husband delicate with other women? Was he affectionate with them after he'd almost beaten her to death? She imagined his hands slipping through the silken strands of an Indian woman's hair. He beat her because she wasn't pure, she was sure of this. Because she couldn't speak Hindi, because she couldn't cook Indian food. But he didn't beat her for working, because in the end they both knew it was the reason he didn't kill her.

They had five children together when Rebecca found out about Avinash. His bastard son was almost a year old.

Arya, the fourth child, was only three months old when Shiva's mother passed, never learning of her son's lewdness. She was bedridden for a long time before that, and Rebecca was her sole caregiver even throughout her pregnancies, changing, feeding, and bathing her, sometimes only hours after giving birth. Before she died, Shiva's mother bought a piece of land for Rebecca, ensuring her daughter-in-law's name was the only one on the deed.

Rebecca and Shiva themselves never had a ceremony, and there was no paperwork to show they were legally married, yet she was his, living in his house, cleaning up after him, cooking his meals. Rebecca told herself that one son birthed from passion couldn't threaten the life she'd pieced together with blood, sweat, and tears. But, and this was a thought that slithered in as quietly as a snake, what if this was a son born out of love? Men had been known to leave their wives for far less.

—*We nevah geh mar-red oh anyting, Krys,* my grandmother tells me, *no ceremony, no nutten. Meh juss move een and dat was dat. Common-law husband and wife. E could kick meh out oh pick up and leave anytime e wahn. When ah hear bout dis uddah chile meh di fraid.*

Rebecca couldn't say anything, and so she pretended Avinash didn't exist, even though she feared he was the one thing that could rip everything from her.

REBECCA OPENED HER EYES. Her belly churned from punches, kicks, and flips. The time for this one was coming close, and the midwife should be called soon.

—*Dere was nutten like goin toh ospital een dem days, Krys,* my grandmother says. *Ah mean people use toh goh, and it wasn't like we was poh, but is bawl ah bawlin like a cow when ah hah toh push dem chilren out een de house.*

Shiva was wealthy, and while many things were kept from his children and wife, some things were also given. Families with money paid poor women to wash their clothes, and Rebecca now had her own washerwoman.

—Dese oman and dem use toh come by de house beggin foh wok. Dey husband gone and leff dem wid chilren hungry. Dey gone een every rum shop toh spend dey paycheck. Fi cent toh wash up de clothes an ting an Mistah Shiva di pay foh it widout ah fuss.

Priya, the washerwoman who'd been coming to them for weeks now, whistled as she unlatched the front gate and walked into the open space on the ground floor.

Becca? Oye Misrez Rebecca, whey yuh dey? Meh come foh meh day wok.

Rebecca was still on the ground where her husband had left her. She rolled to her side and tried to get up. The pain was excruciating. Shiva must've broken a few bones this time. Rebecca wheezed.

Priya gyul, juss siddung dey een de front.

She tried to hold her body together, but it felt flayed, as though she was falling apart. Rebecca held the wooden railing with one hand. One step took her minutes to accomplish.

Misrez Rebecca? Everyting ahright? Yuh wahn help wid someting? Yuh eh sound so good.

Rebecca left a trail of bloody handprints along the railing as she struggled to get to the bathroom.

Misrez Becca? Priya called out again, and this time it was accompanied by tentative footsteps as she approached the staircase.

Rebecca was almost to the bathroom, but to speak she had to stop and fuel her voice with all the energy she possessed.

Priya! she hissed low and slow between teeth clenched, *stop! Goan and siddung oh meh eh goh need yuh suhvices today.*

Priya, a young single mother living in a hut smaller than the one Rebecca had left behind, obeyed. She sat on a bench and waited.

Rebecca pulled her body through the doorway of the bathroom. A new addition to their house, it was an enclosed room made of concrete with a drain in the middle. In a corner lay an overturned bucket. Next to it was a bar of soap on a piece of stone. She grimaced as she turned on the water, the smallest movement inciting pain. Water shot out of the tap hard, fast, and cold. The stream numbed her skin. Blood swirled in marbled patterns until the water ran clear over the rough concrete.

In their bedroom, she didn't glance in the mirror. Steeling herself this way had always worked for her in the past. Downstairs Priya looked at her aghast. At the sharp intake of Priya's breath and the widening of her eyes, Rebecca looked away, not wanting to see anymore of her reaction.

Upstairs hah de hampah yuh coul find all de clodes whey it normahly is. Dungstairs—

Misrez Becca, wah happen? Oh Gawd— Priya cut in.

By her reaction alone Rebecca knew she could never understand. All Rebecca needed was for Priya to ignore what she'd seen and continue with her work. Any other woman or man in the marketplace or nearby villages would know better than to draw attention to what were considered private matters between husband and wife. Domestic abuse was not something that existed in Trinidad during this time, and even later, when it was given a name so it could be reported, it took decades before it was taken seriously.

Priya put her hand on Rebecca's shoulder. It was a gesture so genuine and warm, it almost crushed Rebecca. Despite the pain she knew would shoot through her body, she yanked herself away.

Priya! Yuh muss lun when toh min yuh business and when toh wok. Eiddah goan staht de clodes upstairs oh yuh coul find wok some-place else.

Stung, Priya did not know the language and etiquette of abuse, and she stumbled away toward the stairs. Rebecca called to her, *And doh fohget de fahm tings downstairs and de kitchen towels een de back.*

Now faced with the task of cooking dinner, she had to whip together roti because her husband was not a man for rice. If she chose the easy path of boiling rice, she knew, he would fling the enamel plate and cup to the floor and beat her more. Her children would watch from corners, frightened. She kneaded and punched the roti, violent actions that jerked her body. But she did it to spare her children. Her belly, back, and sides ached from her husband's blows. She sat on a nearby bench and waited for the worst of the searing pain to pass.

In the kitchen, she peeled potatoes, sifted flour, roasted toma-toes. Her children saw the marks on their mother; though still too young to understand, they helped her as much as they could. Panicked hands worked against a ticking clock.

Contractions started. The pain was familiar, and she realized she'd been having them all day. Beneath the throbbing injuries, the contractions had been mild. Now they were more intense. She grabbed onto the nearby kitchen table and doubled over. Rebecca held on to her oldest child. *Goan geh de midwife now!* There was a patter of footsteps. All signs pointed to her giving birth to a boy—pointed belly, carrying high, eating sour, and radiant skin. The midwife fed her these clues, vehemently stating that she was having a boy. No one disagreed with these women; they were elders in the community and had been practicing midwifery their entire lives.

Rebecca felt the urge to begin pushing. Grunting, she squatted in the kitchen and started to push, but something was wrong. The midwife didn't come for at least an hour, for she had to walk miles to get to Rebecca. When she got there, she banished the children from the room. They were to come only when called for.

Labor progressed well into the night, after Shiva had returned home, poked his head into the room, a look of disdain upon his face, and left. Only after baby and placenta had exited her body, after the intensity of birth began to subside, did Rebecca sink into the silence surrounding them. She knew. The midwife had cut the umbilical cord and wrapped the baby in a piece of cloth, but she remained out of view between Rebecca's legs. She and Rebecca knew one another intimately, for she had delivered all of the Singh children thus far. The midwife walked to Rebecca's side and placed the newborn in her arms, tears falling and soaking into the cloth. The baby was blue. She was stillborn. She was the first of four.

—*By di time ah geh toh de tird stillborn chile, Krys,* my grandmother confesses, *meh haht kyant take it no moh. Meh trow two een ah bucket and de lass one ah gih toh dem chilren to trow whey dung de hill.*

LOOK

~~~~

REBECCA WAS ROASTING EGGPLANT on the stove. Sixteen-year-old Arya sat at the table helping her.

Ruuuuuuby.

Their hearts dropped. They didn't even know he was home; he shouldn't have arrived for another couple of hours. Arya urged her mother to run, to get out of the way and hide.

Shiva walked into the kitchen and without a word raised his fist. Rebecca dropped everything in her hands and wrapped her fingers around his neck. It transpired so fast, they all seemed startled by her movements. That was, until words filled the space around them.

Hit meh again and ah will keel yuh, Rebecca said.

She squeezed his throat and didn't let go. His eyes bulged out of his head. His tongue flopped around outside his mouth. He choked. When she finally released him, he fell to his knees and gasped for air. Shiva overturned the tables in the kitchen and threw the eggplant on the floor before leaving.

Mother and daugher looked at one another and an understanding passed between them.

—*So help meh Gawd, Krystal,* says my grandmother, *ah wuddah keel im dat day.*

MY
MOTHER

1997–2007

CHEATED

~~~~~

FROM MY GRANDMOTHER'S KITCHEN to my mother's and back again, we keep cooking together, recreating the oldest meals created on our islands by our various ancestors, from cassava dumplings soaked in spicy curried crab to piles of roti served with dollops of saltfish mixed with lemon juice, onions, and scallions. And all the while, as smoke tendrils rise up all around us, they speak.

As my grandfather withers away in a corner of their shared apartment in Jersey City, unable to walk without help, unable to feed himself, bathe, dress, Arya's and Rebecca's lives dance before us round one table or another. My mother's memories lend understanding to recollections I harbored throughout my own childhood. They tell me stories they never shared with one another. And so, solid memories begin to crack and separate, to reveal the meanings and anguish I couldn't before access.

I'm whisked back to a time when the phone constantly rang. I was ten years old, sitting on a stool in our kitchen in Trinidad. I answered it while twisting the cord around my wrist and forearm. *Hello?* Silence. *Helloooooo.* A whoosh of breath followed by a female voice. *Hi, dis is Krystal? Is Misrez Khan. Ah di cahl before toh talk toh yuh faddah. E helpin meh wid ah case dahlin, e hwome?* I detected insincerity in her voice, but that dissipated when my father took the call, and I was now free to go back to whatever I was doing.

The calls continued for months. Mrs. Khan phoned our house numerous times every week. In the beginning, when my mother picked up, Mrs. Khan would hang up.

Aye Arya gyul, ah din tell yuh bout dis case we appen ovah? my father said. My mother shook her curly head as she cut my sister's stewed chicken to pieces and urged her to eat.

Well wah appen, he said while devouring his own plate of dinner, *is dis oman Misrez Khan entah dis business deal wid so and so. Dey tell she toh meet dem at ah certain location. When she find someting funny bout de exchange, she call de police sta—*

My mother interrupted, *Wait wait wait, yuh tellin me she nevah meet dese people and gone makin business deal wid dem? She leh money pass han and ting?*

Dah is de point, Arya, my father said.

Well who een dey right min goh do dat? My mother took her time on a long, sweet *steups* here. *Yuh eh see de oman dotish?*

Ah was on de case. My father raised his voice. *And when we show up toh de address nohboddy dey. De oman was right and if we din pull up wid police cah and everyting we wuddah find she body somewhey out dey een de foress oh not atall.*

Colette! my mother yelled at my sister. *Eat yuh food, chile, and stop playin before ah hit yuh one slap in yuh backside.*

So now is ah ongoing investigation we hah on we hands and ah is lead on it.

That was how Mrs. Khan of Toco was officially introduced to our home, and it was only after this that she responded when my mother answered the phone. What my mother didn't piece together for a long time was that my father had been on many cases before, but she was the only one who contacted him at home.

———

MONTHS LATER I FOUND MY MOTHER in my bathroom retching and bawling over the sink. Weak sunlight filtered into the room. The elongated faucet curved like the delicate neck of a swan. The silver glinted eerily. Water gushed out of the faucet. She dipped her face into its stream and cried out. My mother often told my sister and me the story of our births and of her guttural screams, *like ah cow givin birt toh dead young one.* She would know, having watched cows give birth her entire life.

I didn't know what to do. The veins in her neck pulsated; her cries were loud enough for our neighbors to hear. I'd left my six-year-old sister in our bedroom down the hall. She'd never heard our mother like this before and was too scared to come.

I can't help wondering now if my grandmother cried the way my mother did. Did her children see her? What did they feel?

My mother grabbed the sink with both hands. She shook it, pressed down on it, rocked back and forth, as though wanting to crack the porcelain with her bare hands.

My father was not home. He'd been sent to America on an assignment, surely now with Mrs. Khan, but I didn't know this and all I could wonder was when he'd call to talk to us. For the past week, my mother'd been on the phone with my grandmother and her sisters who were already living in America. Each time it rang, I thought it was my father, but she never passed the phone for us to say hello. Her sisters had news of my father's doings, and they whispered vicious words in her head.

There were few laws that protected women on our islands. Being married to a policeman who could bend, twist, and break them all was not something my mother had thought about before; her only concern had been how it could benefit her. Once a woman was married and pregnant, a career became nothing more than a memory. Dharmendra couldn't have his wife working on the island; it was an unsavory look for his family. We—my sister, my father, and I—became her life. By the time I was born, she cooked three meals a day; raised chickens and ducks that she killed, plucked, and roasted right downstairs in our house; cultivated the land we lived on, tending to plum, mango, coconut, pineapple, pommerac, pommecythere, orange, grapefruit, cherry, mandarin, and pomegranate trees. Though my parents owned crops, land, an unfinished big house, and a car, they didn't have enough money. Even if she had wanted to work, with no one to help them take care of me, my mother had no choice but to stay home.

My mother strove to escape my grandmother's life, but seemed to follow it closely—with a man she hoped to one day love, no job, pregnant, working the land. The mantra of *house, lan, and motohcah* that echoed from one generation to the next was achieved, but at what cost? Fighting against everything my grandmother was, my mother stepped neatly into her place, serving my father food at the same time every day, packing him hot lunches every morning, prepping his clothes for work, catering to his every desire in the same way Rebecca did for Shiva. My father, like all men on the islands, had a temper and could lash out at my mother whenever he pleased. As a police officer, we all knew, he didn't have to deal with any consequences.

By the time my sister was born in 1991, we didn't even have money for bread. My mother had asked the old man who owned the nearby shop for credit so many times, her name was pages deep in his book. She decided the best thing to do was scrounge up whatever money she could and follow her siblings to America. There she found temporary, live-in babysitting jobs in six-to-ten-month increments. My father's mother took care of us during these absences. The first time my mother left us, my sister was only six months old, and when she returned, Colette was over one. I barely recognized our mother sashaying up our back steps in black pants that slinked to the rhythm of her legs, and my sister refused to even let her touch her.

—*Ah use toh be lock up een a room wid some ah dese families, Krys,* my mother tells me, *takin care ah uddah people chilren while meh own cryin foh me. Boh ah had toh do it oh we wouldn' tah sahvive.*

One US dollar was equivalent to six TTs. My mother kept only enough of what she made to get by in America and sent the rest for our food and clothes. Eventually we could start fixing the unfinished house we were living in.

After working along with her husband to keep and maintain their home, sacrificing the tender years of her children, Arya never thought she'd be one of these women of our islands whose husbands cheated on them, leaving them to weep on the floor before their daughters.

In these moments, did my mother think I was destined to the same and felt powerless to prevent it?

WHEN I WALKED IN ON MY MOTHER crying in the bathroom that day, parts of our cordless phone were at my feet in the doorway. The battery was against the wall; the back plate I would later find beneath a cabinet. My mother splashed water on her face when she saw me. She stopped howling and blew her nose. She splashed more water on her face, washing washing washing as though the cold water could alleviate the pain I saw twisting itself in her. *Come,* she beckoned me with a wave of her hand, water droplets flecking the tiled floor. I handed her a towel, but it hung as limp as her hand at her side. With her back against the wall, she slid down to the floor. Her shirt rolled up, uncovering her back, sides, and a lip of her belly hanging over her shorts. She reached out for me.

I stepped into her arms, and she hugged me, burrowed her face in my hair, bawling in my ears, *Yuh eh know wah e do, Krys, yuh eh know wah yuh faddah do, oh Gawd Krystal, meh kyant believe wah e do, how he goh do dis toh meh, toh* **we**. She rocked us back and forth, side to side, holding me so tight I almost couldn't breathe. I slid my hands down her back and rubbed in small circles, this motion she'd done countless times for my sister and me when we were unwell or sad.

—*Krys*, my mother tells me later, *meh was holdin on toh yuh, chile, meh was holdin on toh yuh foh meh sanity.*

I didn't know that as I sat in her lap, our legs folded the same. The hairs on her skin prickled and scratched me. My mother's tears fell on top of my head and down my face. These tears fell until my hair no long repelled but absorbed them.

Her agitated state made it difficult for her to stay in one position for very long. Soon, she stood up. She wrung her hands, paced back and forth in the narrow bathroom, twisted and turned the doorknob. When she left the room, I followed her to the entertainment center in the living room. She pulled out a photo book. It was their wedding album. She flipped and flipped until she got to the center where there was a large portrait of each of them—my mother on the right, my father on the left. Though separate pictures on their own pages, it appeared that younger Arya and Dharmendra were gazing at one another and smiling. The photographs had been taken at different times, but the photographer captured a moment amid their tedious Indian ceremony where they were each looking at one another. My father was wearing the traditional kurta. A feather protruded from his hat and was caught in mid-flutter. His mustache was trimmed and brushed above his wide smile.

My mother ripped it from its binding. The severed paper curled like a piece of parchment in her hands. She grabbed a lighter.

In the backyard she dropped the picture on the stone cesspit cover and with trembling hands tried to call the flame. She cracked and snapped the picture until it unrolled and she could see his face. I didn't want her to burn my father's picture; even though I was ten, I still didn't fully grasp what was going on. I ran to her and snatched it from among the potted thyme leaves.

Ma, doh do it. Doh do someting yuh might regret, I said.

I wanted to do something that would help her in these moments but felt powerless. Capturing memories on file within albums or to hang on one's walls was an indulgence we couldn't normally afford, even in 1997, and she was about to destroy one of the few photographs we had of them from eleven years before. Never having owned a camera, my mother took us to a studio not far from our home and paid for one picture at a time when she could, and those amounted to only a handful. Whatever tangible memories we owned had been given to us by those who'd been gracious enough to take our pictures, print them, and pass them along. My parents' wedding album was precious, if not to her, then to me, for whatever was lost could never be recovered.

I knew my father loved this picture too. He often held me in his lap as we flipped through the album and always lingered on those particular photos of them, something I couldn't quite reach holding him there a moment longer than any other photograph ever could, and he'd say, *Is de only picture we hah like dis, Krys. Yuh could see de appiness een we face.*

It was evident by his actions that my father loved my mother, and I have never been able to understand why he cheated on her. Akin to my grandfather, he left no room for me to ask, bristling at the mere mention of infidelity. These island men clamped down and resisted being questioned, walking away, shutting me out if I even skirted the subject.

When the lighter failed to flicker, my mother turned to matches; nothing could ever deter her. She struck the head and the flame ignited. It licked a corner of the picture. Slow and purposeful. As though the flame itself was in sync with my mother's emotions. She held it while the fire engulfed the only portrait taken of him on their wedding day. I stood next to her and watched my father's face reduced to cinder, black specks floating in the air and settling in our hair and on our skin. The fire reached her fingertips; she turned it upside down, wanting to hold on to it for as long as she could. My father's forehead fell to the cesspit cover, and the remainder of the print dissolved to gray ash.

Only a week ago my mother had just stepped off the plane after a six-month stay in America. She came back all bouncy-haired, perfumed, and carting suitcases of presents for us and our entire extended family. My father left only a day later, off on another one of his business trips, insisting, as odd as it was, that we didn't need to accompany him to the airport. This was the first time he'd done that. Was it planned this way? In the whirl of excitement of having arrived home after being separated from us, my mother thought nothing of it.

My mother stopped crying. She scattered the ashes with a sweep of a leafy branch, dusted herself off, and took my hand. I slipped my arm around her waist, and she ran her fingers through my long hair. There was a heavy feeling in my stomach and a sadness hovering around us.

We goin toh America now, she said, and I was surprised at how hoarse her voice sounded. *We goan ketch im.*

I became her witness.

REALM

WHENEVER WE HAD TRAVELED between Trinidad and America to visit family, my father would take charge of our documents and arrangements. This was the first time I saw my mother handling our passports, checking and rechecking dates and times, meeting with travel agents to haggle over prices, extracting money from the bank. Everything was done so fast, the whole trip paid for and planned within a couple of days. She did it nervously, chewing at the skin around her nails when no one was looking or winding a lock of hair around her index finger.

Most of the Singh family had immigrated to the states a decade ago. My great-grandmother Jacinta became a citizen shortly after her daughter sponsored her, and in turn she sponsored Rebecca. But when that took too long, my Aunt Reeya reapplied for my grandparents. Once the paperwork was final, my grandmother forsook the islands immediately, leaving my grandfather behind to tie up loose ends with the farms.

Renting out the farms along with the house proved difficult. Unable to drive, my grandfather stayed with us on and off, my father chauffeuring him around every second he wasn't at work. On planning his move to America, Shiva trusted my father to help him orchestrate his rather complicated departure from the island, enlisting his help to lease and rent his properties and even to draw up contracts and agreements. Once it was done, my father even deposited and withdrew money from Shiva's account when he needed him to, the only other person to ever have access to his personal accounts.

Rebecca had been living in America less than two years when we told her the reason we'd be coming. I talked to her on the phone, and she was excited to see us but said, *Undah dese circumstances dahlin is not ah good ting eh love.* The day before our flight, my mother asked one of her sisters to pick us up at the airport. Our flight touched down on American soil around five in the morning. We traveled from JFK Airport in New York to the urban streets of Jersey City, where my grandmother was living in a two-bedroom apartment with a few of my aunts, uncles, and cousins. My grandfather would not permanently relocate to the United States for another year or two.

—*Krys,* my mother says, *we di leave so fass ah din even hah time toh tell Pappy we was goin. If e come lookin foh we, we nowhey toh be found.*

When we arrived at my grandmother's, it was only to toss our one suitcase into her hallway and head up the block to my uncle's. Somehow my father had found out we were on a flight to America and asked his brother if he could stay with him.

My father's younger brother Ram was married to my mother's older sister Reeya. They lived only houses away from my grandmother, and we often had parties there when we visited. My sister and I spent lots of time there with our twin cousins Olivia and Sophia.

We found my father in the basement with Carly, Olivia and Sophia's baby sister, asleep on his bare chest. My mother filled the floor with her quiet anger, but my father refused to give up the baby, wielding her like a shield between them. Soon, almost all of my mother's family was present. They kept talking about my father; my mother said nothing. Protective, I took my sister upstairs to play with Olivia and Sophia, then returned downstairs.

Dharmendra, gimmeh de chile now, my mother said. But he only shook his head, shushed her, and whispered, *Arya, de child sleepin, wah wrong wid yuh?* He was so calm resting there on their basement bed as my mother's sisters pressed into her back as reinforcement. Then I noticed his face was unshaven and his long hair disheveled.

Everyone gathered in the den. They whispered more things in my mother's ear, and her curls shivered as she shook her head. *Divorce,* and the end of the word echoed in my head like the hissing of a snake. Divorce, I thought, was for the people in America, not Trinidad. I told myself that no matter what happened, my parents would stay together.

How much more did I have to see and hear before I understood that these men on our islands would never change?

The more my aunts and uncles talked, the angrier I became. *It eh allyuh business,* I wanted to scream. *Dis eh yuh family.* But they whispered and my mother listened, her upper body collapsing into her lap.

I hung on to every word my mother told her siblings, and it was only then I understood the entire story. My father had lied to my mother, telling her he was on a case and had to travel abroad to America; he even garnished his lie with the appeasement that his department would pay for it, knowing my mother wouldn't check their finances. She was excited because my father had only been sent to neighboring islands before, never to America, and this was perhaps a promotion for him. My father and this woman planned a trip to America together for a few weeks, and the money came out of our account, money that hadn't been there until my mother left her children to work abroad.

Details my mother shared, of packing his suitcase with his favorite items and organizing his papers, pained her. When she realized why he had asked her not to drive him to the airport, her voice cracked, and she tried to rush through the rest of the story. When my mother entered the realm of conjecture, no one stopped her. She thought of my father sitting on the plane with this woman's hand in his, both of them talking about how their spouses had no idea.

We found out that while in America, my father had run into one of his brothers-in-law, and they planned a night of drunken debauchery. In an alcoholic haze, Dharmendra foolishly entrusted his deception to Matthew, Chandini's husband.

My mother found out from the lips of her youngest sister.

—*When Chandini di cahl meh toh tell meh dat back den, eh Krys,* my mother says, *is wit glee een she voice, yuh know. Een dem eyes ah was too happy livin een house and ting wid chilren, nah wokin oudside. Dey di wantah see meh crumple, and e gih dem all dey needed foh dat.*

Eventually my father gave up Carly, and she ended up in my arms. I rocked her back and forth. It took him some time, but he came up from the basement. Silence. No one left the room. There was my mother's side of the room with all her family, and then there was my father standing straight and tall. Everyone glared at him. He did not look down. He did not look away. Uncle Ram, his brother, was upstairs with my sister and the girls. I wondered if my father wished he were here with him, just one single ally. When my father's eyes fell on me, he faltered for a second, his shoulders slumping forward, but he pulled them taut again. I held on to baby Carly like my mother held on to me while she sobbed. I was afraid if I let go of her I would break down and they would crowd around me, using me as a weapon against my own father.

For the same reason my mother took care of the man who brutalized her mother, I now felt sympathy for my father: I was his daughter. That connection was forged deep into my soul, but I also saw regret swimming in the murky depths of his eyes. The realization that he wouldn't do anything to show it unsettled me. After I became an adult, I examined those moments where my aunts and uncles pledged their loyalty to one side, and only then did I begin to understand my mother's predicament with her parents. She didn't choose to take care of her father, who had provided for her, and she didn't ignore her mother's pain and suffering when she did; filial obligation ripped through my mother like a current.

I felt that as I looked at my father. What I would never be able to know is if his regret only surfaced because he was caught.

I had become my mother, and she was now Rebecca.

My mother and grandmother had both fought to prevent so much, to achieve that much more, and yet, in some ways, their fight ended with too many losses. Now I knew and saw their predicaments all too well. Could I help change the outcome? How could I protect both my father and mother? How could I keep our family intact? Was it worth it to do so?

My aunts placed themselves like obstacles between my father and mother, between husband and wife. I walked around jiggling the baby, and voices flared, but I couldn't seem to focus on who was speaking. One aunt turned to me and asked if I had anything to say to my father. What I wanted to tell her was I had something to say to them all, I wanted them to get the hell out, to just give us the space to deal with this as a family, but I couldn't; that would be disrespectful.

I stroked baby Carly's hair and planted a kiss on her forehead. I didn't have any questions. I wanted this whole thing to disappear. Someone took the baby from me, and while I didn't want to give her up, I did. My mother was slumped on the couch, crying, tissues balled up in her hands. She wouldn't look at him. I couldn't bear to see her so broken, and as much as I wanted to fix it, I had this urge to protect my father as well.

Dad, I said really searching his eyes, *yuh rheally do wah dey say yuh do?* I didn't need confirmation. I knew the truth, but for some reason I wanted him to say it. In my own way, I did want to punish him, just not the way everyone wanted me to. While I waited for some kind of acknowledgment, I began to think he was going to ignore me, just as he'd been ignoring everyone else.

Why allyuh hah to bring meh dawtah een dis? Yuh eh see allyuh is nasty wutless people? my father said.

Yuh nasty, Dharmendra! my mother said. *Not **we**. Not **dem**. Yuh is ah nasty stinkin liah.*

Her strength returned for a bit and would continue to fluctuate in the coming weeks and months—rising and waning before me like the tides of the Caribbean Sea.

She was right, he was a liar. But I was his daughter, and her family wanted me to be his prosecutor.

We ended up staying in America for some time—my father at his brother's and us at my grandmother's. My mother used the few houses in between as a barrier.

It was wintertime and, unaccustomed to the cold, all I wanted to do was find warm pockets in the apartment and go to sleep. I prayed for it to snow so I could go back to the tropics and brag to my friends that while they were sweating to and from school, I caught snowflakes on my tongue just like in the Christmas movies that aired once a year in Trinidad. I thought of how they'd stand back in awe and want to hear more, and I'd stand in the middle, under the hot sun, spinning tales, suppressing my pain. Snow never fell, but I spun tales anyway.

My Auntie Reeya's genius idea was to throw a party at her house. My mother ironed a dress for me and laid out white stockings and black shoes with silver buckles. I didn't know where she'd gotten these clothes because I'd never seen them before. Even though I didn't like any of them, I put them on. She pulled my hair into a ponytail and hairsprayed springy tendrils into place.

Though careful with the way my sister and I looked, my mother was not at all mindful of her own appearance. She stepped out of the shower and halfheartedly blow-dried her hair. Her curls tumbled in limp spirals down her back, not buoyant like normal. There was no make-up on her face and no jewelry on her body, save her wedding set on her left hand.

Tumblers and carafes littered the tables and countertops. Rings of condensation from the bottoms of glasses merged to form pools of water. Gyrating bodies congregated in the living room and the den, and outside on the pool deck. Inebriated, friends and family hooted and hollered while kicking back more shots of Caribbean rum. Under different circumstances I would have been dancing up a storm on their makeshift dance floor, making fun of all the adults getting drunk, and playing games with my cousins in the basement. But my father was locked in the basement, tucked away in the farthest room.

I moved from watching drunk people in the living room to watching my cousins and their friends play video games. They didn't ask me to join, and I didn't care. When I found my mother, she was in the kitchen with my aunts. They knocked back shots while my mother nursed a watered-down glass of alcohol.

Lick, slam, suck! they hollered while the golden liquid in the tequila bottle glinted next to them. They tossed bitten wedges of lemon onto the laminated countertop and hissed after each round. They seemed oblivious to their sister moping right next to them. Clumps of people grew smaller and larger around them in the kitchen. They squeezed in and around my aunts and mother, as unconcerned about her as her sisters were.

Some time passed before someone hissed the word *divorce* again, but when I realized it came from my mother this time and I registered the conviction in her voice, I felt something ripping inside me. One of my aunts pointed her chin in my direction to show my mother I'd heard what she said. I turned and pushed people out of the way to get to the bathroom. My Auntie Reeya followed me. She knocked, called my name, coaxed me to unlock the door. I didn't want to. I wanted my mother to come and tell me everything would be okay. I wanted my mother to be the one pounding on the door. I wanted my mother. I wanted my mother to be there smiling with my father when I opened the door. This was not happening, I wanted to tell myself, but it was, and so I pulled myself together and unlocked the door.

My aunt drew me to her and rocked me to the sweet soca music blaring in the background, my face in her bosom, tears soaking her blouse. Her embrace felt awkward; her arms were too thin, and she was too short, forcing me to bend into her so she could comfort me the way she wanted, and all I could think as I let her feel better about herself for doing this was *I want my mother.*

WE RETURNED HOME TO TRINIDAD, but my father slept in the living room, my mother and my sister Colette in the master bedroom in the front, and I slept in my room at the back of the house. In my attempt to not choose a side, I declined my mother's request for me to sleep with her. Colette, my sister, had always slept in their bed, and she continued to sleep with my mom. I envied my sister's role, how everything was so simple for her while I felt tormented. Only six years old at the time, she barely remembered anything from these segments of our lives.

When they fought, it was loud. My sister and I cowered in my room, as far away from them as we could get. During all hours of the night my father pulled us from our beds and stood us before them. *Yuh muddah wantah break up we family. She eh wahn we toh stay togeddah anymoh. She wahn allyuh chilren toh choose who yuh wantah live wid. So choose!* My mother was horrified—eyes and mouth agape. She gathered us up to return us to our rooms.

No, my father yelled, *pick nah. Yuh wantah go wid she oh stay wid me?*

I was troubled because staying with him seemed to mean I'd be home, the only place I'd known my entire life. Where would my mother go? Do I choose my mother or my father? Does that choice mean home or the unfamiliar? My sister let go of my hand and stumbled over to my father, thumb in mouth and doll dangling from her other hand. It was so easy for her as she wrapped her hand around my father's thumb. This proved my mother had been away working too much during my sister's short life. Colette was more attached to our father. My sister called me to follow her, but I couldn't move.

I looked from my mother to my father.

Dharmendra, my mother said, *doh make dem do dis. Ah nevah wanted toh bring dem een de middle ah dis.*

My father had a smug look on his face as though he was thinking, *One dung and only one toh goh.* I saw my mother's pain. I must think rationally, I told myself—if my sister went with my father then I should go to my mother, one child for each parent. Even if that meant leaving everything behind.

I took my mother's hand.

The agony I felt inside was clearly printed on my mother's face, but I had to look closer at my father to see it. He didn't want to do this but couldn't seem to find another way to get my mother's attention. She spoke only to my sister and me, and so he provoked her through us. His actions were learned from men like him who were planted in the sands of our coast and the men who were rooted there in the island from times before. To communicate openly, cross the waters between him and his wife now, and show true emotion went against everything he'd been taught. Better to continue inflicting pain and now extend it to his children.

Yuh gone by yuh muddah? he said. *Dah is yuh choice? Go den. Allyuh goh yuh whey. Me and meh dawtah go stay right hyah.*

My mother took my hand and led me to my room. *Stay here dahlin,* she said. I followed her to the door. She pulled on a pair of sneakers.

Ma, whey yuh goin? I was frightened. It was late. Past eleven. *Ma, do goh, please doh leave we, Ma.* I tugged at the corner of her shirt. I wondered if she realized I uttered the same words to her that she said to her own mother.

Krys dahlin, she said, *ah goh come back. Doh worry meh chile,* and she kissed my head. But I didn't believe her. Couldn't. She was walking out the door with her keys, twisting the lock into place behind her. I barricaded myself in my room and bawled into my pillow.

She left me with my father after I didn't choose him.

After some time, I went to sit by the back door. I turned on the light at the back of the house so she could see when she came home. It was past two now, and I knew how dangerous the streets were at this time.

The crime rate had been climbing, and the news advised people to stay home after six in the evening. We'd even been under curfew a few times. Dole Chadee, one of the most notorious drug lords in the Caribbean, lived in Trinidad. He trafficked cocaine through the islands, buying off whoever stood in his way—judges, policemen, politicians, even chefs if the need arose. And those he couldn't buy, he murdered. To be in the wrong place at the wrong time could mean the death of my mother.

A crisp breeze blew off the river. I rubbed my arms and legs. Sleep and exhaustion from crying tugged and burned my eyelids, but I fought them. Late, after three, I heard footsteps. I tried to see through the bars of the burglar-proofed door. Someone was sitting in the shadows at the bottom of the stairs. *Ma?* I called out, ready to jump backward and scream for my father if it was an intruder. There was a sniffle.

Krys chile, yuh still up? Her voice was heavy. Sadness clung to her every word. She walked up the stairs, and I opened the door to let her inside, tears already springing to my eyes, my body shuddering with relief.

Whey yuh went, Ma?

She told me as much as she thought a ten-year-old should know, and filled in the gaps as I grew older.

Once again, my mother poured herself into me.

My mother had gone to meet the woman's husband. She'd learned he was a pharmacist—*ah rheal nice mahn,* she always said, but he knew nothing of his wife's infidelity. Though late, he agreed to meet her downtown in Chaguanas. We lived in central Trinidad, only one hour from Piparo, where Dole Chadee ruled from his hundred-acre estate. Chaguanas was very much involved in a drug war. My mother told me the pharmacist didn't tell his wife where he was going.

Ma, I said, *e coulda kill yuh, e coulda do anyting, Ma. De mahn couldah be mix up een drugs, wid Chadee evan. How come yuh truss im so easy?* I wondered if my mother wanted to even the playing field between her and my father. I wouldn't blame her if she did, but young, selfish, and terrified for my family, I cast it from my mind. I was not ready yet to think of my mother in that way.

They met to exchange stories. Things fell into place for him much like they did for my mother—the appearance of this policeman, long phone calls, the trip to the States, late nights, frequent absences. My mother felt sorry for him. At least she'd heard from a family member. She, a stranger, changed his world with one phone call. The Khans had four children of their own. While my mother knew she brought pain to this man, she was also the bearer of truth. Doubly satisfying, she wanted more than anything to spin havoc as forceful as a hurricane on this other woman's life.

—*Wah dey does say up hyah, Krys? Bout revenge?* my mother asks. *Dat revenge is ah sweet ting? Ah like de one bout how it does be ah rheal bitch.*

My mother held on to this morsel, delivering it last of the stories she told me.

The husband, Arjun, when told of his wife's infidelity, was devastated. After some time had passed, he called my mother and said, *We should do toh dem wah dey do toh we.*

My mother agreed.

They rented a hotel room in the center of the capital. They flaunted that they were with one another. With the right ears all around them, they knew word would get back to their spouses.

They flirted in the lobby, and Arya flounced her white skirt in the air. As they walked to the elevator, her heels clacked the ground in pleasant clicks. In the elevator, there were other people who knew their spouses. Arya fawned over Arjun, and Arjun doted on her.

As my mother told me this story, there was satisfaction in the curve of her lips and the crooks of her elbows, but I was terrified. My father worked in the Salvatori Building not far from where they were, and what he could have done to her would have left me motherless. There was revenge to have that day, but did she think of the risk she was taking then?

In the hotel room they sat on the bed next to one another, and Arjun put his arm around her; Arya instinctively pulled away, leaving him to reclaim his arm. They looked at their shoes, never at one another. Arjun tried to caress her.

—*Boh when e touch meh, Krys,* my mother says, *it din feel right. Ah couldn't do it.*

Arya said to Arjun, *Ah kyant do dis. Juss because **dey** do it doh mean ah could bring mehself toh do it. It juss doh feel right.*

He was flushed with relief and toppled on the bed. *Meh kyant do it eiddah, gyul. It eh hah nutten hyah.* They waited hours before they left, but when they did, they exclaimed in the corridors, on the elevator, and through the lobby, *Yuh rheal sweet, yuh know. Meh hahd a good time.*

MY PARENTS STAYED TOGETHER, but not out of love or any desire to repair their marriage. Women on the islands strove to attain wedlock, and to reverse that process meant living as a branded woman at best, an outcome in which people shunned you and refused you their services, making the simple act of purchasing food a tribulation. Work became hard to find because you were no longer under the protection of a man, no longer respectable. Too many times, if a woman wanted to leave her husband, he beat her until she changed her mind or killed her for embarrassing him with this stigma.

My father was a high-ranking police officer, and that offered him special privileges. He could cover up actions other men couldn't, and my mother, if she wanted to, couldn't report him for anything. How much did this frighten her? Did it make her flee?

—*Krys*, my mother explains years later when I am old enough to understand, *me eh hah no money, no job, no security. Wah ah oman like me go do on ah island like Trinidad? Ah leave im an crapaud smoke meh pipe, nobody goh even look meh way toh help meh. Ah wouldn't geh a cent, and yuh faddah wid e job wuddah geh toh keep bot ah allyuh. Ah stay foh meh chilren. Boh ah was desperate. Rheal desperate and ah come up wid a plan. Ah wait foh de chance toh goh America. Ah hol on toh dat tight tight tight and when it come ah take it.*

Like my grandmother, who also waited for the opportunity to escape, my mother gathered herself up and was lifted above the islands she'd called home her entire life. She flew to a country quite unlike the place she came from. The land of opportunity, people told her, but she hoped it to be the land where people forgot.

LETTERS

MY MOTHER LEFT TRINIDAD IN 1999. Not a woman to be taken advantage of, my mother knew the only way to reclaim her *self* was to sever ties with the Caribbean and its men.

My mother didn't uproot us solely for selfish reasons; Trinidad was unstable. Dole Chadee, the notorious drug lord, was finally convicted of murder, but that put our country in a tumultuous state. Police corruption was flayed open, and everyone was unsure of who to trust. My father felt the pressure at work, seeing the outcome of dealings with the Chadee gang daily—brutal deaths and the kidnapping and raping of young boys and girls. These families, scared for their lives, couldn't talk to the authorities. If my father was approached for a bribe and refused, my mother wanted us removed from the consequences.

When the untouchable Dole Chadee was arrested for ordering the wipeout of the entire Baboolal family, the death penalty returned to Trinidad and Tobago. He, with eight members of his gang, were hanged in June 1999 over the course of three days. It aired on the news every minute and hit the front page of every newspaper. Try as they might, my parents couldn't hide the violence from me. Because people owed money to Chadee and that money was owed to the Colombians, "kidnap for ransom" became the slogan now, and children were being taken daily. Our plans had been in place for some time, but while doors were being broken in and houses set ablaze, my mother wrapped us up and brought us to the United States.

Because of my father's job commitment, and also because of his pension, he couldn't leave with us. That did nothing to deter my mother, who held our hands firmly at the airport and walked toward the plane, never glancing back at our crying father.

It took me years to acclimate to New Jersey weather. The winters were too harsh and the beaches opaque, riddled with mussel shells that cut our feet. My sister, at the tender age of eight, absorbed everything around her and slipped seamlessly into American culture, losing her accent. At twelve, I never got used to the weather and fantasized about moving back, holding steadfast to my native tongue. With my father still in Trinidad, I hoped we would one day return.

In America, my mother reinvented herself, using the aliases Annie or Annalisa for her babysitting jobs. She embraced her fierceness, stepped out of her husband's shadow, began working full-time again after twelve years, and planted a life for herself and her two girls in stubborn soil. I wondered also if this was punishment for him, one of the only ways she could castigate him for cheating on her. We left our home, our family, and our sense of security—of knowing our place in the world.

In the wake of my father's deception, I thought of my Uncle Avinash. I wondered if my mother ever reevaluated her feelings about my grandfather's unfaithfulness, now knowing firsthand the emotions that came with being deceived. Did she forgive Rebecca for her harshness toward Avinash now that she knew the bite of betrayal?

—Is diffrant, Krys, says my mother, when yuh make meh tink

bout it like dat. Ah know it was moh complicated foh Mammy, boh she was meh muddah and so ah di hol she toh ah diffrant standahd.

We called my father often by way of phone cards, and I begged him to come and get me. *Ah wish ah could, meh chile,* he said. Eventually, the visas we acquired to legally enter the US expired, and we became undocumented. If we went back now we'd never be allowed to enter the States again.

My aunts and uncles also lived here illegally, but years ago when my grandmother became a resident, they filed their paperwork with the United States Citizenship and Immigration Services. With this in motion, their status was pending, and they were protected under an amnesty granted by Bill Clinton for undocumented immigrants residing in America who were waiting for a status shift. We had nothing, no papers to speak of, no safety net. My grandmother was willing to sponsor us, but my mother held off on filing our legal immigration paperwork; I could see uncertainty settle around us on whether or not America was a permanent move. In that crucial period, we lost precious time and wouldn't gain legal status in the US for ten years.

WHEN WE ARRIVED at my grandparents' American doorstep, we traded places with my grandfather, who'd been living with Rebecca for the past year. Shiva's home, along with his farms, had been rented out. With nowhere else to go, he decided to vacation with my father, leaving room for us in the apartment.

—*Dey couldn't stay togeddah long eh,* my mother says. *E come long aftah she done settle een hyah, so de place was she own now. When e feel de itch toh goh back is by we house e gone een. Yuh faddah din seem toh mind.*

Angry, and uncertain of how to direct it, my father yelled at my mother for leaving him behind with Shiva yet again. As over-bearing as my grandfather had been with our family, my father didn't seem to mind when he would stay at our home. What troubled him was his family not being there with him. Shiva and Dharmendra had a deep respect for one another, and my grandfa-ther treated him like a son. What my father didn't realize was that his temper reinforced my mother's will, and so instead of return-ing home, we lingered.

We were lonely. The transplant was jolting and strenuous. We missed our father, our home, our friends, the comfort of our relaxed tongue. My mother was not yet bringing in enough money for us to survive outside my grandmother's apartment. The entire family gathered at my grandmother's at the end of the day, and aunts, uncles, and cousins treated everything as though it was theirs. We had nothing. Not even the room my mother paid for had any semblance of privacy. When they left, we had to clean.

I picked dishes up off the floor, side tables, kitchen counter, and chairs. People were wasteful here, leaving behind chunks of stewed meat or fish, and clumps of pigeon peas. They'd for-gotten how to clean the meat off the bones and suck the marrow from within, and they didn't teach their children to do the same. They left no bite marks on the bones the way my sister and I did, chewing until we splintered them. Tender gristle lay forlornly for the taking. Often, my cousins took mounds of food only to leave it behind and run away to play. It all ended up in the garbage. Because my mother felt as though she'd invaded everyone's ter-ritory, she made an obligatory dinner every day from the dwin-dling funds we had. Her family offered us no help; neither did they care where or how dinner got placed in front of them.

Babysitting jobs were plentiful in the suburbs, but the require-ment for a live-out nanny was a car, and we didn't have that yet.

We scoured the newspapers together, and whenever she had an interview, she depended on one or another sister's generosity to get there. But that required favors, and so on the weekends, while her sisters went out gallivanting and drinking, they left their children for my mother and me to babysit. For free.

Ten years later, we gained residency in America. On traveling back to Trinidad, I sifted through dust, diaries, old schoolbooks, and paperwork in our library. Beneath it all, tied together with rubber bands, I found letters my sister and I wrote to my dad, telling him how much we missed him and how well we were doing in school. I also unearthed postcards and letters from my mom.

In the postcards, from the early days, she says, *Hi Dharmendra, I miss you very much and am thinking about you. I do hope you are taking care of yourself. Please see the doctor if you are not feeling well. The kids miss you a lot. I love you, Arya.*

Eventually my mother found work. Her boss, Caitlin, was a kind Polish woman with an eight-month-old girl and a five-year-old boy. She sometimes asked my mother to work on the weekends, even told her she should bring us. Caitlin rented movies for my sister and me, and left money so we could order dinner. I discovered Caitlin's library and devoured her books while I was there. Once she realized I read the same novels she did, she loaned them to me when she was done. Being in her open, split-level house and roaming her gardens fragrant with blushing roses was the closest thing to Trinidad I could find, and it afforded me a break from the chaos at my grandmother's.

While at work, my mother wrote letters to my father on paper with Caitlin's letterhead embossed at the top. After one of my father's short visits to us in 2000 she wrote this: *So what's new with you? How are you coping with my dad? Please stop the smoking and do some exercise for your stomach. Avoid drinking soda. I would like you to live a healthy long life. We all hope you will come back in April. It is very cold now but haven't seen any snow as yet. Everything is fine here. If you need anything please call me and I am thinking about you all the time in my heart. I will always love you forever my love. Please reply.*

But everything was not fine. My sister and I were not enough to keep our mother grounded, and she felt as unstable as the country she left behind. Her siblings were strangers to us, to her, and the room we stayed in became our island where we shut the door and tried to forget. Colette and I had school, made friends, inhabited a world outside of ourselves, and as much as I didn't want to, hoping for a long time we'd return to Trinidad, we began to put down roots in American soil. I found a best friend, and a boy was interested in me, the *it* boy of school, the one all the girls were swooning over. But my mother was alone and lonely, and with the prospect of us staying that way indefinitely in the US, she turned to the man she had fled. Tears dredged up emotions she'd squelched, and she printed words on paper that, if reciprocated, could pull us from the place we now called home.

Several nights I awoke to use the bathroom and it was locked. I waited, and a woman emerged, a towel not large enough to conceal the rolls drooping down her back and on the insides of her legs. She giggled when she saw me and edged into the narrow corridor, her bleached dreadlocks slapping the wet skin on her neck and back. Her cellulite-ridden buttocks flapped up with the towel, and I just stood in the short corridor as she opened my uncle's bedroom door at the back of the apartment and was enveloped by the darkness.

Many different women paraded in and out of my uncle's bedroom, and I learned to recognize the sharp smell of alcohol prevalent on their breaths. They snuck in late at night with him after work and left with the dewdrops when light touched dark. My mother didn't want us around his night women.

—*E was disgustin, Krys,* my mother says. *Ah couldn't wait toh move out and geh ah place ah meh own whey ah could put dung some rules but we din hah enough money yet. Yuh tink meh wahn meh chilren seein dat kinda nasty behavior? And from meh own bruddah.*

Because of my uncle's behavior but also because of my own, my mother wrote to my father saying: *We started going to church every Sunday because I have to get them involved in something before it's too late. How is my father doing? I still did not receive any letters from you. Still waiting. I bought Rahul's car for $800, it is working good, just good for me to go to work and take the kids around. Love, Arya.*

After school each day, twelve years old now, I walked through the back compound and across the street to what appeared to be a secluded block, my boyfriend's hand in mine. He teetered on the edge of the curb as we kissed, our hands straying beneath our jackets. We became frantic, swallowing each other's faces, often drawing heckles from the passersby.

En route home one day, my uncle recognized me tucked into this block right by the firehouse. He related this information to my mother, landmark and all. I tried to deny it but in the end told her the truth. I was a disappointment now, and I heard the whole immigrant-mother spiel about sacrifice and studying, while all I wanted to do was kiss a boy and have him feel me up.

Without my father as her reinforcement, and this added territory of boys, she turned to church. We started going to the Presbyterian church my grandmother attended every Sunday, because my mother didn't know what else to do with me. It was a semblance of what she grew up with while going to school, a place where she smiled when reciting the prayers along with everyone else, a peaceful calm settling on her face.

She was able to drive us there and back in the car she had bought off her brother, but the windows and air didn't work, so we were stifled wherever we went. I treated the church as I did anything else I was bored with—I showed up, talked to no one, and read a book until we had to leave.

After about a year of being gone, my grandfather returned to the US, and instead of coming back to the apartment to live, he moved in with my Auntie Pooja, about a five-minute car ride away. It was an elegant building with a doorman and vast, spotless floors. My Auntie Pooja needed my grandfather there because it was a senior citizens home. She'd swindled her way into the building with a sob story about my grandfather until he could come back and be there physically. Soon after, he realized his daughter was trying to take credit cards out in his name for her own personal use, so he ended the lease agreement and went back to Trinidad, leaving her to find another place.

I found out the house we rented was being put up for sale by the owner's children as I eavesdropped on my grandmother's conversation one day. Lisa, the wispy-haired old woman who owned the house, lived on the second floor above us and often sat on the front porch smoking cigarette after cigarette with my grandmother.

Sorry, Rebecca, she said to my grandmother. *I didn't want this, but I can't take care of myself, and my children won't take care of me.*

It's not that way in my culture, Lisa, my grandmother replied. *The children are supposed to take care of their parents.*

Companions, they both sat rocking, shaking their heads. My grandmother wouldn't have to put her words to the test for years to come. She would never have guessed the children she bore, birthed, and raised in the face of violence would pledge their allegiance to their father, the man who tormented them all.

———

WITH HIS FARM STILL UNDER LEASE, my grandfather stayed with my father in Trinidad. And so my mother found herself writing: *Recently you are so mad with me and I really don't know what to do. Honey, words can't express how I and the girls miss you. I told my father we are renting out the house, in this way he can remove his stuff. Tell him your niece got a doctor from India to rent. Anything else is your business. Please don't let him push you around. I love you, Arya.*

Shiva had started stockpiling things at our house, and as respectful as my father was, his things had to go. The only way my mother could think to handle this was by telling my grandfather we were renting out our house.

Over the summer, my mother and my Uncle Amrit found a run-down apartment to rent close to the water in downtown Jersey City. It was a much quieter area, a place where you could occasionally hear the birds in the trees.

—*Ah din wahn allyuh chilren rung im wid e behavior,* my mother tells me, *boh ah had no choice. Ah couldn't pay de bills on meh own, so we geh ah two bedroom—one foh e and one foh we. Ah tawk to im bout de night oman an dem and e geh rheal vex, boh e had toh know.*

When my grandfather came back, he stayed with my Aunt Chandini and her husband. They tried to swindle money out of him, and when that didn't work, Chandini told her husband to kick my grandfather out of their house. My grandfather stood at the curb in the cool night air, waiting for someone to come and pick him up.

—*It was one o'clock eeh de morning, eh Krys,* says my mother. *Dat bitch was so nasty. All because e din wantah gih she e own money.*

My grandmother was in the process of finding an apartment in a senior citizens complex. I didn't know if she was given a choice, but my grandparents ended up living together again.

MY FATHER NEVER WROTE MY MOTHER BACK.

—*E nevah did,* my mother tells me. *Wah dat tell yuh?*

The only letter I ever found from him was a cream and gold Hallmark "I Love You" card. It was filled with the clichéd gush of romantic feelings. In it my father wrote, *To Arya my loving wife, for all the pain and suffering you went through for the past few weeks. From, Dharmendra. Love you.*

It was not dated.

My mother never received it.

IN PERSON AND ON THE PHONE, my parents fought about my grandfather needing to learn his place, that my father was not his personal driver. But my mother couldn't stand up to her father, had never been able to, and so she allowed her father to gnaw away at what was left of their marriage. In turn, to punish her, my father refused to pick up the phone when she rang and never, not once, answered the letters she wrote to him.

We all knew my mother never asked for her father's help the way his other children had. My father provided for her from the moment he took her as his wife. They were indebted to Shiva in no way, something my grandfather didn't seem to comprehend, as everyone he'd ever known had owed him something at one point or another. His days of dominance had officially come to an end, but people still remembered him in all his supreme glory, especially his family, and I was sure it was hard for him to let go.

CRUSHED

WE PULLED INTO THE DRIVEWAY of Chandini and Matthew's house around eight one summer night. Chandini migrated to America when she was eighteen, six years older than I was when I came. Because her husband was a successful garbageman, they could afford a house in suburban New Jersey. It had a back and front yard, even an aboveground pool. As usual, her husband yapped about landscaping this and that as though I understood what he was talking about. He didn't walk me through his yard this time because it was too dark, but with their new installation of lights, I thought he might. We had to do things a certain way at her house—tread carefully, not eat in the living room, not touch anything. Once I grew up and saw other houses, I realized her place was small, cramped, not even in what was considered a good suburb. But compared with my grandmother's dank apartment, it was grand and spacious.

After living in Trinidad without us for four years, my father forfeited his retirement money and finally moved to America to be with us; he'd now been living with us for some time. Chandini invited us over for dinner, yet when we arrived it was to a kitchen full of stuffed grocery bags she'd gotten for free from the local store she worked in as a clerk.

I'd never lost my accent, and when I spoke, Chandini said

in her forced American way, *Oh Arya, look how cute she sounds.* My mother tittered. In her family, it had always been a race to see who could lose their accent the fastest, who could sound more "white."

My mother started clearing the countertops.

Oh no Arya, keep those out, they're for the salad and that's for the chicken. My mother held up a bag and said, *Dis ting?* before catching herself and switching to her American accent. *You didn't start dinner yet?*

My mother raised her eyebrows. Chandini either ignored or didn't notice my mother's incredulous look, and continued on about the kitchen. *Arya gyul,* Chandini said, *you cook so well, how do you make your fried rice? Show me nah.* And with that, Chandini plopped her generous backside on the couch and filed her claws while my mother took over the kitchen. When she was out of earshot, my mother muttered, *Yuh mean toh tell meh she invite we ovah foh dinner and is make ah hah toh make it foh meself? Bettah we di stay hwome.*

Exasperated with my aunt's routine of *show me how to make this,* or *teach me how to make that,* I set out to help my mother to get this night over with as quickly as possible. While Chandini kept up a constant stream of gossip about everyone in our family, my mother slaved in her kitchen. I couldn't help but appreciate how beautiful my mother was, the ferocity of her movements, calculated yet graceful, sweat enhancing the umber color of her face.

My parents had been fighting this week, so I was surprised that my father had come along. Matthew and my father, despite what happened years ago, were now on friendly terms, and they retreated to the basement, where Matthew had set up a bar.

In the kitchen, I chopped and diced, julienned and sliced, sautéed and fried, mashed and mixed until I was a sweaty mess.

Having arrived fresh from a shower, I gave Chandini the evilest eye I could muster as she sat yapping away at the table, first filing then polishing her long fake nails. My mother slammed pots and pans around the kitchen, but her frustration was lost on my aunt, who fanned herself with flaming tips of hot pink.

Chandini, my mother says, *oh Gawd gyul, how yuh does even wipe yuh ass wid dem claws? Yuh doh cut yuhself?* I felt satisfied hearing my mother laugh this insult into a joke. Chandini joined her in laughing. *Oh my goodness Arya, where do you get this stuff from, girl?*

When I was done, I joined my sister in the living room, where she was watching television. My aunt called after me, *Please don't forget to wash your hands before sitting on the couch.* Colette rolled her eyes with me. *Meh do it ahready mahn,* I called back, and said only to Colette, *Right een front yuh big ass.* Colette picked her nose and rubbed it on the cushion. *How's that for washing hands?* she said to me, and we laughed. At twelve, my sister already had a mean streak; even I steered clear.

There was a computer downstairs, and we wanted to play games on it. As a teenager, I could work my way around any electronics. But my aunt, from her hawk's perch, followed our every movement.

Auntie Chandini, I said ever so sweetly, *do you mind if Colette and I play a game on your computer downstairs?* Her spiel began: how to set it up, how to use it—and behind her back, we rolled our eyes.

My father and Matthew sat on the other side of the base-ment, and we heard them shuffle the chairs around the bar when they left to go outside for a smoke. No one called us upstairs for dinner, so we didn't budge. Angry voices erupted. Our parents were fighting. It was a familiar sound by now. I was not surprised

Chandini and Matthew had caused them to start again. The back door slammed.

Did Mom leave? Colette asked.

I listened at the top of the stairs, but all I heard was the whirring of the vent above the stove in the kitchen. Then I heard their heated voices outside and joined them in the backyard. My parents were standing a few feet apart from one another. Muscles and cords rippled on their necks and arms. I was trying to hear why they were fighting, but Chandini stepped in front of me.

Come sweetie, Chandini said, *let's take you inside. You don't need to hear this.* I looked around her. She tried to put her fleshy arms around my shoulders, and I sidestepped her. My parents were fighting right next to the pool; the water was still and black.

My mother flung herself to the ground and snatched two of the decorative stones that formed a path around the pool. She placed her engagement ring on one. The gold and diamonds caught the faint porch light and gleamed for a second before vanishing. Holding the other stone high above her head, she brought it down with all her might and smashed the ring between them. Her ring jumped and skittered across the path. She scrambled after it and brought it back to the stone. It seemed untouched.

My father started to clench and unclench his fists. My mother looked at him. He said, *Arya, yuh is ah ass oh someting? Dotish awah? Stop dis nonsense right now.*

Calling her an imbecile gave her the strength to dent the part with diamonds and flatten the band. It was a grotesque sight. I was afraid she would regret this later, but then I saw the fierceness in the glittering coals of her eyes. I knew she would never regret this. Never had I seen such power in a woman, and I didn't want to stop it.

The wedding band was not spared either. My mother pounded

and ground while we all stood aside and watched. Sweat cascaded down her face. She stopped. Her rings were reduced to lumps of shimmering dust that glowed white in the night. My father turned and strode through the back gate, leaving the wooden door flapping wildly, like laundry forgotten in a hurricane.

Back in the kitchen, my mother and her sister sat at the glass kitchen table sipping drinks. Their words fell like rain around me.

E eh know whey e goin, my mother said. *Meh worried.*

I imagined my father walking briskly up and down a grid of streets, fists stuffed into his pocket, his face untamed fury. Then my mother muttered, *E goh kill eself.*

The father I knew had only cried twice in front of me—at his mother's funeral and when we left him behind. But the words *kill eself* washed over me again, and I was reminded of my father's suicide attempt during their courtship.

As the wait around the kitchen table continued, I hoped my father would return soon. All the talk of suicide around the kitchen table was starting to scare me, and I imagined him floating facedown in the still, black water of my aunt's pool. When the adults weren't paying attention, I slipped outside via the cellar doors in the basement and checked the pool for my father's body, just in case. Relieved that I didn't find him there, I unlatched the gate and looked up and down the quiet street, but there was no movement, not past twelve at night.

My father finally returned but refused to enter the house when my uncle unlocked the door for him. My mother told Chandini and Matthew she'd take it from here, but they wouldn't excuse themselves; they sat at the table with their hands clasped around their glasses, intrusive as always, as though they had staked a claim on my parents' marriage when Chandini told my mother Dharmendra was cheating on her.

Chandini said to me, *Krystal, why don't you go and lie down with your sister?* The litany of curses that sandstormed in my head was one that continued against her for years.

No, I said to her and walked out the door to my father. When he was angry like that, the only person he talked to was me, and I enjoyed this special privilege. Much like Shiva, my father was very much a product of our twin isles, and though they were different men, they sometimes seemed like the same person, and both saw something in me. I seemed to carry the essence of an old world, one they wanted me to take and carry for them.

Lewwe goh, he said. I gathered my sister and her things and pulled her out the back door. On our way to the car, I had only to tug at my mother's hand for her to follow us. Our parents taught us to thank our hosts and hostesses for their hospitality, for the food and drinks, and for an all-around good time, but since none of those things transpired that night, Colette and I didn't even glance back.

Though my parents ended up staying together, their fingers remained devoid of rings.

—*E di take care ah me when ah had nutten, no questions ax,* my mother says, *and now een dis country whey we hah to fend for we-self, it was my tun.*

WEIGHTED

2007–2010

MEMORIES

I THINK OF MY GRANDPARENTS as one coiling length of rope—she the rope unfurling for infinity, and he all the kinks and knots.

After my grandfather is deposited into the reluctant hands of my grandmother at the end of summer in 2007, about eight months after his brain surgeries, my mother and I visit often. I watch as she brushes his teeth, cuts his hair, clips and files his fingernails and toenails, and even gives him sponge baths but stops short of his crotch, saying to my grandmother, *Ma yuh goh do dey, boh do rough im up eh.*

Having been on the side of the siblings who insisted on his surgery, my mother can't stop blaming herself for how he ended up and so continues to devote all of her time to him. She and her father mirror one another, both ending up as echoes of their former, vibrant selves.

On the day I stumbled upon him in the bed, covers off, hands clawing at his uncovered crotch, his birthmark swimming before my tearful eyes, I ran away. The wild and crazy look I saw had never been there before, and so each time I saw him powerless, it destroyed a part of me. The man I knew as Shiva Singh was tall, silent, and powerful. He commanded every room he walked into, and the people in it. I admired that. I admired him. Admired how he could instill fear in others. Could that man ever return? After all the stories, did I really want him to?

The violent stories surface only after my grandfather is incapacitated. It is almost as though these two women need him to be debilitated before they can part their lips and tell. But with my grandmother taking care of Shiva, I need to tread delicately when asking questions, bearing witness to her as she conjures memories long quelled. These stories are of a past these women strove to forget, to raze. Now they surface in a new home, far removed from who they once were.

As these long-suppressed memories simmer to the surface, I overhear my grandmother saying to my mother one day, *It een de drawer, Arya. De knife juss cahlin meh. Ah could juss do it.*

She wants to kill him after everything I've made her remember.

—*We take she back toh ah bhad place, Krys,* my mother says to me, *and we hah toh be rheal careful.*

We must all be careful.

We take it slowly.

FUNERAL

MY MOTHER, POOJA, AND GITA help my grandmother make a will for my grandfather. In it, Rebecca retains power of attorney and Arya continues to be his legal executor. They wait until Shiva has enough strength to sit up by himself, though he still can't hold a pen and sign his own name. We think a thumbprint may suffice, but don't know for certain if it will.

—*E was suppose toh be een e right frame ah min,* my mother says, *boh ah dunno how dis lawyer see im fit so. By some act ah Gawd de lawyer ax im ah string ah questions an Pappy move e head up and dung yes for each and every one, Krys. Meh wouldn't tah believe it if ah wasn't dey mehself.*

The new will shares everything equally among his children and Rebecca. With this document, my grandmother has security and all other wills are rendered useless against it. My mother helps her sell a piece of his land in Trinidad for close to one million Trinidadian dollars; my grandmother splits the money evenly among her children. Among many other stipulations, Rebecca includes savings for her and Shiva's burials and medical bills.

Burden is the word my grandmother uses when she is done writing the will. *Meh eh wantah be ah burden on anybody wid dese tings.*

———

I WAS WITH MY GRANDFATHER when I saw death for the first time. He was standing in a pressed white shirt and khaki pants starched till the folds formed tents along the front of his legs. Behind him the familiar pomegranate tree bloomed on a little mound with ruby orbs ready to be snapped from their branches. My grandfather's long hair was slicked back; the black strands shone beneath the midday sun. When he entered the car the sweet smell of coconut oil came with him. He displaced my mother from the front seat, and she was shoved in the back to sit with my sister and me while my father continued to drive, already Shiva's chauffeur.

We were taking him to the airport for his trip to America, one of many as he planned his transition from the Caribbean to the States. We snaked our way off the property by way of the only road that led in, gravel grinding beneath the rolling tires. In the midst of a heated battle of hair-tugging with my sister, there was the rumpled sound of a crash. Through the windshield, we saw, not far in front of us on the main road, a body floating into the air, above the trees, and hovering momentarily before drifting back down, past our line of vision. It seemed serene within the humming of the car, windows up, crunching gravel, the stillness of our breaths, the only movement my mother's clamping her fingers over my sister's eyes.

We drove past. A man lay facedown on the roadside. There was a fissure where his face had once been, blood pouring onto the asphalt, the contrast of red and black striking under the sun. His body was deflated, the inside of skin touching skin, no organs left to fill the space. His insides gushed from a gaping hole in his hip.

Drive nah, Dharmendra, drive! my mother hissed, worried that my sister and I had seen.

My grandfather was unperturbed by it all, looked amused, a smirk playing at the corners of his mouth. He expressed no concern, displayed no other reaction, and made no move to cover his mouth.

My grandfather. The uncontested patriarch of our family. Did I see the true glimpses of who he was and, like everyone else, choose to pretend it didn't happen? I wrestle with two images of this man, wanting to know more, needing to discover as much as I can to make sense of him, of us all, for allowing him to dominate our lives.

For four years after his surgeries, our family struggles with Shiva's life. Finally, pumped full of morphine, my grandfather passes. I don't cry. His death is expected; we know what the procedure is like in hospice; we are warned more than once. I come to think my family held on four years too long. I stop visiting. He recognizes no one, though they say otherwise. *Meh see ah spak in Pappy eye when e see meh. Pappy, yuh know is me? Shake yuh head yes, Pappy.* They choose to ignore his constant bellowing of *No-No-No-No-NO-NO-NO!* unable to bring themselves to listen to the doctors when they say he can't come back from this, that the damage is irreversible.

The first time I cajole him into looking at me, I am sure his answer will be different. I am sure he will stop flinging his head left and right, his eyeballs sliding in all directions. I am certain he will arch his gray-and-black-speckled brows in concentration like he used to, turn to me, and though he can't talk, he will nod. I have that surge of power running through me whenever I am around him, an electric spark I feel that happens only in connection to him.

We are in my grandparents' apartment. Aunts, uncles, and cousins are littered throughout, but they all look at me when I go up to him, place a hand on either arm of his chair, bring my face close to his whipping head, and say loudly, *Grampa? Grampa. Yuh recognize* **meh**? His response to me has to be different from the response he gives the others. Instead he swings his head to and fro and belts out his seven *NO*s. I hear someone snicker and know it has to be one of my cousins. It stings. I don't ask again, can't bear to. My grandfather is no longer mine, hasn't been for a long time, and now everyone knows it.

I am waiting for his death. Only twenty-two years old, I already know I don't want to be present when it happens, probably can't be with school and work and a new married life myself.

My mother can't control herself when she calls to tell me he is gone, can barely get the words out of her mouth. *Ah know*, I interrupt, saving her from having to utter them. *Shhhh, meh sure e gone een peace.* Doubt starts its seep, and I am not sure I believe this. She is with him until his final breath shudders his body in ripples, until the pronouncement of his death, until the machines are turned off, until they cover his black body in a white sheet from head to toe.

They—my mother, grandmother, and aunts—sit outside the room on the hard plastic chairs, unable to pull themselves away from this place. Rebecca fills out paperwork, signs in multiple places, and when she is done, she is ready to go.

My mother notices the sudden lightness in the way Rebecca moves her body and the happiness that touches the corners of her eyes and edges of her mouth. It angers her that her mother has discovered joy at her father's death, and she pushes from her mind all she's witnessed, the burden her father has been these last four long years, the tyrant he's always been. Arya lashes out at her mother, her tongue like a blade just sharpened on a stone. *Ma, wah appen toh yuh? Yuh eh hah no shame? Yuh could geh up so and twiss and tun like e eh just dead? Dah is true hahtlessness.* Rebecca has just breathed the crisp air of freedom, an openness she comes to only at the end of her life, at seventy-three years old, and as Shiva's daughter, with her father's death fresh in her mind, my mother can't bring herself to understand this.

Rebecca stands once again frozen before her children. She watches them bind together as they'd done throughout his sickness, and their impregnable accusations make a wall around her. Defeated, she closes in on herself once again and waits until they are no longer present so she she can embrace a life without Shiva Singh.

I ATTEND THE WAKE WITH MY FAMILY. At the door of the funeral home, my father somberly greets one of my uncles. In a hushed voice, my uncle tells my father there is a bar up the street, and my father says he doesn't need to be told twice. This, they agree, is what men do in times like these.

We'd been to this funeral home already, knew the family who ran the place—both times for the deaths of my cousins, one a stillborn baby and the other a twenty-year-old. The lighting is dim and yellow, its softness fit for grieving. Everyone is meticulously dressed, hair coiffed, nails lacquered, make-up pristine. Our heels puncture the plush carpet as we walk around greeting one another. There are two rooms, one with the body that hasn't been opened yet and one without. The chairs are gold with cream pouf tops; I sink slowly into one. People weave their way in and around us, stopping to offer their condolences, first to my mother and then to me.

The walk to any dead body is always long, endless almost, and once I am upon it, I can't escape fast enough. But with so many eyes on me, I can't scramble away for fear of what the tongues will cluck. I stare down at the body of the third of my grandparents to die, and it hits me that only my grandmother is left. I will cherish this woman, I say to myself.

The powder on my grandfather's face is too light, his hair is combed to the wrong side, and he is beginning to thaw, beads of water forming on his face. His hands rest on his chest, his fingers overlapping; they should be in fists at his side. I can stay no longer because I don't even want to be there to begin with, but also because my mourning time with his body has expired; I feel people pressing behind me, waiting their turn, agitated at others who take too long, this grotesque queue now winding down the aisle.

Wakes in Trinidad are done differently, collectively. We do not gather in halls with soft lighting where people, primped and proper, stroll around politely tipping their heads. We flock to the home of the deceased to help their families. We do not visit nail salons before a wake or take the time to apply meticulous make-up so that someone will stop to say how pretty we look. We show up, whole families after work or school if it is a weekday, or first thing on a weekend morning. We place our brown bags next to those the neighbors and other family members have already started to unpack. We see the tears in mourners' eyes, the pain in their forced smiles, their cumbersome footsteps, and we do not pretend phrases like *Please accept our condolences* or *I'm so sorry* or *Let me know if there's anything I can do* will suffice. We lead the bereaved to their bedroom and say, *Ress. Take ah sleep dey nah. Bade or juss relax, doh worry we goh take care ah everyting before people staht toh show.* And we do. People band together and work seamlessly in the house—a kitchen team preparing food for later that night, a cleaning crew straightening and dusting every corner and crevice, and the organizers who call the family pundit to make sure he is coming and arrange flowers, thaalis, havaan cone, conch shell, and offerings for the prayers. By the time they emerge from their rooms, somewhat rested and clean, their house sparkles, food is prepared, and meals for the week sit prepped in the fridge. No thank-yous are necessary, for we know when the time comes, they will do the same for us.

In Trinidad the body is brought to the house the night before the funeral. Because we are all Hindus in my family, it is customary for the casket to be wrapped in white and for the body to be draped in traditional whites—saris for the women and kurtas for the men. In the living room, people hold hands and support one another, approaching the dead. The next day the body is transferred to a makeshift stretcher constructed of bamboo, the whites of everyone's clothing, the color of our mourning, dazzling beneath the sun. We go to Waterloo at the southern tip of Trinidad, to the temple at the sea. The men of the family lift and carry the stretcher to the pyre of wood prepared on one of the concrete cremation sites. We follow, gripping one another. We watch as the eldest male lights a cube of camphor on a silver spoon and places it into the mouth of the dead. Sometimes the eldest, broken in grief, can't do it and a younger brother or a friend steps in. Fire licks the lips and curls around the mouth. The men, their muscles straining from the weight, slide the body into the center of the pyre. Bamboo hides the body from sight. With torches, the men touch the four corners of the pyre, and fire leaps from one place to another. We wait and watch. We visit the temple and touch the feet of gods, extending offerings as we pray for the lives of our family members and our own. Only when we hear the explosion of the skull do we leave, making sure all are taken care of and have a ride home.

Early next morning the family returns to the site of the cremation, and whether or not they do this alone is something they decide. They gather the ashes and set them free into the ocean. Prayers mingled with sobs escape their lips, and while they are tempted to let the sea swallow them as it has the remains of their loved one, they will turn around and trudge on. They are not the only people to lose someone, and we all know the pain, like everything else, will fade.

My grandfather can't be cremated by the water's edge, can't be taken to his home for a viewing of the body, doesn't have his prayers and ceremonies. We've all now scattered in America, and his traditions and customs are lost, forgotten. Instead he is incinerated, and no one is allowed to watch as he is shoved into the cold steel fortress of the crematorium.

One of his last surviving sisters makes the trip from Trinidad to attend his funeral. Traditions and customs are held intact within her—she knows the Puranic songs and chants from their shared childhood, the length of the mourning period, the funeral rites in the correct sequence for the days and even months after he is cremated. Though she and my grandmother are polite to one another, between them is a deep rift that can never be mended.

At the wake, someone invites us to the front of the room to sing bhajans and utter prayers. My mother urges me forward, physically pushes me, knowing I am the only other one besides my father who knows the words by heart. I stumble into the aisle, and a few people turn back to look at me, their gazes inquisitive. *No,* I say firmly. *And doh push meh again. Ah will sing from right hyah, Ma.*

My mother is taken aback at my resistance and sways by my side to the familiar songs. My grandfather's sister is the only one singing; her voice follows the swell and fall of ancient words. She falters, and the swaying crowd stops. I pick up where she's left off, and my cousins glance at me through slits of eyes. They think I'm showing off, but I am only trying to give my grandfather a semblance of the end he should have, what we all know he would have wanted.

In Trinidad, we do not live shut up in our houses. We see the outside of our homes more than we see the inside. It often rains without thunder and lightning, and on those days we laugh and talk in the rain. The island is small, tiny even, and we are bound to see each other often. While in America, we escape to our city or town or house for years before we see one another again. On the islands, death affects us differently, drawing people from their homes to pay their respects to the dead. It is a place where grief falls in wails and thickens the flat blades of grass and earth around the deceased's house, the same earth we will eventually trample when visiting again.

But in the funeral home in Jersey City, we stand in rented space and time. And so when my cousins and I cross paths, everything is tainted; we exchange sneers or simply ignore each other as we pass by. I look at them as they flounce away as a pack, and I don't understand what has happened to us, that as adults we have come to face death and loss with anger and pride. Maybe in Trinidad there would have been more room for forgiveness; maybe we would share stories about our grandfather, and I could apologize for welcoming his favoritism, explain to them that I didn't understand how he could be so hurtful. We would hold one another tightly, chest to chest, exchanging tears in our embrace. But there is too much isolation in America, too many miles and people between us. We yearn to be apart instead of together, preferring the darkness of our homes to the wails that unite us.

These nights of the wake are torturous; it goes on for days, and I can't bring myself to go to all of it. Instead I bury myself in my work, immersing myself in the poetry of Frost and Tennyson and letting the language of Hardy consume me.

EULOGY

I HAVE NO REGRETS about not attending my grandfather's funeral. I lie to my family and tell them I have a midterm I can't miss. *Yuh teachah goh undahstand,* my mother says. And she is right, of course, but we are reading Thomas Hardy, and that is more appealing than roiling in my seat at his funeral while speeches are made about how perfect my grandfather was. Hardy makes love to language in his descriptions of landscape; his work is rich and enticing, paragraphs pregnant with succulent words, a world I want to succumb to, even if only temporarily.

My grandfather's eulogy—my cousin wrote it, considering it her right as the eldest grandchild—starts off saying he is a "magnificent person, and awesome dad," then continues to extol him as though he is Christ returned to earth: "Our father, Shiva Singh, was a very loving, compassionate, caring, hardworking..." No attempt to marshal some measure of truth.

At the wake, I stewed while the same group of adult cousins bawled their eyes out, snot dripping from their noses, voices cracking as they spoke of this man they knew nothing about, didn't even bother trying to find out anything about. Yet they spoke of him and remembered him without truth, without glancing at his wife, their grandmother, who sat through their performance without a teardrop forming in her eyes. My grandmother struck up hearty conversations with people around her and laughed her throaty laugh that resonated deeply in her chest. A free woman now, she could grin as she wanted and wherever she pleased.

I still wonder how my grandmother must have felt when she heard these words at the funeral:

> *Family meant the world to our father. He treated his family with respect, and dignity. He cared for his family so much more than words can describe . . . He cared for his wife like no other. He treated her as if every day was his last, and even did in his last moment.*

In his last moments, when my grandmother approached him at his bedside, he screamed the familiar string of *no* we'd all learned to endure—*No-No-Nonononono!* Eventually even this reaction dropped away. When my mother asked him, *Pappy, yuh know meh?* there was no response. When I asked him, *Grampa, yuh know who dis is?* there was no response. Yet every time my grandmother opened her mouth, or someone said her name, he'd muster up enough energy to scream his string of *no*'s.

> *His grandchildren meant a lot to him in all aspects of his life. He treated every one as if they were his own. Helped raised them all and taught them every life's moral he taught his children.*

Shiva's children were, in his view, destined either to be nothing like him or everything he embodied, nothing in between. That is what he taught them. He shunned the grandchildren he called *wutless and bhad,* told them, *goh from hyah, meh eh wahn to see yuh,* yelled at their parents, *take dem chilren away wid dey nasty behavior.*

Given the chance to write that eulogy, in front of family and friends, I promise I would have told the truth.

EPILOGUE

My first time back in Trinidad since leaving twelve years before, I find myself alongside Uncle Avinash, planting my toes in the soil while we sit in the shade of a coconut tree. My family and his lie in the sand just where the water pools at your back, then recedes, the calmest point of intersection between sea and land.

Only a few seconds before I'd been playing with my teen-aged cousins—Avinash's son and daughter—and talking of our shared interest in music. They were quite involved with American pop culture, while I was more interested in the rhythms of the island, each of us yearning for the other side of the divide.

And then I saw Avinash sitting off to the side, everyone occupied with someone except him, at ease by himself, loneliness his company, much like his father, my grandfather. How complicated it must have been for them all with Avinash's entrance into their lives. Young Arya was unable to understand the depth of her father's betrayal. Avinash's existence posed a threat to the life Rebecca had fought so hard to preserve, the life she was providing for her children. Rebecca must have felt that giving her children permission to physically harm another child was an act of self-preservation. And yet this child who grew into a man, who became more of an uncle to me than some of my full uncles, is kind and generous, but I do not know if this stems from the favor my grandfather showed me as well.

And so we sit and watch the ocean before us, one of the most glorious beaches in the Caribbean—Maracas. It is a natural bay etched on unblemished terrain, waters pristine and picturesque, that aquamarine blue that tapers off and meanders around mossy green mounds and emerald waters, where stray dogs trudge along the sand picking at bits of fried bake and shark, dried roti chunks, congealed pieces of breadfruit, and pigtail people have left behind. We cook on these beaches over open fires, taking the day's catch and dousing it in lime and pepper sauce, drying fish and shells on pieces of galvanized metal before roasting them over the fire. The waves are tempestuous, exactly the reason we've traveled through the mountainous region for an hour to arrive at this gem of ocean nestled deep down in the valleys. For us, comfort lies in the least calm waters.

Today the notorious Maracas waves pulverize the shoreline; the coconut trees dance as nuts shake loose from their bunches, and a pain sprouts in my heart as I look into Avinash's face. What I want from him, I realize right there in that moment, is for him to be my grandfather because he looks so much like him. His eyebrows threaded together across his handsome face, the gleaming darkness of his skin, his free locks blowing in the breeze. He looks the way I once remembered Shiva—tall, fierce, and dark. I yearn for the moments of gruffness my grandfather had toward others and how I was capable of turning his mood around with the suggestion of a checkers game or a story. Avinash is my grandfather incarnate. The child he never meant to have is the man who will carry forth his legacy.

Krystal, Avinash says as he digs in the sand. His voice sounds so much like my grandfather's I cringe from him for an instant.

My mother is talking to Avinash's wife, Delilah, and her eyes keep flicking to us, to him. When she locks eyes with me, I know she is thinking the same thing.

Yuh know wah dis is, Krystal? He says my name in that same voice, in that same way my grandfather always did. Uncle Avinash reveals a translucent creature scrabbling in his cupped hands.

We does call dem sea cockroach, he continues, oblivious to my reaction, speaking more to himself than me. *We use toh ketch dem plenty and ross dem right hyah on de beach back een de day.* I look at the creature lying supine and kicking its many legs, trying to flip over, the wet sand around it holding it down. *Me and yuh faddah use toh come all de time and cook dem,* he says, *dat an chip-chip.*

My father, mother, and Avinash. They had good times once. Before Arya married and moved away. Before my mother had me and my sister, catapulting her first into motherhood, then onward to America. They didn't forget one another in the interim, the obligatory appearances at weddings, funerals, baby showers, births, and celebrations bringing them together, but not in the same way they had once listened to music and drunk beer, tumbled in the waves and wrapped themselves in the sweetness of their stolen time as friends.

Avinash still lives in Trinidad, working as a maxi taxi driver, the only one of Shiva's children who didn't witness his demise.

Yuh nevah try it before? he asks, inviting me into the conversation the same way my grandfather would. Right here is where I want to say so much to him, lean my head on his shoulder in the most familiar way and tell him everything I know, but now I don't know which him I would be talking to—my grandfather or Avinash.

I shake my head and choose to say nothing as he talks more about sea animals and cookouts on the beach. Such a mundane conversation told in the dangerous bass of my grandfather's voice, one that makes me feel as though I am slipping into velutinous darkness. He asks me another question, and I venture a *no*. He laughs the same soft *heh-heh-heh* my grandfather used to laugh so amiably with me. Uncle Avinash's laugh conveys I've missed out on an important Trini ritual, and try as I might to look past his laugh, the sound swells in my mind, becoming louder than the waves crashing in the background.

Uncle Avinash closes his hands over the sea cockroach for a moment, and I stiffen. He opens it and closes it again. My stomach twists. Open. Close. I cringe. He's going to kill this tiny thing right in front of me, right in the middle of his hand, he's going to squash it to death, I think. For no reason.

But then he opens his hands like a clam displaying a pearl, and the defenseless critter scuttles around before leaping from the sand bed in his palm. It arcs elegantly through the air before plummeting to the beach, then skips and hops its way to the sea, where it burrows deep into the ocean bed.

My grandfather would never have let it go.

What remains is this: long after Shiva has withered away and died, cooking remains the sacred ritual binding my grandmother, my mother, and me. For many years I watch my mother and grandmother become stronger, powerful even, around the fire. We continue to gather together often, and eventually he seems almost to not matter anymore. As my grandmother briskly spins spinach seheena balls in the center of her palm, my mother sears brown sugar in oil for jerk pork, and I boil bits of dasheen tossed with habanero-infused smoked herring; and when we all partake of a meal, our fingers soaking roti bits in curry—we build together. These familiar smells release our inhibitions, draw us closer, and around the tantalizing aroma of food, comforted, these women whisper their stories for me to weave together, to make sense of our lives, healing and understanding passing from one generation to the next.

WE FOLLOW THE FRACTURED ROAD that spirals first up, then down the mountain. The foliage along the hills is incandescent, the coarse tree trunks almost black from morning dew. After so many years away, each time we jump into our rented car to visit a place of distant memory, the energy is electric, coursing through us and crackling the air. The streets are wide enough for one car only, and when there is an oncoming vehicle, my father pulls aside on the grassy embankment of a drain to allow the other car to pass.

My mother and I want to go back to the place where she grew up, to walk through the estate, touch the walls of our childhood, find something familiar in this country that has changed so much while we were gone. We make stops along the way to eat in the shade of shacks, to visit with old friends who still live off pathways where cars can't drive, like my grandmother's childhood home. They live in houses constructed from corrugated tin, clothes flapping on lines outside their home. My parents remember these roads that veer off paved streets and channel down steep inclines. We must pull off the main road and leave the car to walk down a path to get to these friends, people they've not seen since school days but who remember my parents in an instant.

Seeing my mother's curled hair and carefully made-up face, painted nails, designer blouse and jeans, these women shy away, gulping her in with their brown eyes. Their skin is greasy, their hair oily and flat against their heads, the clothes on their bodies ragged and torn. When they smile they cover their mouths to hide their rotted teeth or toothless gums. Nevertheless, the hospitality remains the same, and they draw us into their homes, offering drinks they do not have or cannot afford. We decline collectively and opt for water, and while our glasses sweat in the incredible heat and our make-up melts off our faces, we rediscover these lives.

These houses are far removed from the fortress I grew up in, but the poverty is familiar. To look upon the faces of people we once knew and see their pain wrenches something from deep within. I clutch these women and men, friends of my parents, in a tight embrace; I wish them well. I kiss their sweaty cheeks and wrap my arms around their thick necks. They are surprised and step away, as though scared to wrinkle my colorful sundress. Tears glitter in our eyes as we leave them behind. I start the hike back to the car, allowing my mother to linger and slip them money they refuse to take but which she leaves anyway; American bills, an oddity, a luxury.

We resume our journey to Sangre Grande. I place TT bills on my skirted lap, and Colette unrolls US currency on hers. I straighten the bright reds, greens, purples, and blues. They are luminous against my white clothes and prismatic in the sunlight compared to the muted greens, yellows, and grays of America's money.

We reach, my mother says, and I cock my head as I look out the window. The mountain along the gravel road, once teeming with trees, has been shaved. Atop it is a garish steel structure fenced in by a swaying chain-link fence.

No doubt dat fence goh electrocute yuh, my father says as he maneuvers the car over the bumpy road and rolls to a stop in front of a wooden house.

Who lives here? my sister queries.

I answer her because my mother is already out of the car, looking for the owner of the lopsided house.

Is Grampa nephew, Sachin.

His house is the first people see before reaching my grand-father's. Memories of Radica, Raj, and me scooting across the yard flash before me. I see the bed in the dilapidated room where the whole family slept. We played hide-and-seek, tag, scooch, anything we dreamed up, a friendship forged despite the rivalry pulled taut between our families.

I open the car door and hesitate before stepping out. The ground is muddy; the grass is wet; my sandals will be soiled, ruined. Sachin, Mitra's boy and my grandfather's nephew, is in ratty farm clothes, his boots caked with manure. He wields a cut-lass in one hand and a rope in the other.

Aye, Arya gyul, dah is you? he asks, pushing his head forward to peer at her. *Aye gyul yuh diffrant, rheal diffrant,* and he eyes us all in the same way everyone else does, like tourists who've traipsed into unknown territory. A swarm of flies buzz around him.

Krystal? Lil Krystal? he says, then hesitates, wipes his hands on his pants, and extends them. I pull him into a hug. Memories between us and our families have never been pleasant, but I look at this place that has fallen to despair, where loneliness and death are draped so casually all around, and I feel a need to connect with him. I want him to hug us all, for him to know that though years have made us strangers, we still remain family.

Dah eh no lil Krystal again, yuh know. Dah is big Krystal now, my mother jumps in and we all laugh. Sachin is as gruff as I've remembered, a smile never crossing his soured face. His son remained to help him, his wife is gone, his daughter has eloped.

We come toh see de house an ting.

He looks toward my grandparents' old house and says roughly, *Yuh kyant go dey. Watch nah, de cah hah toh stay right hyah. Yuh goh dey and yuh eh sure toh come out.*

My mother and I turn to the house for the first time. We stumble toward it, mud squelching between our toes. The further we walk, the more the earth yields until my steps are exaggerated as I pull my feet from its suction. We've come to an impasse. I push forward, but she holds me back. The trees around the house grow slanted as though reaching to claim it as their own. Vines trellis the windows and doors, sealing each entryway. The kitchen has caved in, and the whole structure of the house leans heavily to that side. Still, I want to venture forward, but my mother again pulls me back. *Yuh kyant goh dey*, she whispers and points with her chin to the trees. I squint and try to see what she's pointed to. Along the top of the calabash tree is a canopy of snakes. Tails dangle from the trees like wispy branches, unblinking eyes a glassy onyx between the viridian brush, scales glittering like jewels in the rays of sunlight that penetrate the leaves. On the tree trunks, iguanas stare with beady eyes. I search no more, wanting to discover nothing new.

We clutch each other, not a word uttered between us. Chickens skitter and peck at our feet; emaciated cows, goats, and donkeys amble around us. The path that dips into the valley, leading to the chicken coops and fields, is overgrown. No one has set foot here in years. We turn around and walk away. My mother slips her arm around my waist, and we incline our heads at the temples as we saunter back to the car.

Ma, I start, *yuh tink yuh could evah move back to Trinidad?*
Nevah.

ACKNOWLEDGMENTS

To all the women like my great-grandmother, grandmother, and mother, and to the women before them, your sacrifices have not been in vain. Without your strength and conviction, I shudder to think where we would be today.

To my mentors at New Jersey City University—Edvige Guinta, Ethan Bumas, Joshua Fausty—this book started there. Because of you, I had the courage to continue. You helped me create and foster the space in which to start. This was the most important lesson of all: foundation.

My deepest thanks to the ReCollective, our beautiful writing community that started at NJCU and grew after. And a few special words to my dear friend Kathy Potter, the glue of our group, who is no longer with us. I finished, my friend. I did it for us all. May we be rigorous in our collection of memories.

My friends who were generous enough to donate their time to reading this book in its many stages: without you, Angel Lemuel Eduardo, Amy Kandathil, and Renee Clemente, there could be no shape. Together, we sculpted. But especially you, Angel. Without your steadfast friendship, sharp mind, constant questioning,

I would be unmoored. I find respite and harmony in our long, meandering conversations. May that never change.

My short time at Hunter College blessed me with a writing partnership that propelled me in the years after. We did good, Cecilia Donohue and Jessie Male. Our teachers there made sure we were armed and ready. Thank you, Kathryn Harrison, Louise DeSalvo, Alexandra Styron, and Roxana Robinson.

To my oldest friends in this country—Robert Queenan, Joseph and John Gancia—you unflinchingly showed up to things you didn't even understand. I'm honored to have you as my friends. You first knew me as a girl and supported me through it all as we've always done for one another. May our international food nights stretch well into our old age as our self-proclaimed family grows.

My sister: my first ears, my first editor, my first everything. There are not enough words in this world to describe how much you mean to me. You are the audience everyone hopes for, the editor everyone dreams of, and the person I grudgingly share with your husband. We are connected in ways no one will ever understand.

Sylvie Greenberg, you are the special agent who entered my life swiftly and with purpose. It was exactly what I needed at the time, and you seemed to understand that better than anyone. May we look to the future together.

From my heart to yours, Alane Mason, you are one of the most brilliant people I've had the pleasure of working with. Wading through this book again and again was never as painful as when

ACKNOWLEDGMENTS

I did it by myself; in fact, it was exciting. From being tangled in titles to chiseling out the perfect word, your patience and care with what has been a book-in-progress for ten years has shown me just how lucky I am to have worked with you. To touch other books in the ways you've done this one is only a sliver of who you are as a human being.

Whether it was over the flicker of candlelight in a windy backyard, a yawning reading hall, or special Tudor house in New Jersey, we've gathered to tell our stories, and as one who was invited to share, I want to warm the hearts of Edvige Giunta, Annie Lanzilotto, and Rosette Caportorto for drawing me in, along with the others who have been blessed to be a part of this clan.

My beautiful partner, my husband, Pawel Grzech, I love you. Thank you for creating a beautiful family with me.

And to all women, may your stories always be told.